Strategic Financial Planning

Strategic Financial Planning

A Manager's Guide to Improving Profit Performance

Harold Bierman, Jr.

with epigraphs by Florence M. Kelso

THE FREE PRESS
A Division of Macmillan Publishing Co., Inc.
NEW YORK

Collier Macmillan Publishers
LONDON

The Free Press
A Division of Macmillan Publishing Co., Inc.
866 Third Avenue, New York, N. Y. 10022

Collier Macmillan Canada, Ltd.

Library of Congress Catalog Card Number: 80–1058

Printed in the United States of America

printing number
1 2 3 4 5 6 7 8 9 10

Library of Congress Cataloging in Publication Data

Bierman, Harold.
Strategic financial planning.

Bibliography: p.
Includes index.
1. Corporations--Finance. I. Title.
HG4011.B473 658.1'5 80-1058
ISBN 0-02-903560-0

Contents

If you're running out of time,
Just skip the text and read the rhyme.
FMK

Preface

This is a book on corporate financial strategy. The objective of a corporation is assumed to be a maximization of the well-being of its stockholders, taking into consideration the interests of its employees.

The style of the book is qualitative rather than quantitative, though at times symbols are used and frequently numerical examples are used to illustrate the argument that is being made. Generally, absolute statements are not made unless proofs are available for backing up the statements, but the proofs are not presented in this book.

Frequently in finance we do not know and cannot prove that one decision is better than another. We can always point out the relevant considerations, and occasionally we can make definite recommendations.

If a firm currently has a capital structure with 35% debt and if a bond rating agency has promised to change the bond rating of the firm's debt from a double A to a single A if more debt is issued, we can describe the costs of adding more debt. We can describe the financial consequences of issuing preferred stock rather than adding more debt. It is very unlikely that we can prove that it is more desirable to issue preferred stock than to add more debt.

Frequently in the strategy area the world is simplified so that the "correct" decision seems to be obvious. A conclusion follows naturally that a product which dominates a rapidly growing market should receive investment funds rather than a product which has only 10% of a nongrowing market. But a conclusion such as this (which is intuitively appealing) may be completely wrong, if significant considerations are omitted.

Strategy decisions are important. They are too important to be left to excessively simplified generalizations.

My thanks to Larry Hastie, Bill Straight, Bill Strong, and Paul Tregurtha for many solid lessons in practical business finance and strategy.

Harold Bierman, Jr.
Cornell University
Ithaca, New York

Chapter 1

Strategy and Decision Making

Though BCG would milk the "cow"
In point of fact no one knows how.
FMK

In discussing corporate financial strategy, the question can well be asked as to how strategy differs from more modest decision making. There is no completely satisfactory answer to this question, since there is an extensive intersection between those activities that we label decision making and those we label strategy formulation. We could resort to a distinction and have decision making become the application of the basic strategy, but generally decision making has a broader interpretation. Peter Drucker has stated, "The effective executive does not make many decisions. He solves generic problems through policy."[1]

Let us consider an actual business situation that illustrates the point Drucker is making. A university administrator was spending a lot of time approving or disapproving requests for travel. This was a nuisance to professors who had to wait for approval and who resented the requests that were rejected, and a waste of time for the administrator. In addition she was using up her good will with the professors. After several months of this situation it was decided to change the travel *policy* so that requests would be submitted only for a reduced list of eligible trips and the professor knew the approval was automatic as long as the request was consistent with the policy. A well-thought-out policy was substituted for a series of ad hoc decisions. Good policies and strategies can greatly reduce the number of decisions that have to be made.

Elements of Strategic Planning

We shall consider five elements of the strategic planning. There is no question that the list to be presented is not unique. In fact, before reading on, you might well want to prepare your own list of five elements of strategic planning and compare your thoughts with the items to follow.

The number one element in developing a strategy is the identification of the problems and opportunities that exist. A successful firm will have a fertile idea-generating environment. What problems and opportunities are there? Problem and opportunity identification is one of the more important outputs resulting from good strategic planning. You cannot solve a problem or seize an opportunity unless you know it exists.

The second element is to set goals (objectives). Goal setting is not independent of the identification of opportunities. If the goal is to achieve growth in sales of 15% per year, it will be necessary to spend more resources generating ideas than if the goal is to avoid growth. Some would argue that top management should stop with the setting of the goals and leave everything else to the operating managers. For example, top management might set the goals to earn at least 25% return on investment (ROI), to maintain a 15% growth rate per year, and to corner 20% of the total market as the firm's profit goals. Operating management would then establish the details as to how the goals would be achieved. A popular form of managerial style is to "manage by objectives." If one manages by objectives, the goal is set by the top, but the specific method of getting to the goal is not controlled. The results are important, not the method of getting to the results. Performance measurement is substituted for detailed supervision. Thus goal setting becomes a crucially important element in the strategic planning.

We now have problems and goals defined. The next step is to have a procedure for providing possible solutions, or "paths" the firm can follow to find a solution.

For example, the current energy situation can be defined as a problem or an opportunity. The goal might be to achieve energy independence or to make a given return on investment. Assume a firm has decided to enter the energy industry and has to decide what kind of energy it will develop and how it will go about it. For example, it might consider solar, wind, tide, and fossil and then decide to go with solar.

Having decided to enter the solar energy industry, the corporation might decide to spend large sums on research or alternatively might decide to acquire a firm that already has valuable know-how and thus accelerate its entry into the industry. The setting of tactics follows the setting of the basic strategy for entering the industry.

The basic decision is to "enter the solar energy industry." The goals that are set can be to earn 25% ROI, increase earnings 15% per year, and gain 20% of the total market. Top management of the corporation might then leave the details of how this is to be achieved to the managers operating the solar energy division. This is an extreme form of decentralization and "bottom line management." The more normal procedure is for top management to oversee the more important decisions that are made, especially those involving large investment outlays or other large commitments.

Now we have problems, possible solutions, and the goals defined. The fourth element of strategic planning is to choose the best solution, given possible solutions and the firm's objectives. On what basis will the best solution be chosen? The goal might have been established to maximize the well-being of the stockholders. This is easy to state, but given a large number of ways to enter the energy industry, which method should be chosen? It might be decided to choose the path with the largest net present value. But then risk considerations should enter analysis. Choosing the best solution, even with well-defined goals established, is a difficult job.

The fifth and final element of strategic planning is to have some type of review procedures to check how the best solution has actually performed. How this review function is executed will depend on the preferences and style of management.

The above five elements of strategic planning do not reveal anything about the style in which they (and the resulting plans) will be implemented. They are broad enough to encompass a wide range of financial decisions. For example, if the goal is to have reasonable growth but little risk, the amount of risk that is acceptable to the owners of the corporation (or in their absence, to the board of directors) will greatly affect the amount of debt that is used to finance the corporation.

A major planning question not yet answered is to what extent the interests of the organization come ahead of the interests of the different groups of employees. If you were a college president, would you fire your football coach on Christmas eve? What sort of performance measures will be used, and what happens when goals are not met? Will excuses (explanations) be listened to, or will there be an insistence on performance? Managerial style will circle back and affect things like idea generation.

Strategy Is Not Fun

Herbert Simon has written that there is a Gresham's law of planning: "Programmed activity tends to drive out non programmed activity."[2] The decision to buy a new energy-saving piece of equipment is a lot easier to discuss and analyze than strategic investment decisions. In the case of the energy-saving equipment, cash flows can be estimated and the decision to buy or not to buy can be made based on well-known capital budgeting techniques. The basic capital budgeting techniques are "programmed activities" in Simon's law. Strategy issues are a lot softer and a lot less satisfactory to write about and to read. However, it may well be that strategy issues are much more important, even if they are not fun to consider.

Strategy leads a firm to enter the energy business. That is the first and most important decision. The firm might then have to value a prospective acquisition as a means of accelerating the entry into the industry, but without the strategy decision it would not be necessary to value the acquisition.

Abstractions

All business decision making is based on abstractions from reality. We have to simplify in order to make decisions. We can delay decision making by insisting on more information, but when the more information is obtained, there will still be more information that could be obtained if you were willing to defer action. Sooner or later one has to resist the opportunity to get more information, and one has to make the decision.

Herbert Simon has said this best:

> Administrative theory is peculiarly the theory of intended and bounded rationality—of the behavior of human beings who *satisfice* because they have not the wits to *maximize*.[3]

And as additional explanation:

> Whereas economic man maximizes—selects the best alternative from among all those available to him, his cousin, administrative man, satis-

> fices—looks for a course of action that is satisfactory or "good enough." Examples of satisficing criteria, familiar enough to businessmen if unfamiliar to most economists, are "share of market," "adequate profit," "fair price."[4]

The substitution of the word "satisfice" for "maximize" is not necessary if we are willing to consider the costs of information, search, and delay in the decision to maximize. In a sense we can conclude that Simon is suggesting that it is better to make decisions, even imperfect decisions, than to endure the long wait until the perfect information and perfect decision processes are available. "In an important sense, all decision is a matter of compromise."[5]

An Important Assumption

While Simon's "satisfice" description is an extremely useful device for describing how managers operate, we shall find it convenient to collapse Simon's "satisfice" and profit maximization into one expression.

Throughout this book profit maximization (where profit is defined in terms of risk-adjusted present value) is deemed to be the primary objective of the firm. More is better.

You can assume that the profit maximization objective includes the information cost and cost of search so that it is consistent with Simon's satisfice (we are not rejecting the "satisfice" concept).

The assumption is that decisions should be made from the point of view of improving the well-being of the stockholders. This is a reasonable point of departure, but it cannot be the entire message. Managers, employees, customers, and society in general have interests in the results of a firm's operations. We must also consider the impact of decisions on the well-being of these groups. You might object to this conclusion, but realistically such considerations are being included by successful firms.

No manager submits an investment or other decision proposal without carefully considering the impact of the decision being reviewed on his or her well-being. Even the board of directors will consider the well-being of managers if for no other reason than that managers are likely to be on the board. Employees also must be considered, since an obvious and continuous disregard of their interests will cause them to insist on the right to protect their interests. Customers also gain their right to be considered by the economic power they wield, not in the board room directly, but indirectly via the right of a consumer to avoid buying a corporation's product.

The rights of society can to some extent be ignored by a corporation for a short period of time, but continuous implementation of a "public be damned" philosophy is likely to bring forth a string of government legislation. The interests of society must be respected if only to avoid such legislation. A corporation should do "right" either because it is the proper thing to do or because it is in its own best interests to behave in such a fashion.

Approaches to Strategy

We will consider four approaches to strategy. The first uses brilliance and is unstructured, while the second uses dramatic simplifications and broad generalizations. The third relies heavily on statistical data, and the fourth is a theoretical approach that is correct, but may not always be practical.

Approach 1: Brilliance

Under this approach each situation is unique and the problem solver applies brilliance in arriving at a strategy. There is an unstructured analysis. A systematic approach to thinking about strategy can be learned (one can practice strategy decisions via cases and games), but there are few if any generalizations. A listing of the five elements of strategic planning described above is an illustration of an attempt to systematize thinking about strategy.

One can read a strategy recommendation for a firm and admire its wisdom, but still not be able to tell a computer how to do the next analysis.

Approach 2: Broad Generalizations

The Boston Consulting Group (BCG) has developed an amazingly simple to understand and attractive approach to strategy (this is not to imply that this is the group's only contribution to strategy development). Figure 1.1 shows the basic classifications used by BCG.

The best of all worlds is for a product to have a high market

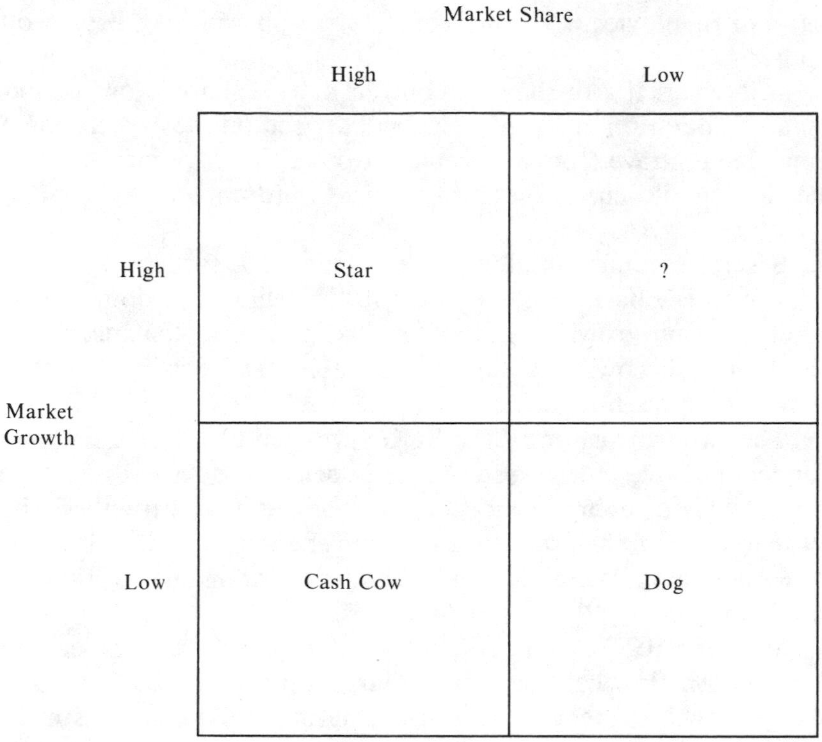

Market Share

	High	Low
Market Growth: High	Star	?
Market Growth: Low	Cash Cow	Dog

FIGURE 1.1

share in a high-growth market (be a star). Thus the implication (recommendation?) is that a firm should maintain dominant market position in a growing market (the market segment may be very limited) or the firm should abandon the activity.

To some extent this recommendation is based on theory. To be in a monopolistic position is a desirable state from the point of view of profit maximization. Secondly, if you are producing more than your competition, you are apt to be further along your learning curve, and thus your costs are likely to be less than those of your competitor.

It is assumed that the incremental costs reduce with the number of units produced, and there is evidence to substantiate this assumption.

If you have a high market share but slow growth in the market, you have a cash cow. Do not invest in this market, but drain off the cash.

If both the market share and market growth are low, you have a dog, and the advice is to find some fool who will take it off your hands.

If the market growth is high but the market share is low, the box contains a question mark. Strategy will depend on the expectation of being able to move from a low market share to a high market share. The firm should either spend to achieve stardom or get out of the market.

Several recommendations follow from this strategy format in addition to the basic strategy of trying to achieve stardom. A firm should plan on growing with the market. Also, a "balanced portfolio" of cash cows and stars is desirable. The cows are used to finance the growth of the stars.

The basic attraction of the BCG approach is that it is simple, it is understandable, and it seems to make sense. It does not bog down in the details of complex models and massive sets of numbers, but rather focuses on the broad strategic considerations. What firm does not want to have essentially a monopolistic (dominant) position in a growth market?

With the BCG system resources are allocated to stars and discounted cash flow calculations are largely meaningless. One establishes a growth strategy instead of evaluating individual investments spread over many different product lines.

There are many questions unanswered. What happens if three firms in the same market all spend massively to achieve a dominant market position?

Would BCG advise Wendy's to challenge McDonald's? Or Toyota to challenge Fiat, Volkswagen, and General Motors? Or Avis to challenge Hertz? Certainly, it is reasonable to enter a market and compete if you have some "edge." Consider a strategy of a business that is defined in terms of earning a satisfactory return on investment (this is consistent with General Motors' strategy). If the return is satisfactory or better, do it. Otherwise the activity should be terminated. This is a clearly defined, theoretically correct strategy.

Approach 3: Statistical Analysis

The third approach is to perform statistical analysis using industry data. Regressing the data, one draws conclusions as to the optimum strategy to be followed.

For example, one might conclude that quality is very important in slow-growth markets. This conclusion is intuitively appealing.

Customers are apt to become choosy in a situation where there is excess capacity (the market is growing slowly).

The difficulty with this basic approach is that one can determine associative relationships (quality is shown to be important when there is low growth) but not causal relationships, and certainly there is no reliable implication as to the decision that should be followed. If high quality is desirable in a low-growth market, one does not conclude that low quality is desirable in a high-growth market (you might be better able to get away with low quality, but it might still be a bad long-run strategy).

The statistical analysis and comparisons should be of some use in setting profit goals. The profits of the other firms can help set the profit targets of your firm.

Can the data be used to judge the effects of changes in strategy of a firm? Can the data be used to determine the strategies and decisions that will lead to optimum positions? There are many firms that are betting that the statistical analysis of industry data can be used for these purposes.

Approach 4: A Theoretical Approach

The final approach is a purely theoretical approach. It is consistent with widely accepted economic and financial theory. It bypasses the broad generalizations and focuses on the details of the decisions. The basic strategy is to insist on detailed facts and evaluation of the alternatives, using conventional profitability measures.

Consider the resource allocation decision. Expansion of production in a given market is desirable as long as the marginal revenue of a product is larger than the marginal cost of producing and selling it. A project is undertaken as long as the discounted cash flow is larger than the cost of money (the net present value is positive).

Yes, it is nice to be further down the learning curve than your competitors. That is to say, it is better to have some sort of advantage (a good position on the learning curve being one) that leads to your having lower costs than your competitor. This preference is a fact, not a strategy consideration.

In addition to exploiting marketing cost advantages, a firm should take into consideration a wide range of institutional factors. These include the tax laws, trade arrangements, the availability of tax-exempt bonds, and government programs aimed at helping your industry (sometimes the legislation is not aimed at helping an industry but is interpreted in such a manner that it does help).

It is recommended that the definition of diversification be extended by us from the limited interpretation of obtaining cash from cows to supply stars to a consideration of risk factors arising from different mixes of product lines. This type of risk analysis is a complex subject that will be considered in more depth later.

Based on the details of decisions, one can consider a wide range of different strategy factors. For example, we can focus on the identification of a gap in the market and set out to supply a product to fill the need. The need may be in the form of better service or better quality. The strategy is to identify situations where such needs exist.

Which Approach Is Best?

If we interpret the BCG strategy as exemplified by Figure 1.1 as a systematic approach to the type of theoretical considerations described in approach 4 as well as the brilliant insights of approach 1, maybe all four approaches can be reconciled and we do not have to choose a best method of formulating strategy. If BCG were to only use Figure 1.1 and the naive conclusions that follow when a product is a dog or a question mark, we would then reject the approach. But we should not attribute that degree of naiveness, because even if it existed at one time, it would not be a stable position. In like manner the brilliant insights of the first approach have to be based implicitly on theoretical considerations. Basic principles of economics, finance, marketing, etc., must apply, if not for all situations, then enough so that the so-called brilliant insight approach is not completely isolated from the more conceptual theoretical approach.

The theoretical approach without an occasional stepping back in order to see where specific decisions are taking the firm would merely lead to a series of decisions without form or purpose. The decisions would not necessarily be consistent with each other. Thus the theoretical approach is not being recommended here in its pure form.

Any strategy that ignored statistical evidence concerning the financial affairs of its competitors would be deficient. It was useful for Wendy's to note the profitability and scope of McDonalds before entering the fast food market. We tend to project the past into the future.

Evaluation of a Strategy Plan

The first question to be asked about a strategy plan that has been prepared is whether it is understood by the managers who have to implement it. Just because something is said or written does not mean it is understood.

The second question is to determine whether the plan is consistent with the firm's resources (e.g., money and managerial talent) and consistent with the objectives of the firm and the capabilities of top management. Recognize that the objectives can range from profit maximization (and there are many ways of measuring profits) to just plain survival.

The final step in the evaluation is to determine whether any crucial information or consideration has been omitted. For example, is the action legal?

It is easy to fall into the trap of too simple generalizations. Assume a glass fiber factory has excess capacity and the plant manager is using the plant to process cotton textiles. This additional activity generates incremental business and incremental profit.

Should top management terminate the contract to process textiles since the corporation is in the glass fiber business and does not want to dilute the specialization and expertise that is its competitive advantage? Or should top management recognize that marginal revenue exceeds marginal cost and accept the textile business as long as there is excess capacity? One position is that the firm is in the "processing business" and it does not make any difference what it is processing as long as it makes profits and the product is legal.

In a real case like the above situation the plant manager was told to cease the activity. The textile business was thought to be inconsistent with the broad corporate strategy. The plant manager, whose salary was affected by the amount of profits made by the firm, was extremely upset by the loss of profits that resulted.

Extreme Strategies

Extreme strategies are not likely to be sustained through time. They are apt to change either because management changes its mind or because the composition of management changes.

A one-product firm might be a reasonable strategy if resources are limited and if the market for the one product is growing rapidly. The existence of rapid technological change might require that management focus its entire attention on the one product.

Sooner or later the threat of product obsolescence, a slowing down in growth, or even the accidental discovery of a new product or technique will lead to the firm expanding its product line. But as important as the above factors is the fact that a corporate strategy of producing one product is likely to be rejected by the next generation of managers who want new worlds to conquer. A chairman of the board who had a bad experience with a bank may resolve never to use bank debt, but when that person is replaced, you can expect to have banks used as a method of financing.

Extreme strategy positions are frequently the result of one very unusual talented person heavily involved in the organization of the firm. When the genius is replaced by the professional managers, they are more apt to employ normal strategies similar to those employed by other firms in the industry.

Just because the extreme position is not likely to be maintained, a firm should not necessarily move to a so-called normal position. Drucker said it well:

> The job of management, therefore, is never to be concerned with restoring or maintaining normality, because normality is the condition of yesterday. The real task of management in the effective business is that of re-directing and re-focusing activities towards what are the right economic realities for today and for tomorrow.[6]

Two Styles of Planning

Let us consider two different styles of planning.

Style 1

The first step is to set a growth goal. The second step is to inventory the tools that will enable you to reach the growth goal. Will the present set of products and markets do the job? If so, the plan is simple: ride the growth curves of the present products. If more growth is needed, the second possibility is to expand the technologies and markets of the firm. Again, if this satisfies the growth objective, the search is stopped; if not, we proceed to the next step. This final way to achieve the growth objective is to find new products not closely related to present products and technologies.

Style 2

Style 2 differs from the above by first inventorying the profitable investment and marketing opportunities. Only after this is done is an expected growth rate computed consistent with the optimum set of decisions. The resulting expected growth rate may be more or less than some target growth rate that is in the mind of the chief executive.

If the expected growth rate is not satisfactory, there is not a change in the operating plans of the next year, but rather a look is taken at the administration and budget of the research and development efforts.

The two styles differ greatly. With style 1 a growth rate is set, and then the ways of achieving that goal are found. We can expect there to be a forcing of numbers in the forecasts in order to meet the preestablished goals. With the second style of planning the focus is on all profitable opportunities. A zero growth rate is acceptable if that is consistent with the present opportunities. But a zero growth rate might also give rise to new research efforts that will mean that in the future the likelihood of having profitable growth opportunities will be increased.

There is an implication with the first style that good opportunities will be placed on the back burner if the target growth can be achieved without them. Equally bad is the fact that the expected profitability of bad investments may be made to look good so that the expected growth is equal to the target growth. Style 2 planning eliminates these two objections but introduces one of its own, an implied willingness to live with a low expected growth rate if that is what is indicated by the available opportunities. The answer to this objection is that this acceptance of a low growth rate is consistent with the fact that all alternatives presently available have been investigated and the firm has no alternatives that will lead to profitable growth. Profit (net present value) is a necessary condition for a prospect to be accepted. Without profit, growth is not desirable. Having found an expected zero growth, if growth is desired, the next step is to spend resources to develop profitable opportunities. Zero expected growth does result in changes in resource allocation if growth is desired.

Does your firm use style 1 or style 2 planning? With some slight changes they come together and become identical. But without the changes, they will lead to different attitudes. Long live style 2!

Conclusion

Managers have a tendency to like that which is easy to understand and reject that which is complex. Since consultants tend to tell managers what they want to hear, this has resulted in a lot of advice that is excessively simplified and as likely to lead to wrong decisions as to right decisions.

Consider a division of the states of the world into high and low relative market shares and high and low real market growths. It does not take a genius to conclude that one would prefer a high relative market share in a market that is growing in real terms. It is a fact that a high market share in a growing market is better than the other alternatives, all things being equal.

But this is not a decision. It is a description of a preference (wanting more compared with less). Business decisions in this context are of the type "Given this relative share of the market, where we forecast that the market is going to grow at X%, then we should do. . . ." The decision involves determining the amount of expenditures to affect market share. Knowing the current state of world (the current share of market) does not tell us what amount should be spent on the product.

There is virtue in simplicity. Let us be careful not to give it a bad name by moving to excessive simplicity and ignoring well-known and accepted facts.

We shall make an effort in this book to consider corporate financial strategy. We shall define some of the paths a corporation may take and point out the advantages and disadvantages of the different paths. Frequently we shall find that we know how to analyze the situation, but we will not necessarily know which specific decision is the correct decision. For one thing, that conclusion is going to depend on the objectives of the firm. Since the firm is managed by people, the conclusion will depend to a large extent on the subjective preferences of the decision makers who have sufficient power or influence to set the financial policies.

Chapter 2
The Cushion: Common Stock

Issuing blocks
Of common stocks
Absorbs shocks.

FMK

The holders of common stock are the owners of a corporation. With a privately held firm it is easy to see the relationship between owning shares of common stock and controlling the corporation. The owners exercise control. With a company the size of the General Motors Corporation the connection between ownership and control is less easily seen. A person holding 100 shares of stock in GM is not apt to be able to tell the president of GM to modify an operating decision.

Thus in the modern corporation there has tended to develop a separation between ownership and control. The stockholders receive dividend checks and a yearly proxy form, but rarely do the stockholders effectively band together and directly influence operating decisions.

The function of the stockholders with the modern large corporation is not to manage, but rather to supply capital. In return for supplying the capital, they hope to receive cash dividends and appreciation in stock price. If these expectations are realized, they will receive a return that will reward them for placing their capital at risk as well as forgoing safe investments such as government notes and bonds or relatively safe corporate bonds.

If we look at the corporation as a separate legal entity, then from the viewpoint of the corporation (and its managers) the use of common stock is a very attractive way in which to raise capital. The primary advantage of common stock as a form of capital is that there is no legal obligation for the corporation to pay cash dividends in a given year. The declaration of dividends is a discretionary act on the part of the firm's board of directors. If it is deemed desirable to cease paying a dividend, there is no threat of bankruptcy. There is no maturity date for the common stock; thus management does not have to be concerned with meeting at a given date a balloon payment as with debt. The common stock capital is the cushion. When operations are not going well, it is the common stockholders who act as the shock absorbers. They bear the brunt of downturns in the economic well-being of the corporation.

Those who complain about excessive corporate profits should buy shares of common stock in a few corporations. They will find that for the stockholders of many firms returns do not exist either in an accounting sense or from the viewpoint of stock appreciation plus dividends. Since the stockholders have no protection either from downturns in the company's activities or from downturns in the overall stock market, the holding of common stock is like riding a roller coaster. There are inevitable ups and downs. Common stock is a risky investment.

If common stock is a risky investment, is it also a rewarding investment? There are stories that abound about the person who held 100 shares of IBM in 1924 and is now a millionaire. And there are also stories about the persons who advocated buying Penn Central's common stock right before it went bankrupt because it owned valuable property in New York City (the property was leased for long periods of time and thus not a liquid asset of a large amount). There is evidence that over the long haul (say 1920 to 1980) investors have earned a fair return by investing in stocks listed on the New York Stock Exchange for the amount of risk they are undertaking.

The crucial question in any year is, What is going to happen to an investment made now in common stock? Is it better to buy now or to wait for prices to go lower? These are difficult questions for either a financial adviser or an investor to answer.

The corporate financial officer has an equivalent question to answer. Is it better to issue common stock now, or is it better to wait until the price per share goes up?

There are interesting psychological traps awaiting the financial manager. One is the "trend trap." If the stock has been increasing in value, it is easy to fall into the trap of thinking that the price tomorrow will be higher so we should not issue the shares today.

The second trap is the "looking back" trap. If the price yesterday was higher than today's price, the stock today is assumed to be undervalued. It is incorrectly concluded that the firm should wait until the stock returns to its historical high; otherwise the stock will be issued at a depressed price, harming the interests of the present stockholders.

If these two traps reflect the actual thinking of management (or more exactly the board of directors), then the firm will tend not to issue common stock in any year. Either the price is increasing and we should wait for it to go higher, or it is depressed and we should wait for it to increase.

Theory to the rescue! There is a way out of the box if management will listen. The theorist says the market is efficient and at any moment in time reflects all the information that is available. In addition, the short-run changes in the stock price from the current price will be random. The current price is an accurate reflection of the firm's value at the present time unless the market does not have significant information available to management. Thus the board of directors thinking of issuing common stock should not worry about whether the stock is going to go up or down in the future, as long as the investors have all the relevant information. Any day is as good as any other day to issue the stock.

It is true that in some cases the development of events will indicate that a wrong decision was made, but there is no way today to forecast the results of such a decision made today.

Stock Prices and Interest Rates

In a period of high interest rates managers may say that their stock is depressed, but this neglects the fact that high interest rates lead to discounting of the future, especially future growth. Consider the use of a popular valuation formation:

$$\text{Stock price} = \frac{\text{annual dividend}}{\text{cost of equity} - \text{growth rate}}$$

If the growth rate is .10 for the year, the dividend is \$1, and the cost of equity is .11, we obtain a value of \$100:

$$\text{Stock price} = \frac{1}{.11 - .10} = \$100$$

Now if an interest rate increase forces the cost equity up to .15, we have:

$$\text{Stock price} = \frac{1}{.15 - .10} = \$20$$

The managers who see their firm's stock price decrease from $100 to $20 are going to find it difficult to believe there is not a faulty evaluation taking place if the operations of the firm are just as profitable and growing this year at the same rate as in the past. However an increase in the cost of money can cause the decrease.

While special information available only to the board might well lead to a decision to defer the issuance of common stock, there is an important reason for arguing that the stock should be issued. Assume the expected value of the use of the cash to be received is positive. In this case even if the common stock were to be somewhat undervalued in the market, this underevaluation will tend to be equalized by the increase in the net value resulting from the use of the cash receipts made possible by the stock issue.

Some corporations will raise interim capital using short-term debt while they wait for the common stock price to increase. This strategy would be reasonable if there are real reasons for thinking the common stock is undervalued. A second strategy is to issue long-term debt as a substitute for the expensive common stock.

A Stock Valuation Model

Previously we used the relationship

$$\text{Stock price} = \frac{\text{annual dividend}}{\text{cost of equity} - \text{growth rate}}$$

to illustrate the effect of increasing interest rates on stock prices. The relationship is obtained from summing an infinite series of dividends where the dividends of each year have the same growth rate and all cash flows are discounted at a rate of discount called the cost of equity capital. It is necessary that the growth rate used be less than the rate of discount; otherwise the formulation is not valid. Also, the model assumes a constant growth rate (thus increasing investment through time). If it is desired to use changing growth rates through time, we could have a much more complex model. Also, if the current dividend is equal to zero, the model in the form presented cannot be used. But the basic formulation using the present value of *future* dividends can be used, even if the resulting formulation is more complex than that presented.

Some observers object to the use of the dividend valuation

model, since they know that investors buy common stock not only because of dividends but also because of the prospect of capital gains. This complexity is easily resolved. If the future price is based on value, the dividend model completely and correctly incorporates the price appreciation. If it is expected that the stock price will be higher than the value based on future dividends, we again would have to shift from the model presented. But for the model not to be valid for this reason, the future price would have to be based on "the greater fool theory." Someone next period will have to pay more than the dividend-based value because another fool is around the corner. Basing business decisions on the assumption that the market is not rational and will continue not to be rational in the future is not an attractive strategy.

Previously we illustrated the change in stock price value arising from a change in interest rates. Now we will hold the discount rate constant at .11 and change the growth rate assumption. We obtained a stock value of $100 with a growth rate of .10. Now assume an expected growth rate of .01. The stock value is now $10:

$$\text{Stock price} = \frac{\text{annual dividend}}{\text{cost of equity} - \text{growth rate}}$$

$$= \frac{1}{.11 - .01} = \$10$$

A change in the expected growth rate from .10 to .01 results in a change in the stock value from $100 to $10. Growth rate expectations of investors are extremely important in setting stock prices. When a company's stock is valued based on high-growth expectations and those expectations change, the stock price is going to be driven down dramatically.

Growth Rate Expectations

There are many reasons for the earnings of a company to grow. The reasons can include raising (or lowering) prices, increased efficiency, improved business conditions, new products, etc. But after all of these factors are implemented, the next improvement in growth must come from new investments. If debt is equal to zero, then we obtain the following relationship:

$$\text{Growth} = \text{retention rate} \times \text{return on investment}$$

The relevant return on investment is the return expected on the new investment. For example, assume a firm is currently earning \$100 and retaining .40, or \$40. If the firm can earn .25 on new investment, the expected growth rate is:

$$\text{Growth} = .40 \times .25 = .10$$

The \$40 of investment will earn .25, or \$10. The \$10 new earnings added to the basic \$100 of earnings is \$110, which is a growth rate of .10. The dividends will also increase .10 from \$60 to .6 of \$110, or \$66.

If the firm is using debt, the expected growth rate is more complex than that given. Growth then becomes a function of the retention rate, the expected return of new investment, the amount of leverage, and the cost of debt.

The types of models presented in this section move the estimate of growth from a purely subjective "wish" of management to an estimate based on such decisions as retention rate and amount of leverage as well as such other variables as the earning opportunities available to the firm and the cost of debt.

If the president of an already efficient, well-managed firm forecasts a .20 growth rate when the firm is retaining .40 of the earnings, with zero debt the president is implicitly assuming a return on new investment of

$$.20 = .40(\text{return on investment})$$

$$\text{Return on investment} = .50$$

If the president does not think new investments will earn an average return of .50, the estimated growth rate should be changed, or alternatively the retention rate should be changed. Following the logic of this section, estimated growth rates result from basic estimates of the economics of new investments. We derive growth rates from information and analysis. They are the end result of analysis, not the starting point.

Cost of Common Stock: A Graphical Approach

Figure 2.1 shows the cost of common stock as the amount of leverage increases (substituting debt for common stock).

The cost of common stock with zero debt is of interest, since

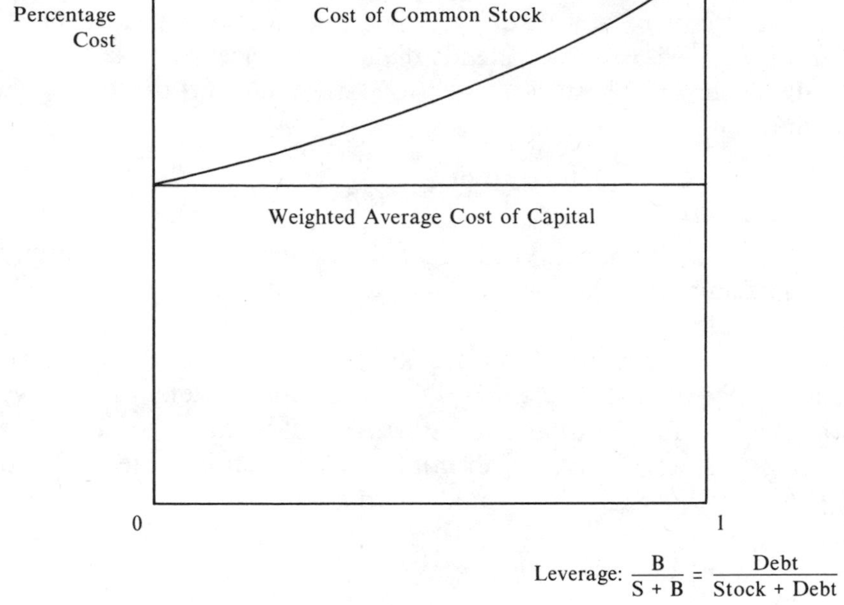

FIGURE 2.1

logically at that point the cost of common stock is equal to the weighted average cost of capital (common stock is the only security outstanding). As the amount of leverage increases, the cost of equity increases. The stockholders require larger expected returns as the amount of leverage increases. The *actual* return might actually decrease, but the *required expected* return increases.

When we discuss the cost of debt we will find the cost of debt curve is everywhere below the cost of stock equity. This occurs because debt is senior to common stock, meaning that the debtholders are ahead of common stockholders on "payday." Since debt has less risk than common stock, we can expect the holders of common stock to require a higher expected return than with debt (the tax laws could require a modification in this generalization).

Cost of Stock Equity

If we manipulate the dividend stock valuation model presented earlier we obtain:

$$\text{Cost of stock equity} = \frac{\text{annual dividend}}{\text{stock price}} + \text{growth}$$

An important conclusion resulting from the above formulation is that the cost of stock equity is not generally equal to earnings divided by price, or the dividends divided by price. For example, if the dividends are \$1, stock price \$100, and the growth rate .14, we obtain:

$$\text{Cost of stock equity} = \frac{1}{100} + .14 = .15$$

To use the dividend yield of .01 to estimate the cost of equity would be an error. The cost of equity is actually .15, if we accept the model and the given facts.

Some financial people prefer to use earnings rather than dividends. Since annual dividends = (1 − retention rate) earnings, we can substitute the right-hand side of this equation in the equation for the cost of stock equity. For example, if the retention rate is .2 and the earnings are \$1.25, we would again have:

$$\text{Cost of stock equity} = \frac{(1 - .2)1.25}{100} + .14 = .15$$

It makes no difference if we use dividends or earnings as long as we do not ignore the growth factor and do adjust the earnings for the retention factor.

Common Stock Issuance: Basic Strategy

We want to consider the basic strategy considerations entering into a decision to issue more common stock.

A prime consideration is control. If the issuance of more shares will increase the likelihood of loss of control by the stockholders presently controlling the corporation, you can expect a high reluctance to issue those shares. Since the only way to insure control of a corporation is to own more than 50% of the shares, the holders of 50% of the shares are not likely to want shares issued that will reduce their ownership to less than 50%, if they have alternatives.

The second consideration is the direct economic effects. We could determine the economic consequences by a conventional capital budgeting analysis, but for purposes of illustrating the effects on the common stock, we will take a different approach.

Assume a situation where a firm has 1,000,000 shares of common stock outstanding and the stock has a market price of \$40 per share. Management has information that leads it to think that the intrinsic value of the shares is $50 per share. The company is thinking of issuing 500,000 shares at a price of $40 to finance an investment. Should it do so, given that the shares are undervalued?

One strategy would be to issue debt until such time as the market recognized the intrinsic value of the stock. We will bypass this alternative, not because it is not worthy of consideration, but in the interest of simplicity. Assume that there are good reasons why the firm cannot issue debt.

While there is a real incentive not to issue the common stock given the depressed stock price (a value of $50 and a market price of $40), there is need for additional information before a decision can be made.

Assume the $20,000,000 of capital raised with the issuance of 500,000 shares will lead to an increment in value (real and perceived) of $30,000,000. Each new share of common stock will add $60 of value. Since the current intrinsic value per share is $50, there will be an increase in the intrinsic value of the currently outstanding shares, and the issuance of the new shares is desirable.

While the above explanation is sufficient to justify the stock issue, we can give other calculations. The $30,000,000 of new value added to the present market value of $40,000,000 gives a total value of $70,000,000 for 1,500,000 shares, or $46.67 per share. This is larger than the present market price of $40 per share; thus the shares should be issued. Comparable calculations could be done using the present intrinsic value per share, and the same conclusion would be reached.

If the value resulting from the issue of the new shares is $22,500,000, or $45 per share, the decision is less clear-cut. The $45 is less than the $50 per share of intrinsic value; thus the value per share will be diluted. The total value per share after issue will be reduced from $50 per share. On the other hand, the $45 is larger than the $40 market price. If the market believes the value added is truly $22,500,000, we can expect the market price to increase from $40 to $41.67 (the $64,500,000 of total value divided by 1,500,000 shares). Thus if the value per share added to the firm is greater than the market price but less than the intrinsic value, the correct decision is not obvious.

If one is willing to assume an efficient market, where it is assumed that the market has access to the same information as management, then the $50 measure can be assumed not to be relevant.

The shares should be issued as long as the new value per share is larger than the current market price.

We have assumed that the market will be able to measure the change in value arising from the new investment and that the market's measure is exactly equal to the value measurements of management. If there are wide differences, we may again not be able to arrive at a definite decision that the issue of common stock is desirable.

A "Fair" Profit

In November 1979 the Mobil Corporation took out a full two-page advertisement in the *New York Times* to explain and justify the level of its profits. Among the justifications offered were the return on average capital, return on shareholders' equity, profit per dollar of revenue, profit per gallon, and a comparison of the level of profits and the amount of investment expenditures.

If we were determining the reasonableness of the profitability of a regulated firm operating in a regulated industry, for purposes of setting the next period's prices we would certainly want to consider some of the above measures. But let us consider a competitive firm operating in a competitive industry. What is a fair level of profits, assuming the firm has operated in a manner consistent with the laws of the state? Many persons would respond that the firm should be allowed to earn as high profits as it can. If the profits are excessive compared with those earned in less profitable industries, capital will flow into the industry with excessive profits. Excessive profits serve the very useful function of attracting capital that will reduce the excessive profits to a normal level. This is how the free enterprise system is supposed to work, and it is how it will work if government does not interfere with the process.

Unfortunately, a large number of persons do not trust the above mechanism, but rather place their faith in the judgment of "public servants" in establishing the fair level of profits. They say that the industry is not competitive because there are not an infinite number of competitors or because the prices of the products being sold are now high compared to past prices. The fact that high prices act both as a rationing device and as a signal that more capital is needed is either ignored or cast aside.

It must be recognized that common stock is a highly risky

security. If profits are made, the stockholders may earn very high returns, but losses may also occur. Many common stock investments lead to negative returns. The common stockholders are last in line when the firm is distributing assets to its capital contributors. The payments to the stockholders are the first to stop in times of difficulty. The cushion offered by the flexibility of common stock is valuable to a firm interested in survival.

A Different Approach

In a previous section the formulation for the cost of stock equity was based on a definition of the cost of equity as the rate of interest that equates the present value of all future dividends to the stock price.

There is a different approach which can be used based on a theory called "the capital asset pricing model." Essentially the model adds to the default-free government borrowing rate a factor reflecting the risks of the firm. The firm's risk that is relevant for this model is based on the degree to which the affairs of the corporation are linked to the return earned by investing in the overall market (more exactly the risk is measured using the correlation of the stock's return with the market's return). It is argued that this correlation is the only risk for which the market demands compensation (all other risks can be diversified away).

Theoretically the cost of equity obtained using the capital asset pricing model will be equal to the cost of equity obtained using the dividend valuation model. Problems of estimation will cause differences to result, but this does not mean that the two models are inconsistent.

Conclusions

There is nothing easy about analyzing decisions involving common stock. While the cost of debt is merely a matter of calculation once we have the contractual terms and the market price, with common stock there are no contractual terms. All we have are estimates of market expectations. It is difficult to determine exactly the cost of equity capital.

It will be shown that debt has obvious tax advantages (the interest is tax deductible), but the advantages of common stock are more subtle.

Common stock's retention of earnings delays the payment of taxes by investors, and offers the possibility that the gain resulting from retention will be taxed as a capital gain.

The primary justification for issuing common stock is that the presence of the common stock and the cash received with its issuance tend to be risk reducing for the present investors. The amount of benefit associated with the risk reduction is difficult to quantify in terms of dollars. Thus justifying the issuance of common stock rather than some type of debt alternative is apt to be a difficult task. Nevertheless, when the going gets rough, management will greatly appreciate the fact that common stock was used rather than debt (to the extent it was used). Common stock capital is truly a cushion protecting the corporation against the disruptions of bankruptcy.

Chapter 3
The Amplifier: Debt

The theory is sound. We defend it.
You have to have money to spend it.
If conditions are good,
Go in debt as you should.
Just borrow at less than you lend it.

FMK

Debt is easy to understand, but the consequences of debt are difficult to keep in mind. Debt is an amplifier where the amplification can be good or bad. Instead of "amplification" the terms "leverage" and "gearing" are widely used.

Imagine a situation where a firm with $50,000,000 of common stock can have the following two outcomes:

	PROBABILITIES	COMMON STOCK EARNINGS	RETURN ON INVESTMENT
Good business conditions	.6	10,000,000	.20
Bad business conditions	.4	2,000,000	.04

While having only two outcomes is artificially simplified, the example could be extended to a continuous spectrum of outcomes with no change in the basic method of analysis.

Note that in this example even with the bad event the firm has positive earnings. An investor in the common stock will always earn something. Now let us substitute $30,000,000 of .10 debt for $30,000,000 of common stock. The debt pays $3,000,000 interest. Continuing the above example, now subtracting the interest the following outcomes can occur:

	PROBABILITIES	COMMON STOCK EARNINGS	RETURN ON INVESTMENT
Good business conditions	.6	7,000,000	.35
Bad business conditions	.4	– 1,000,000	loss

The good return increases from .20 to .35, but the bad return to the stockholders is now negative. Negative returns in one or more years imply there is a risk of bankruptcy.

Of course, normally there is the possibility of a firm having negative incomes even if there is zero debt. But that does not change the fact that the addition of debt tends to increase the probability of the earnings to the common stockholders being negative.

Fortunately a small increase in debt might leave the probability of negative earnings relatively unchanged (for example, $2,000,000 of debt would not change the probability of loss) and in fact might decrease the probability of loss if the funds obtained were invested in highly profitable real assets with little or no risk. But in most realistic situations where debt is substituted for common stock we can expect an increase in the probability of loss.

So far we have concentrated on the negative aspect of debt, the fact that debt increases risk. We also need to stress the positive leverage aspect. The good outcomes are amplified in such a way that debt can appear to be very desirable. In the example, the return on investment was increased from .20 to .35 for the good event. If the probability of this event were .99 instead of .60, we would have a very strong case for the substitution of debt for the common stock in this situation.

Frequently the variance of the outcomes is used as a measure of risk. Variance is a measure of spread or dispersion. The more spread out the outcomes, the more risk there is. We can use the example to illustrate the way that debt affects the variance of the outcomes. Without debt there was either a .20 return or a .04 return. With debt there was either a .35 return or a loss. The debt increased the range of the returns on investment. We could make comparable calculations using earnings per share and find the same type of increase in variance (the variance can be defined exactly mathematically, but the notion of spread is adequate for this discussion).

Debt is most attractive when the analysis assumes there is one highly desirable outcome. For the current example, if we assume the earnings before interest are $10,000,000, the substitution in turn of $30,000,000 and $40,000,000 of debt causes substantial changes in the return on stock equity investment (see table, p. 29).

Moving from $30,000,000 to $40,000,000 of debt increases the ROI from .35 to .60. This process is called "trading on the equity." The example illustrates well the way that debt can be presented as an attractive means of financing.

	ZERO DEBT	30,000,000 OF DEBT	40,000,000 OF DEBT
Earnings before interest	10,000,000	10,000,000	10,000,000
Interest	0	3,000,000	4,000,000
Earnings to stockholders	10,000,000	7,000,000	6,000,000
Investment	50,000,000	20,000,000	10,000,000
Return on investment (ROI)	.20	.35	.60

Assume that initially (zero debt) there are 10,000,000 shares of common stock earning $1 per share. The $30,000,000 of new debt is used to retire 60% of the shares, so that after the debt issuance there are only 4,000,000 shares outstanding and the earnings per share become $1.75. With debt of $40,000,000 there are 2,000,000 shares outstanding, and the earnings per share are now $3 per share. Again, as long as we assume only one desirable event is possible, the arguments are very strong that debt should be used. Even when it is well known that more than one event is possible, corporate financial analysts sometimes prepare reports and reach conclusions as if there were only one possible event.

The use of debt should be considered by all firms, but the decision as to how much debt is optimum is not as easy, as implied by the above examples.

The Cost of Debt

The cost of debt is generally defined as the internal rate of return of the debt cash flow stream. A bond paying $100 interest per year for 50 years and $1,000 at maturity issued at a price of $1,000 has a cost of .10. If we discount all the cash flows using .10, the net present value of all the debt flows including the initial cash receipts is equal to zero.

Despite the seeming simplicity of defining the cost of debt, there are some interesting complexities. For example, assume a firm has $300,000,000 of .05 debt outstanding, and if it issues additional debt, the cost will be .14. What is the cost of debt? A public utility regulator would use the embedded cost of .05 in setting rates. The .05 is not relevant to the decision making of a manager of a firm engaged in normal nonregulated business activity unless there is a possibility of retiring the debt. If there is .05 debt outstanding and if the next best use of funds to the firm is .04, then it might be desirable to retire the .05 outstanding debt. The .05 becomes a form of opportunity cost, and this opportunity cost is relevant to a decision to retire the debt at its face value.

But if the firm has investments yielding .07, the .05 cost is not of any relevance in deciding whether or not to undertake those investments if new capital is needed. If external capital is needed, one would not want to borrow at .14 to invest in projects yielding .07. The .14 becomes a minimum necessary return for new investment. Unless the investment yields more than .14, it must be rejected (this is inexact, since the risk characteristics of the investment might lead to its acceptance, but the conclusion is correct with no uncertainty and no taxes). The average cost of debt, including the embedded cost, does not affect the investment decision.

In the above discussion we ignored taxes and the fact that debt interest offers a tax shield. With a .46 corporate tax rate and a borrowing rate of .14, the after-tax cost of debt is:

$$(1 - .46).14 = .0756$$

If the firm found that it could not use its tax shield to reduce taxes (say that its losses were so large that it was not paying taxes), the cost of debt would then return to .14. So a firm borrowing at a cost of .14 could expect its after-tax cost of debt to be between .0756 and .14 depending on its tax status. A change in tax rate would be another factor causing a change in the after-tax borrowing rate.

Debt Cost and Leverage

Previously we have assumed the debt cost to be a constant. We can expect the cost of debt to be a function of the amount of equally senior debt that has been issued or can be issued. Figure 3.1 shows the cost of debt as a function of the amount of leverage. We define the amount of leverage as the amount of debt (B) divided by the amount of stock (S) plus amount of debt (B).

Note that the cost of debt curve goes up as the amount of debt increases. We do not know the exact shape of the curve, but we would expect the cost of debt to increase as the amount of leverage increases. For example, if with zero debt the cost is .08, with .5 debt the cost is .10, and with 100% debt the cost is .12, then the cost

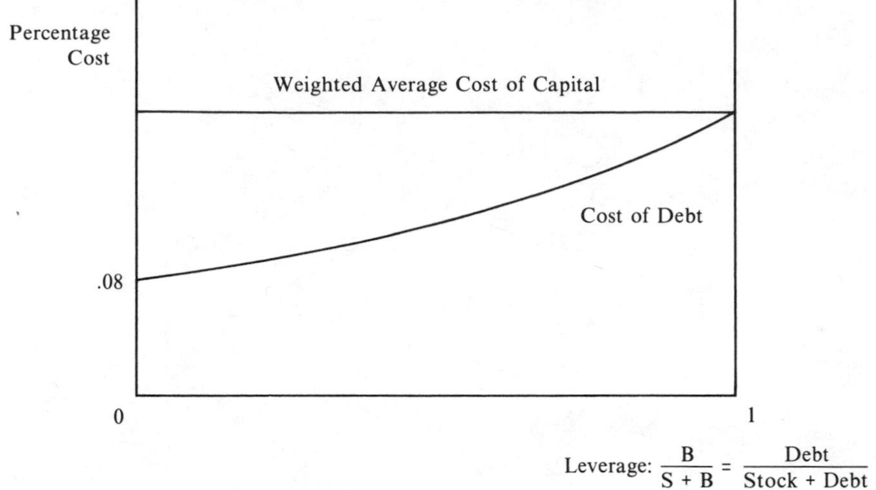

FIGURE 3.1

curve would be linear (a straight line). While a firm with 100% of its capital in the form of debt is difficult to find, the extreme situation is useful for defining the debt cost of a 100% debt firm as equal to the cost of stock equity for a zero debt firm (the debt is essentially common stock). At 100% debt the cost of debt is equal to the weighted average cost of capital.

One has to be very careful in saying the cost of debt is represented by the curve of Figure 3.1. In a sense it is and in another sense the curve does not represent the true cost. The fact is that the issuance of debt increases the cost of common stock (as well as the cost of other more subordinated debt) and thus has a cost in excess of the explicit contractual interest cost.

Consider a situation where with zero debt the addition of $1 of debt costs .08 and the addition of $1 of common stock costs .12. It would appear that debt costs less than common stock. However, assume that the issuance of debt leading to a capital structure of .5 debt results in a cost of debt of .10 and a cost of common stock of .14. With a capital structure of either zero debt or .5 debt, the weighted average cost of capital is .12. Figure 3.2 shows the situation.

We do not know whether Figure 3.2 accurately represents how the weighted average cost of capital changes as one adds debt, but we do know that both the cost of debt and the cost of common stock increase as the amount of leverage increases. It is inaccurate to state

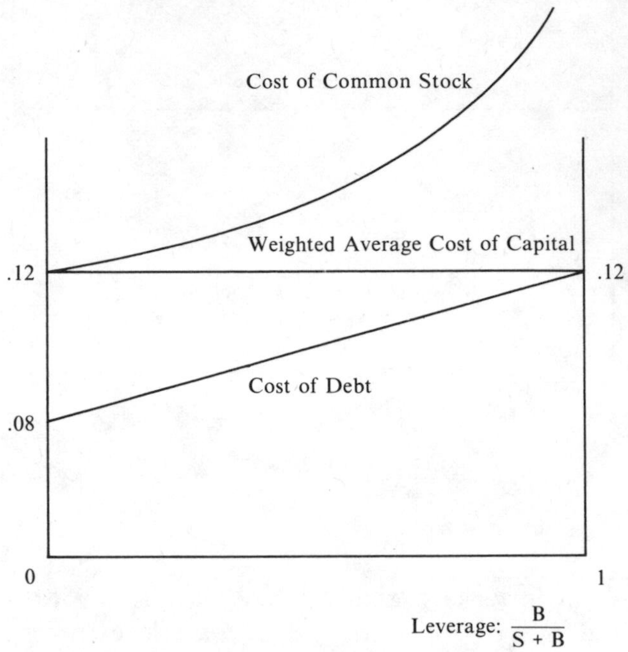

FIGURE 3.2

that the yield of a debt issue represents the cost of the debt, since the cost of common stock is affected by the issuance of the debt.

Using Debt to Reduce Risk

There are two ways of using debt to reduce risk to the stockholders. One is to use a large amount of debt, thus reducing the total amount of capital committed by the stockholders. In some situations the amount of capital committed by the promoters of the project may be close to zero.

A second type of risk reduction takes place when the investment being undertaken has very little risk. Thus the addition of the investment, even where there is a large amount of debt added, still reduces the risk to the firm. Imagine a situation where an investment earns $1,000 per month and the debt payments are $800 per month. If the $1,000 is certain, the overall risk of the firm is reduced by the $200 net increment, which can be used to pay other bills. The same conclusion follows if there is just a little risk, but does not hold as the amount of risk becomes large.

Debt Characteristics

Each characteristic of the debt contract affects the cost of the debt. For example, each of the following characteristics has a direct bearing on the interest rate the firm will have to pay if the debt is going to be issued at par:

1. Length of time until maturity (or the duration of the debt)
2. Degree of protection (e.g., a mortgage) or subordination to other debt
3. Length of noncollectability and the call price
4. Financial protections (minimum current ratios, working capital, etc.)

The way that the debt contract is written will depend on the strategy considerations of the firm. For example, if it is important that the firm not be locked into a high-cost debt contract, the firm will want to make the debt callable as rapidly as is feasible.

Also, if the funds are going to be used to finance long-lived assets, the firm will prefer the use of debt with long maturities. It is important that long-lived assets be financed with long-term debt in order to keep the level of risk at a manageable level, and to increase the likelihood that the cash is available to pay the debt. It is a risky financial strategy to use short-term debt to finance long-lived assets. The debt comes due before the assets have generated the cash flows necessary to repay the debt. The firm is then at the mercy of the lenders. While theoretically other lenders should be willing to step forward and supply the financing, one might not want to risk the situation where management knows the prospects are good, but the lenders do not have the same view of the world.

Nonconsolidated Subsidiaries

It is conventionally assumed that the debt of a nonconsolidated subsidiary corporation is not attributed to the parent firm. This has led to the financial strategy of forming financial subsidiaries that are highly levered but where the financial affairs of the subsidiary are not consolidated with the affairs of the parent. Usually the financial subsidiary's primary interest is to finance the receivables of the parent.

In addition to financial subsidiaries, foreign corporations and corporations where the percentage ownership is relatively small also are not consolidated for financial reporting purposes. There is a tendency to use a large amount of debt in these nonconsolidated corporations, since the debt does not appear on the parent's balance sheet.

It would be surprising if form were more important than substance. A financial subsidiary might be a useful form, but it must be for reasons other than bad financial reporting. If a corporation has sold its receivables to a financial subsidiary and thus lost a large percentage of its noncash liquid assets, its ability to borrow will be reduced. Thus the parent's debt capacity is reduced at the same time as the financial subsidiary is issuing debt. Also, many analysts will ignore the accounting profession's failure to consolidate and will prepare pro forma statements merging together the financial affairs of the several corporations.

Probably the benefits arising from having a captive finance company are relatively minor to the extent that we are looking for benefits from the nonconsolidation of financial position. If substantive benefits are to be found, they are likely to be found elsewhere.

Captive finance companies are said to increase the debt capacity of the parent and to accelerate the receipt of cash by the parent. It is true that the captive borrows cash and buys the receivables from the parent; thus the parent receives the cash earlier than if it kept the receivables and did *not* borrow. However, if the parent kept the receivables *and* borrowed, it would have the same amount of cash if it borrowed the same amount as the financial subsidiary borrowed.

It is far from clear why a captive finance company accelerates the cash receipts of the consolidated firm or increases the debt capacity of the joint firms. If such an increase exists, the explanation must be in some unexplained advantage of limited liability or a tax advantage resulting from having a financial subsidy.

Buying Insurance

In 1978 a major U.S. corporation approached 10 banks with an interesting proposal. If a set of the banks would be willing to lend anytime in the next five years $100,000,000 at a cost of 9½% per year, the company would pay the banks an immediate fee. The fee was to be negotiated.

Six of the banks said no. There was no fee likely to be paid that would compensate them for the risk of being stuck for a period as long as 5 years with a low-interest note receivable. Four of the banks agreed to negotiate a fee and a deal was struck.

The strategy implications are interesting. The banks that said yes could win if interest rates stayed the same, went up a little, or went down. Given the specific contracts, the corporation would win if interest rates went up by more than ½ percentage point (50 basis points).

The banks that said no to the possibility of discussing terms were obviously averse to the types of risks associated with a financial innovation. These banks accepted conventional risks, but they were not willing to accept a new type of risk. They might have invested $100,000,000 in a new hotel in Atlanta, but were not willing to risk having a 9½% loan outstanding if alternative loans were yielding more. But this type of situation occurs with noncallable long-term loans with fixed interest rates all the time. There should have been a fee large enough so that the six negative banks would be willing to say yes. History has shown that the fee had to be large (the prime lending rate soared above 19% in 1980).

The Investor and Debt

The issuer of debt should have an appreciation of the risks that an investor faces. The investor has many risks. The primary risk is the risk of default. Not being paid back the funds which have been lent is the worst fate in the minds of most lenders, but there are several close contenders.

With long-term debt an increase in the market rate of interest will result in a decrease in the market value of the security. While the loss might not be recorded, it still exists. Each period the investor has a loss of interest revenue arising from being locked into a low-paying security.

A comparable loss arises from having invested in a fixed-income security when a period of surprise inflation occurs. The loss in purchasing power might not be avoidable, but it is still a loss.

With more and more investors considering investments in other countries, the risk of loss from exchange rate changes becomes more significant. The fact that FAS 8—Financial Accounting Standards No. 8 of the Financial Standards Board—requires the recording of such losses has made the business community more sensitive to their existence.

If the investor has a security paying a high interest rate, the risk of having the security called by the issuing firm is real. A bond that is noncallable has protection against a situation where interest rates go down. Without that protection an investor is apt to find a high-yielding bond replaced by a new low-yielding bond.

Why Use Debt?

Why should a corporation use debt? The most obvious reason is that it needs an infusion of capital. But why debt rather than common stock?

Obtaining debt from a bank where the firm has a line of credit or a credit agreement may be a very rapid process, as is the issuance of commercial paper.

An important reason for using debt is that it is a fixed claim; thus its use offers the possibility of large gains to the stockholders if the investment expectations of profits are realized. This "trading on the equity" is a powerful reason for using debt. Debt amplifies the returns to stock equity capital.

It is conventional wisdom that debt costs less than common stock because of the tax laws. One has to be careful before accepting this conclusion, but there is no question that the tax shield of debt interest is very attractive. Aside from the tax shield, debt will appear to cost less than common stock because the conventional calculation omits the effect of debt issuance on the cost of the common stock.

In a situation where the present stockholders do not want their ownership control to be diluted, debt is a useful form of capital. Also, the existence of the capital need may be viewed as relatively short term, and debt gives flexibility, since its retirement on maturity automatically shrinks the size of the firm.

Once debt is issued, the cost of the debt capital has been defined by the contractual cash flows. This is useful where the revenues are also well defined, and one does not want to risk an increasing cost of capital.

A frequently offered reason for using debt is that it is a bad time to issue common stock. The common stock price is temporarily depressed, or the price/earnings (P/E) ratio is too low. The lack of faith in an efficient market is widespread. It is not unusual for management to think the market to be efficient (the stocks are reasonably priced) for other common stocks but not properly priced for its own stock. A much more acceptable strategy, in the absence of significant insider information, would be to conclude that the market has considered the same factors as management and, given all factors (including current interest rates and business condition expectations), has set the market price. Thus "timing" would be downgraded in importance in determining whether debt or common stock should be issued.

Temporary Debt

If management wants to bet that the market for its common stock is temporarily depressed, then a strategy of issuing short-term debt as a temporary source of capital is reasonable. When the market price of the common stock approaches its intrinsic value, the debt is replaced by the common stock. The objection to this strategy is that one does not know when this increase in stock price is going to occur. In fact, it is not clear the common stock is actually depressed. It might just be that management's expectations are excessively optimistic. Thus an alternative strategy is to issue common stock directly rather than first issue debt.

Arguments against Debt

The primary argument against the use of debt is that debt may cause the stockholders to lose their ticket to future profits if an unforeseen bad event occurs. The variance of the outcomes to stockholders (both ROI and earnings per share) is increased, with the result that a bump can throw off the stockholders. This prospect is not pleasant, and unfortunately its occurrence is inevitable (not for any one specific firm in a given year, but over a long enough period for several firms, the probability of financial difficulty becomes large with significant amounts of debt).

In addition to the increase in the amount of risk, there is the loss of managerial freedom. It is a rare debt covenant that does not restrict the actions of management in a manner that management would prefer did not exist.

A primary reason for not issuing debt is that there is a loss of financing flexibility as debt is issued and the firm approaches debt capacity. Management frequently will prefer a margin of safety (flexibility) that means the firm can issue more debt if it needs more capital.

The above paragraph implies the existence of barriers limiting the amount of debt a firm can issue. These barriers may exist in the minds of management (a formulation of corporate financial strategy), or they may actually be specified by the outstanding debt contracts. The preference of the bond rating agencies may also be highly significant. There are many types of barriers. For example, a firm might not want more than a .35 debt/equity ratio (debt divided by common stock) or less than a three times interest coverage ratio ($75 million of income before taxes and interest divided by $25 million of interest, or some variation of this). Once these barriers have been set, they preclude the issuance of debt that will violate them. Perhaps the exact limits cannot be justified, but they are effective.

Conclusions

We have discussed the nature of debt, why debt should be used, and why debt should be avoided. It is hoped that as many questions have been raised as have been answered.

In the U.S. Navy there was a saying that one never wanted a brilliant navigator, who tended to always *know* where the ship was. A less brilliant person was apt to be unsure and to check position constantly. In like manner a treasurer who is a bit uncertain about the use of debt is apt to better serve the financial objectives of the stockholders. Once this uncertainty of understanding is recognized, a corporate treasurer can move to the formulation of a financial strategy using debt in a manner that will tend to maximize the well-being of the stockholders.

Chapter 4

The Stew: The Weighted Average Cost of Capital

*My heart leaps up when I behold**
A profit I might make.
*Contrariwise my blood runs cold***
At risks I'd have to take.
For risk, as such, I've no desire,
But profits—there's the carrot!
The pot of gold I might acquire
Inspires me to dare it.

FMK

The financial officers of a firm are likely to be interested in four questions involving capital structure:

1. How is the overall cost of capital of the firm changed by decisions affecting the capital structure?
2. How much debt should a firm have and how will the firm's value be affected as debt is added?
3. What is the firm's cost of capital?
4. What is the relevance of the cost of capital to investment decisions?

Answers to the first two questions influence the types of securities that are issued to investors to finance expansion. The answer to the third and fourth questions conventionally impact the investment decisions. The cost of capital is frequently used as the cut-off rate (or the rate of discount) for investments, and this is of crucial importance. But the correct answers to all these questions are not obvious, and it is likely that a manager reading the literature pertaining to these questions will become confused. The chapter will attempt to

* This line is from William Wordsworth, "My heart leaps up," *An Oxford Anthology of English Poetry* edited by H. F. Lowry and W. Thorp, Oxford University Press, New York, 1933, p. 642.

** This line is from Ogden Nash, "Song to be Sung by the Father of Infant Female Children," *Verses from 1929 On,* Little, Brown and Company, Boston, 1952, p. 117.

clarify the issues and to offer some suggestions. First, we need some definitions and basic relationships.

Definition of Cost of Capital

Define the cost of capital as the cost to the corporation of obtaining funds. With zero taxes it would be equal to the average return that an investor in a corporation expects to earn after having invested proportionately in all the securities of the corporation. To simplify the discussion, assume the rates at which the corporation can borrow and lend funds are .10 and if the corporation has an investment that earns more than a .10 internal rate of return then it should accept the investment. Unfortunately the decision rule and the definition of cost of capital both gloss over considerations of uncertainty and risk preferences which we cannot ignore if we expect the decision rule to be operational in the real world.

The weighted average cost of capital (WACC) is equal to sum of the costs of several different types of capital each weighted by its proportion in the capital structure. Thus if the following capital structure and costs apply (there are zero taxes), we obtain a cost of capital of .10:

	Amount of Capital	Proportion	Cost	Weighted Cost
Debt	20,000	.4	.08	.032
Common stock	30,000	.6	.113	.068
			WACC	.100

Since the famous Modigliani and Miller article on capital structure and the cost of capital in 1958, a continuing controversy has raged about the sensitivity of the cost of capital of a firm to changes in its capital structure.[1] The controversy is of importance to financial officers, since the effect of capital structure on the cost of capital affects the debt versus common stock decision, and the determination of the cost of capital affects the cut-off rate that is conventionally used to determine which independent investments are acceptable. In addition, with corporate and personal income taxes, the capital structure affects the cash flows available for investors.

The broad assumptions made by the several parties to the discussions are worthy of review. The capital structure debate implicitly assumes that:

1. There is a definable something which we can label "cost of capital."
2. It is possible to compute the cost of capital with reasonable exactness and meaningfulness.
3. The cost of stock equity capital is the factor used (either explicitly or implicitly) by an investor in common stock in making investment decisions.
4. Different risk classes of firms have different costs of capital.
5. We can take the cost of capital and use it in making investment decisions. Using the present value method of making investment decisions, it is the rate of discount to be used in choosing the best of a set of mutually exclusive investments, and it is the cut-off rate for accepting or rejecting independent investments. Comparable statements can be made if the firm uses the internal rate of return to evaluate investments.

These assumptions are convenient, since they enable us to implement the very logical present value procedure, which works in excellent fashion so long as we do not ration capital or bring uncertainty into the analysis.

Although assumption 1 may be satisfied, there is no reason for assuming that the other four assumptions hold under conditions of uncertainty. No one has shown in a logical manner that the cost of capital can be computed in such a manner as to be used as a general method of evaluating investments, if the factor of uncertainty is taken into consideration. We will attempt to determine the effect of leverage on the cost of capital and on the value of the firm, but will not be able to determine the exact weighted average cost of capital to be used in investment evaluation. An average cost of capital of a firm cannot be used to evaluate all investments of the firm.

The Optimal Capital Structure

How much debt should a company have? It would be nice if we could answer that question in a simple definitive manner, but unfortunately the answer is complex and inexact. In this chapter we shall suggest some approaches to the basic type of capital mixture question, aiming to eliminate some misconceptions and suggesting some useful methods of analysis.

First, we will assume there are zero taxes. While this is an unrealistic assumption, it is useful in highlighting the necessary conditions for one or another forms of capital structure.

It can be shown that in the absence of taxes the value of a firm is not affected by its capital structure.

No Corporate Taxation

Assume there is a zero corporate tax rate, no costs of bankruptcy, no benefits from limited liability associated with being corporated, and all firms and individuals borrow funds at the same interest rate. A firm's value should not change because of a modification in its capital structure. The invariance of a firm's value to capital structure changes will be illustrated assuming an individual investor can borrow at the same interest rate as the corporation or is willing to purchase a well-designed mixture of debt and equity, or by buying a mixture of the stock of firms to attain a given risk level. In a sense we assume the investor consolidates the affairs of the two corporations in which she owns stock as well as with her own financial affairs.

EXAMPLE: Assume a woman has $4,000 to invest. She wants $1 of debt for each $1 of stock equity. The stocks of two firms are available for acquisition. The before-interest earnings of the two firms are identical. The characteristics of the two firms are as follows (assume values are being measured):

	A	B
Assets	10,000	10,000
Debt	0	8,000
Common stock	10,000	2,000

To satisfy the requirements described above, the investor could buy $1,000 (or .5) of B's and $3,000 (or .3) of A's common stock.

The financial position of the investor's pro rata share of the two firms is shown below. We assume she owns .3 of A and .5 of B.

Instead of buying a mixture of A and B, the investor could have borrowed $4,000 and invested all $8,000 in A. The financial position

	A	B	Total "Consolidated" Position
Assets	3,000	5,000	8,000
Investment:			
Debt		4,000	4,000
Common stock	3,000	1,000	4,000

would be identical to that indicated in the total "consolidated" position column but the column is now a consolidator of corporate and personal position.

Assume A and B both earn $2,000 and that debt costs .10. When the investor owns both A's and B's common stock, we have the following income statements:

	A		B	
Income	2,000		2,000	
Interest			− 800	
	2,000		1,200	
Percentage of ownership	× .3		× .5	
	600	+	600	= 1,200 income of investor

If the investor bought .8 of A at a cost of $8,000 and borrowed $4,000 at a cost of .10, she would have:

Earnings of A	2,000
Percentage of ownership	× .8
	1,600
Interest	− 400
	1,200 income of investor

In both cases the investor's income is $1,200. There is no reason to think the investor would pay a premium for B's common stock compared with A's stock.

The investor has accomplished arbitrage by borrowing on personal credit and by purchasing combinations of firms to obtain the desired financial mix (as well as the desired asset mix).

A third possibility for eliminating capital structure effects is for the investor to delever B by buying a mixture of that company's debt and common stock. Assume that B's common stock is selling at a discount because of the excessive use of debt. Assume A's common stock can be purchased at $10,000, and B's common stock can be purchased at a cost of $1,800. The investor can purchase .4 of A's common stock and when the company's earnings are $2,000 the investor has claim to $800 of these earnings.

Now assume the investor buys .4 of B's debt and .4 of B's common stock. The cost of the investment is:

Debt, 8,000 × .4	3,200
Common stock, 1,800 × .4	720
Total investment	3,920

The investment in B costs $80 less than an investment in A. In each case .4 of the firm's capital is owned. With $2,000 of earnings for B, we have:

Total earnings	2,000
Interest	−800
Common stock earnings	1,200

The earnings of the investor holding .4 of the debt and .4 of the common stock of B are:

Interest,800 × .4	320
Common stock, 1,200 × .4	480
Total earnings	800

The $800 of earnings are exactly equal to the earnings resulting from investing in .4 of A's common stock. This equality will hold for any value of corporate earnings (as long as the earnings before interest of A and B are equal). The same earnings are obtained by investing in B as in A, but the cost of investing in B is less by $80. This is a disequilibrium condition that cannot continue to exist. The market value of B must increase, or the market value of A must decrease. The values of the two firms must be equal.

Until we bring in taxes, there is no reason why the possibility of changing the capital structure should lead to the possibility of increasing the value of a firm. The strategies of buying the firm's debt and common stock or buying a mixture of low levered and high levered firms can delever firms using a large amount of debt. Also firms using too little debt can be levered by the use of personal debt to achieve leverage. Only when taxes or bankruptcy costs are introduced is there a logical justification for expecting there to be a value increase from classification of ownership claims as debt rather than common stock.

Corporate Income Taxes

In the last example we showed that without income taxes the value of a firm could be independent of its capital structure. With corporate income taxes and no personal taxes the value of a firm is greatly affected by the fact that interest is deductible for tax purposes and dividends are not.

EXAMPLE: A firm is considering a $2,000 investment earning $200. Debt is available at a cost of .10 per year. There is a .4 marginal tax rate. With different financing arrangements, the results would be as follows:

	100% Stock	50% Stock, 50% Debt	100% Debt
Earnings before tax	200	200	200
Less interest	—	100	200
Taxable income	200	100	0
Income tax	80	40	0
Income after tax	120	60	0
Plus interest	—	100	200
Total contributions to capital	120	160	200

There is a larger after-tax distribution with 100% debt than with any other financial arrangement. If the stockholders buy the debt, there is no additional risk to the stockholders, compared with raising the required capital using common stock. Since the total payoff to the capital contributors can be increased by using more debt, the value of the firm can also be increased. In reaching this conclusion, there is an implicit assumption that the capital structures will not be changed in the future time periods, and the investors holding the securities do not pay taxes.

The question as to whether or not the overall cost of capital of a firm is changed by decisions affecting its capital structure is answered with a yes if the assumptions are valid. If it were not for the income tax laws, the answer would be no. The present tax laws allowing interest on debt but not dividends on stock to be deducted in computing taxable income result in a bias in favor of issuing debt. The reason for this bias is most easily seen where the debt is purchased by the common stockholders. In this situation there is no increased risk to the stockholders, since they own the debt, but the tax treatment of the distribution of earnings is changed.

With all the capital in the form of stock, the cash distributions to the owners would not result in a tax deduction. With all the capital in the form of debt, an amount equal to the tax rate times the cash distribution would be a tax saving. In order to avoid being identified as a "thin corporation," the firm would want less than 100% debt, and to avoid arousing the Internal Revenue Service, it might not want to issue all its debt to the stockholders. But assuming the firm did not go too far, in the presence of income tax laws allowing interest as a deduction one can change the value of a corporation's earning stream by changing its capital structure. The clearest illustration of benefit arises when we merely change the form of the distribution (a dividend changed to interest) and the payments are made to the same capital contributors. Where the payment is made to a third party who is not presently a stockholder, the analysis becomes more complex since the risk changes, but the same basic logic applies.

A corporation that has debt outstanding or is issuing debt is better off with interest being deductible than not deductible, for tax purposes. For example, assume that interest is deductible and that debt is outstanding with an interest rate of .10 and the marginal tax rate is .4 (the after-tax interest rate is .06). We will further assume that the before-tax time value of money of both stockholders and bondholders is .10. In this situation the deductibility of interest for tax purposes enables the firm to undertake investments for the benefit of the stockholders with yields of less than .10 (but with after-tax yields of at least .06). Without the deductibility of interest, investments yielding less than .10 would be rejected.* The investments are desirable with after two yields exceeding .06 because of a combination of tax deductibility of interest and trading on the equity.

With an investment yielding over .10, financed by the .10 debt, the stockholders again benefit, but with investments yielding over .10, we have a situation of pure trading on the equity and acceptability of the investment is not the result of the tax deductibility of interest (though the fact that interest is deductible will make the investment more desirable).

* Insurance-type (risk-reducing) investments are not being considered here.

EXAMPLE: Assume $1,000 of debt paying $100 of interest is issued. The amount available for stockholders is illustrated assuming three different after-tax earnings (independent of financing):

	Situation 1		Situation 2		Situation 3	
After-tax returns (before interest)		60		90		110
Interest	100		100		100	
Less tax savings	40	60	40	60	40	60
Net gain to stockholders		0		30		50
Total amount distributed to capital contributors		100		130		150

There is no gain to stockholders when the investment returns just the after-tax yield of the bond. In the second situation there is a net gain to the stockholders of $30 that would not exist if the interest were not deductible for tax purposes. In the third situation the stockholders are $50 better off; $10 is a result of trading on the equity and $40 is a result of the tax saving.

If the investment had been financed by common stock funds, the amounts available for distribution in the three situations would have been $60, $90, and $110 instead of the $100, $130, and $150 distributed to the capital contributors when the $1,000 of debt is used.

A Graphical Analysis

Figure 4.1 shows the costs of debt and common stock and weighted average cost of capital for different amounts of leverage.

There are several points of interest. At zero leverage the cost of stock is equal to the weighted average cost of capital, and at 100% leverage the cost of debt is equal to the weighted average cost of capital. There are logical reasons for assuming that the cost of debt and the cost of common stock capital both increase as the amount of leverage increases.

We cannot be sure of the shape of the weighted average cost of capital curve. With zero taxes there are good reasons for assuming that the weighted average cost of capital is constant for all amounts of leverage. Given taxes, conventional wisdom among financial executives is that the WACC curve goes down and then goes up. That

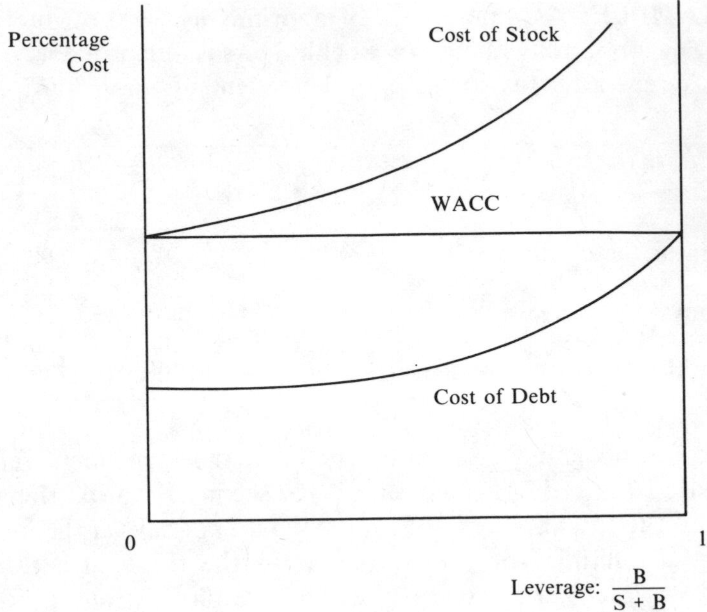

FIGURE 4.1

is, there is an optimum capital structure and management should aim to find the mixture of debt and common stock that leads to a minimum weighted average cost of capital.

The location of the minimum point of the WACC, in fact the existence of a minimum point, is heavily dependent on the corporate taxes and taxes on investors, the mix of investors, and the institutions connected with bankruptcy situations. Under certain conditions (e.g., zero taxes and zero bankruptcy costs) there is no minimum to the curves and the value of the firm is indifferent to all capital structures. With corporate taxes but no taxes on investors there are logical reasons for assuming that 100% debt is the most desirable capital structure. With more realistic assumptions, it is less clear that either one of these two positions is correct.

Certainly the evidence represented by the financial statements of corporations indicates a general belief that the use of some debt is desirable, but not anything approaching 100% debt (though banks certainly use a large percentage of debt).

The fact that an increase in the amount of leverage increases both the cost of debt and the cost of common stock is important. If with zero debt the first dollar of debt costs .10 and common stock costs .18, it is not obvious that debt costs less than common stock even though .10 is less than .18. For example, if the leverage were to increase to .5 and the average cost of debt is now .14 and the cost of common stock is .22, we have a situation where the weighted average cost of capital was .18 before the issuance of debt and after the issuance of the cheaper debt the weighted average cost of capital is still .18. If the new cost of common stock was just a bit above .22, the new weighted average cost of capital with increased leverage would be increased even though the cost of debt of .14 was significantly less than the cost of common stock.

Consider an operating financial executive attempting to decide whether it is desirable to move from a leverage of .35 to .40. An analyst can indicate the effects on earnings per share and the increase in risk, and can offer an evaluation of the effect on the firm's bond rating, but cannot give definite answers as to whether or not .35 or .40 debt is desirable. In some situations it is useful to know where exact conclusions cannot be reached, instead of pretending that exact answers are possible when they are not.

Tax Considerations and Costs of Different Capital Sources

Assume for illustrative purposes that holders of bonds, preferred stock, and common stock of the ABC Company all require a return of .10 and there is a .4 tax rate. There is $1,000 of each security outstanding (the return to each type of security is $100).

In order to have $100 to distribute to each type of security, the company will have to earn $433.34 before tax (See Table 4.1).

TABLE 4.1

	Before-Interest, Before-Tax Earnings	1 − Tax Rate	Necessary After-Tax Earnings
Bonds	100.00		100
Preferred stock	166.67	.6	100
Common stock	166.67	.6	100
	433.34		300

Since the bond interest is deductible for tax purposes, we only need $100 of before-tax earnings to satisfy the interest payment to the bondholders.

If we take the ratio of the necessary after-tax earnings to the capital contributed, we find the cost of each type of security is .10 (we would also say that the return to each type of investor is .10).

But let us consider more exactly the after-tax cost of debt. The $100 of interest results in a tax saving of $40; thus the net cost of debt is $60, or .06 (60/1,000 = .06). We extend Table 4.1 to show the after-tax cost of each security in Table 4.2.

TABLE 4.2

	Necessary After-Tax Earnings*	Tax Saving†	Net Cost to Corporation
Bonds	100	40	60, or .06
Preferred stock	100	0	100, or .10
Common stock	100	0	100, or .10

* From Table 4.1.
† Equal to the tax rate times the tax-deductible interest.

We have three sets of costs. These are set forth in Table 4.3.

TABLE 4.3 Costs of Each Type of Capital: Same Contractual Costs

	Necessary Earnings before Tax*	After-Tax Distribution as a Fraction of Capital*	After-Tax Cost†
Bonds	.10	.10	.06
Preferred stock	.167	.10	.10
Common stock	.167	.10	.10

* The earnings from column 1 of Table 4.1 divided by $1,000.
† From Table 4.2. Each number in this column is .6 of the number on the same line in column 1 of this table.

Instead of assuming that the returns of each type of security are equal we will now assume the returns are .10 for debt, .15 for preferred stock, and .20 for common stock. The magnitude of these costs are consistent with real world experience. Table 4.4 shows the cost of the alternative sources:

TABLE 4.4. Costs of Each Type of Capital: Different Contractual Costs

	Before-Tax Necessary Earnings	After-Tax Distribution	After-Tax Cost
Bonds	.10	.10	.06
Preferred stock	.25	.15	.15
Common stock	.334	.20	.20

In the current example the common stockholders require twice as large a return as the bondholders, but the before-tax cost is more than three times as large. The difference in cost between preferred stock and bonds is also interesting. The preferred stock is more than twice as expensive as the bonds despite the fact that the return to the preferred stockholders is only .15 compared with .10 for bondholders.

The differences in the cost would be less dramatic if a tax rate less than .4 were used. A higher tax rate would make the cost differences more dramatic.

The example aims at illustrating the different costs arising from the different tax treatments of the different securities as well as different costs arising from the different risks. One has to be careful before assuming that debt costs less than common stock because the after-tax cost of debt .06 is less than the .20 cost of common stock since the issuance of debt affects both the cost of the next dollar of debt and the cost of common stock. In addition, personal taxes makes the conclusion more complex than a comparison of .06 and .20.

The Time Value Factor and Investment Evaluation

All investments have three basic elements that an investor is likely to take into account in some fashion:

1. The time value of money; funds at different times have different values.
2. The fact that the outcomes are uncertain; attitudes toward risk are relevant.
3. The value of the information; the uncertain flows are spread

out through time, and at present we do not have the information as to the outcome.

It is not surprising that there are markets that enable different individuals to attain their own preferences relative to the three elements listed. We may have a person whose near-term plans are completely independent of the actual outcomes of an investment, who thus would pay nothing for information relative to the outcomes of an investment. Other persons (say two parents planning the education of their children) may be very concerned with the fact that they will not know the outcome of their investment for a number of years. The same types of differences among individuals with respect to time value of money and risk lead to a conclusion that exchanges will take place if there is a market for such exchanges. Now we shall discuss the time value of money and how it should be incorporated into the evaluation of investments.

Time Value of Money

The conventional present value method of making capital budgeting decisions takes the time value of money into account using the firm's cost of capital as the discount rate. This might be called a risk-discount approach to the cost of capital. The essence of this approach is that the average cost of a particular source of capital is defined in terms of investors' required return. This is the discount rate that makes the present value of the expected proceeds that will be received by the capital supplier equal to the market value of the securities representing that capital. With a business corporation, proceeds expected to be received by the capital supplier have some degree of uncertainty. This is clear in the case of equity capital; and so long as there is a probability of default, it is also true of debt. The excess of the cost of corporate capital sources over the discount rate that applies to default-free cash flows presumably reflects an adjustment for risk. Raising the discount rate to compute present values of cash flows of different time periods may not be an effective or useful way of allowing for risk. The use of a default-free rate of interest is not dependent on the cash flows of an investment being riskless. It may be used to accomplish discounting for time with uncertain flows, though the necessity of incorporating an adjustment for risk remains.

The Interest Rate

The classical approach to the description of the interest rate is to state that it is determined by the interaction of two forces which may be represented by schedules. On one hand is the schedule of consumption preferences through time given different rates of interest. On the other hand is the schedule of production opportunities which are acceptable for different rates of interest.

A dollar available today for consumption or investment is more valuable than a dollar available one period from now assuming investment opportunities exist.

Assume we can exchange $1 now for $1.10 of return one period in the future; then we may exchange some consumption today for a higher level of consumption next period. If the return were higher than $1.10, we might defer (or save) an even larger amount. What determines the amount of future consumption which we can obtain for deferring present consumption? One factor is the productivity of capital (i.e., the expected return of invested funds). There are two primary reasons why capital can generate an interest return:

1. Some types of capital increase in value through time because of changes in physical characteristics, for example, cattle, wine, and timber.
2. There are many work processes where roundabout methods of production are desirable. If you are going to cut down a large tree, it may be worth investing some time to sharpen your axe. If you are going to dig a hole, you might want to build or buy a shovel, or even spend the time to manufacture a back-hoe.

These characteristics of capital lead to a situation in which business firms can pay interest for the use of money. If you invest $1 in an industrial firm, the firm may be able to pay you $1 plus interest if your savings enabled the firm to use some roundabout method of production or to delay the sale of a product while it accreted in value. The interaction of the schedule of consumption preferences at different moments in time and the productivity schedule (supply and demand for capital) determine the interest rate, with both schedules being affected by the supply of money.

This discussion ignores the fact that both the present outlays and the future benefits may not be certain. If investors with reference to a specific uncertain investment indicate they require a .20

return, this does not indicate that their time preference for money is .20 per year. It remains for us to decide how a firm should transform future benefits and outlays back to the present, collapsing all the cash flows to one measure.

It is interesting to note the effects of a corporation erring on the side of using too low a rate of discount (i.e., the estimate we use is less than the unknown "true" or appropriate rate of discount):

1. More investments are undertaken by the corporation than should be undertaken. This company grows faster than it would otherwise grow. The effects on the economy would depend on the number and scope of companies which used the too low discount rate. Conceivably it could result in more total investment than would otherwise be undertaken.
2. Less money is returned to the stockholders than should be returned (some stockholders in higher tax brackets may be pleased by not receiving the funds at this time).
3. Longer-lived investments (or investments with more cash flows in the future) have a better competitive position in the decision process than shorter-lived investments (or investments with more cash flows in the early years).

One would expect the stock price of such a corporation to become depressed, with the ultimate result that the present management would be challenged by new owners and management willing to return excess funds to the owners of the firm.

The Discount Rate

The capital supplier expects payment from a corporation for two primary factors:

1. The utilization of the funds through time
2. The risk element associated with the possibility of the corporation failing to repay the capital or the interest on the capital

The cost of capital combines these two factors into one measure, a percentage. This percentage is then used in a basic discounting formula. It is assumed that a stockholder should multiply a future cash flow by $(1 + r)^{-n}$ to find the present value. The validity of this computation can be shown where r measures the time value of money. It has not been shown to be correct if r is a combination of two factors, a time value factor and a risk factor.

There are several ways in which we can show how a compounding formula applied to future cash flows fails to take risk effectively into consideration. For example:

1. Look at the effect of discounting $100 one period and 50 periods at two different rates. The effect of changing the discount rate is not easily forecast:

TIME	INVESTMENT A, .05	INVESTMENT B, .20	RATIO OF COLUMN 1 TO COLUMN 2
1	95.24	83.33	1.1
50	8.72	.01	872

Does the risk of B increase relative to A the further the cash flows are from the present?

2. Consider the situation where the immediate outlay is uncertain but future flows are certain. Should we use a high discount rate? A variation of this situation occurs when all the events occur immediately (or in a very short time period). The use of a high discount rate will not affect the present value of the cash flows, since $(1 + r)^{-t} = 1$ when $t = 0$.
3. It is possible to have a high expected present value and still not have a desirable investment. Increasing the discount rate may make the investment less desirable, but there is no reason to assume that it will effectively take risk into consideration.

The cost of capital implicitly incorporates a risk adjustment that is added to a time value factor. When the cost of capital is inserted in the relationship to compute the present value of an investment, this risk factor is then compounded. This may not be a correct way of incorporating risk considerations.

The rate of discount used in computing the present value of cash flows should not attempt to take into consideration risk preferences or aversions. It is appropriate that the time value factor is the result of a compounding calculation, it may not be appropriate to assume automatically that risk is the same type of compounding phenomena.

One possibility for the choice of discount rate is the default-free interest rate (say the appropriate rate on government securities). However, it can be shown that where the borrowing rate of the firm is higher than this rate, an investment with a yield less than the borrowing interest rate is not desirable if the cash flows of the investment are known with certainty, and if the funds have to be borrowed.

EXAMPLE: Assume the marginal borrowing rate of ABC Company is .10 and the rate on one-period governments is .06. Assume the firm has an investment that promises to yield with certainty the following cash flows with a .08 return:

Period:	0	1
	−1,000	1,080

The use of the default-free rate of .06 as the rate of discount would result in a positive present value, but a large number of these "desirable" investments financed at a borrowing rate of .10 could bankrupt the firm. Investments with certain cash flows and yields less than .10 should be rejected by the ABC Company if the funds have to be borrowed. If the funds are currently on hand, then a .08 investment is better than certain investments available to the stockholder yielding .06. But the funds cannot be borrowed at a cost of .10 to finance the .08 investment. If the cash flows are not known with certainty, then risk characteristics of the proposed investment, their effect on the risk characteristics of the current investments, and their effect on the cost of raising funds must be considered.

A problem in using the interest rate on government securities as the rate of discount in making investment decisions is that we have to decide on the maturity of the debt used as our bench mark. The interest rate effective at any time is a function of the length of time until maturity. We could choose the interest rate of securities of the same duration as the life of the investment. Another possibility is to use the long-term debt interest rate.

Another problem with using interest rates on government securities is that they are greatly influenced by government-controlled (or government-inspired) actions. Thus the interest rate on these securities may reflect bureaucratic decisions rather than consumption or production opportunities. This means that we cannot automatically accept the interest rate on government securities as a measure of the time value of money to the economy. From the point of view of the individual investor it does set an opportunity cost or minimum return that would be required from other investments.

The Corporate Tax Consideration

Assume that we are dealing with a company that is paying no corporate tax either because of the peculiarities of its business or because it is operating at a loss and expects to operate at a loss in the future. The government security interest rate is .06, and the firm can borrow funds at .10. The investment we are considering has certain cash flows. A correct decision rule would be to use the present value procedure. Investments with a positive net present value using .06 as the rate of discount are accepted if the firm does not have to borrow at a cost of .10. If the firm accepted investments with a yield of less than .06, its investors would be worse off than if the firm returned the funds to the investors.

Now we will assume that the firm is being taxed at a marginal rate of .4. How does this alter the decision process? It is commonly agreed that the cash flows used in the investment analysis should be on an after-tax basis. The corporation must be interested in what it has left after the tax bill is paid in order to compute the net benefit to the stockholders. With the cash flows on an after-tax basis, it is reasonable to assume that the discount rate should also be on an after-tax basis. If the company can borrow at a cost of .10, it can deduct the interest from its taxable income, thus reducing its tax bill. With a .4 tax rate, the net interest cost to the corporation will be .6 of .10, or .06. The .06 assumes there is no possibility that the firm will have losses for a series of years and not be able to use the interest tax deduction.

EXAMPLE: Assume a certain investment promises the following before-tax cash flows:

Period:	0	1
	−1,000	1,120

The after-tax cash flow of period 1 assuming a .4 tax rate is $1,072. (The tax is $48.) The after-tax cash flows are:

Period:	0	1
	−1,000	1,072

Using a .10 rate of discount, the investment would be rejected. Using the after-tax borrowing rate of interest of .06, the investment has a positive net present value and should be judged to be acceptable. The stockholders are better off if the investment is undertaken than if the investment is rejected. The corporation's net income and asset position will be improved by accepting the investment. With certain cash flows the decision rule for an invest-borrow situation would be simple: "Use the after-tax cash flows and the after-tax borrowing rate cost to compute the net present value. Accept if the net present value is positive."

If the investment is to be financed by stock equity funds as well as debt, we have a complication. The dividends paid to stockholders are not deductible for tax purposes. We would have to take a weighted average of the costs of the two sources.

EXAMPLE: Assume the time value of money of all capital contributions is .10 and that cost of both debt and stock equity funds is .60 before tax considerations. The capital structure is .7 stock, .3 debt. The tax rate is .4. The after-tax cost would be:

	Cost of Funds	Tax Factor	After-Tax Cost	Capital Structure	Weighted Average
Stock	.10	1.0	.10	.7	.070
Debt	.10	.6	.06	.3	.018
					.088

If all capital structures are possible, the after-tax cost can be as high as .10 and as low as .06. This cost only considers the tax effects, not risk.

EXAMPLE: Assume the borrowing rate is .10 and there is a .4 tax rate on corporate earnings. The firm can invest in a one-period investment costing $1,000 that will give cash flows in period 1 of $1,120 before tax. The taxable income is $1,120 − 1,000 = $120. The net after-tax income is $72, and the cash flow is $1,072. The following cash flows are after tax, but before financing cash flows:

0	1
−1,000	1,072

If the firm can finance the investment entirely with .10 debt, the investment is marginally acceptable. The financial-type cash flows will be:

	0	1
Debt (principal)	+1,000	−1,000
Interest		−100
Tax saving from interest deduction		40
Total	+1,000	−1,060

The investment cash flows are more than sufficient to repay the debt. The .06 is the minimum acceptable rate assuming 100% debt financing. Now assume the investment being discussed is financed 100% with common stock (the dividends are not deductible for tax purposes). The cash flows associated with the investment would result in $72 of additional cash being available for dividends. Assuming the investment is financed entirely with stock, the stockholders would receive a return of .072. This is not a satisfactory return to them, since they could have earned .10 in bonds or stock of a comparable corporation. With 100% stock financing the rate of discount should be .10 of the stockholders' time value of money (the opportunity cost to the stockholders). This assumes that the stockholders are not subject to tax on the dividends they receive.

We will now incorporate in one example the two complexities that have been introduced (taxes and availability of cash). Assume the marginal borrowing rate is .10 and the rate on one-period government securities subject to tax is .07. There is a .4 marginal tax rate. The following table shows the after-tax cost of obtaining new money issuing stock at a before-tax cost of .10 and by issuing bonds (also at a before-tax cost of .10), assuming a capital structure having .3 debt.

	Cost of Funds	Tax Factors	After-Tax Cost	Capital Structure	Weighted Average
Stock	.10	1.0	.10	.7	.070
Debt	.10	.6	.06	.3	.018
					.088

Now assume that the firm is holding cash that is available for investment. The best certain return available to the investors is .07. If the distribution would not be taxed, unless the firm can earn a certain return equal to or greater than .07, the funds should be returned to the investors. With debt outstanding the firm could retire the debt. This would be a .06 return after taxes, and this is not as desirable a yield as returning the funds to the stockholders on a zero-tax basis. If the distribution is taxed, the analysis is more complex.

WACC and Investments

The use of the WACC as a hurdle rate for accepting or rejecting investments has great intuitive appeal. For example, assume that debt costs .10 and common stock costs .16 in a situation where equal amounts of debt and common stock are used and there are zero taxes, so that the WACC is .13. Basic logic dictates that if an investment yields .13, the investors will obtain the return they wish. For example, assume a $2,000 investment will return $2,260 one period hence (a .13 return). The investors obtain:

Debtholders	1,100
Stockholders	1,160
Total	2,260

The investors receive the returns they require. The use of the hurdle rate of .13 insures that both sets of investors receive their required returns. The use of the WACC to evaluate the investments is effective in this simplified situation.

The difficulty with the use of the WACC occurs when the risk of the investment being considered is different from the normal risk of the firm or where the timing of the cash flows is such that the WACC does not reflect effectively the costs of time value and risk of the specific investment. The normal investment has a life of more than one year and has unique risk characteristics, so the use of the WACC as a discount rate is questionable.

Conclusions

This chapter has considered the basic nature of the weighted average cost of capital and the question of the appropriate manner of incorporating time value considerations in the evaluation of investments. The use of a default-free interest rate and the borrowing rate is suggested. However, it should be remembered that if the investment passes the time value test, it must still satisfy the risk criterion. So far we have considered the problem of adjusting for time value, not adjusting for risk.

Business decision making is constantly searching for rules that will lead to clearly defined accept-or-reject decisions. It is reassuring when we can direct our attention to one number and justify the decision using this number. One could recommend taking the cost of capital and accepting only those independent investments that have positive net present values. Unfortunately this is an incorrect decision rule. We do not know that one should automatically reject investments that yield less than the estimated cost of capital; in fact stockholders may want firms to accept many such investments where the investments are relatively safe or where they have risk characteristics that reduce the overall risk of the firm. In like manner many investments yielding more than the cost of capital should be rejected because of their risk characteristics.

The use of debt in the capital structure of a corporation does enable the firm to reduce its cost of raising capital, since the interest payments are deductible for tax purposes. The desirability of debt compared to common stock is dramatized when the debt is purchased by the common stockholders, since in this situation there is no increase in the risk to the investors. One could be led to the conclusion that a firm should issue as much debt as possible, with the stockholders purchasing the debt if they fear an excessive increase in risk arising from the highly levered capital structure. However, the tax authorities are likely to limit the amount of this type of debt that a corporation may issue and too much debt may result in the distribution being relabeled as dividends. The addition of debt, even where the debt is a relatively cheap source of capital because of the tax structure, does add risk. If there is no taxable income, the full cost of the interest falls on the corporation and ultimately on the stockholders. Thus we can conclude that the present corporate tax structure offers strong incentives to issue debt but that there are forces (the risk of bankruptcy and the conventions of the investment banking community) that restrain the corporation considering the issuance of unusually large amounts of debt compared with common stock. In addition, there is the complexity of personal income taxes.

We conclude that with the institutional facts of taxes and bankruptcy costs the cost to a firm of obtaining capital is a function of its capital structure. Thus with real-world institutions the cost of capital is a variable dependent on decisions of corporate managers. The rate of discount to be used in evaluating investments should measure the time value of money and not include risk adjustments, as long as risk is taken into consideration separately.

If we assume that the firm has optimized its capital structure and if we omit situations where the firm is not willing to enter the capital market, its time value of money is determined by the money market. The discount factor to be applied to a specific investment may not be equal to the weighted average cost of capital, which by definition includes an adjustment for risk. The cost of capital expresses in one measure the return required on the average by the investors. It does not express investor preferences for a unique investment opportunity with different risk characteristics than the average risk characteristics of the firm.

In future chapters we will again discuss the strategy considerations involved in choosing different capital structures.

Chapter 5
The Compromise: Preferred Stock

Preferred stock-we really wish you'd
Understand just why they're issued.
But never buy such stocks preferred
*If you've done so, you have erred.**

FMK

What does a firm do if it cannot issue debt but wants to use leverage? What if it wants more stock equity but does not want to dilute the position of the common stockholders? The security which supplies an answer to these objectives is preferred stock.

The issuance of preferred stock is a method of financing that, from the short-run point of view of the stockholders of an issuing corporation, has less risk than bonds and more risk than common stock. It is a fixed-return type of equity, but the dividend is optional. While one would expect the yield on preferred stock to be higher than bonds to compensate investors for increased risk, because of peculiarities in the law the before tax yield of preferred to investors is frequently less than that of bonds issued by the same firm, even though the bonds have less risk.

Comparing Debt and Preferred Stock

Preferred stock is similar to debt in that a specific annual payment is specified. With debt the payment is called interest, and with preferred stock the payment is called a dividend. The company's legal obligation to pay interest on debt is much stronger than its obligation to pay the preferred stock dividend. Failure to pay interest leads to bankruptcy, but failure to pay dividends does not;

*Please excuse the poetic license. There is a reason for corporations to buy (the 85% dividend received credit). There is much less reason for individuals to buy for their personal account. Author (not poet).

thus debt is said to be more risky from the viewpoint of the issuing firm.

All bonds currently being issued by corporations have maturity dates, and some bonds have sinking funds. Preferred stock may or may not have maturity dates and/or sinking funds. Obviously the inclusion of these characteristics moves the preferred stock in the direction of being more like debt than like common stock. There have been recent issues of preferred stock with provision for repurchase each year for a sinking fund or with provision for mandatory redemption.

A maturity date is considered by the tax courts to be a necessary condition for the security to be classified as debt (though there is no essential reason for this requirement). If there is a maturity date, there must be some provision for retiring debt. Provision is commonly made in the form of a sinking fund. A maturity date imposes more risk of being unable to pay on the borrower. If the firm does not have the funds for repayment at the maturity date, it may be forced into receivership. Preferred stock has no such risk if no provision is made for retirement, and even where the preferred stock has a maturity date, it is difficult for the preferred shareholder to force the issuing firm into bankruptcy.

The investor holding a debt instrument in a given corporation is subject to less risk than someone having an equal dollar investment in preferred stock of the same corporation, since the debtholders have prior claims to assets in case of liquidation and have first claim to earnings. The counterpart of this is that the stockholders of a corporation issuing debt have more risk at the time of issue than the stockholders of an otherwise identical firm issuing preferred stock. The statement requires two explanatory qualifications. First, the average life or duration of the two securities may be different. Secondly, while the issuance of debt results in more risk to the corporation's stockholders as long as it is outstanding, the after-tax cost of debt is likely to be lower than the after-tax cost of preferred stock, since dividends are not generally deductible. Assume the bonds and preferred are both issued to yield .10 and there is a .46 corporate tax rate. The after-tax costs are:

	Contractual Yields	Tax Savings	After-Tax Yields
Bonds	.10	.046	.054
Preferred stock	.10	0	.10

To pay the .10 contractual interest, the corporation would have to earn .10 before tax. To pay the .10 dividend, the corporation would have to earn .10/(1-.46) = .185 before tax (the tax would be .085 and the after-tax return would be .10).

Corporations can frequently issue preferred stock at slightly lower yields than they can issue debt at, since there is a tax advantage to corporate purchasers of preferred stock compared with bonds. The corporate investor receives a .85 taxable income credit for dividends received; thus only .15 of the dividends received by a corporate investor are taxed. An insurance company wanting fairly certain (predictable) returns has an incentive to purchase some preferred stock rather than debt, since $100 of preferred stock dividends will result in only $15 of taxable income but $100 of interest will result in $100 of taxable income.

The existence of the dividend-received credit does not necessarily imply that debt does not have a tax advantage compared with preferred stock. It is sometimes incorrectly concluded that the dividend-received credit makes it desirable for corporations to issue preferred stock rather than debt. The credit makes it easier to sell (issue) preferred stock, but the credit cannot overcome the tax deductibility of the debt interest.

EXAMPLE: Assume a firm has $100 of net revenue (before tax). The corporate tax rate is .40. Compare the net returns to a corporate investor if $1,000 of bonds were issued to yield .10 with those from $1,000 of preferred stock to yield .06.

	Calculation for: Preferred Stock	Bonds
Net revenue	100	100
Tax	40	0
Dividend (interest)	60	100
Amount taxable to investing corporation	9	100
Tax (.4)	3.60	40
Net return	56.40	60

The bonds lead to a larger conservation of cash for the joint affairs of the issuer and investor than the preferred stock.

Comparing Bond Risk and Preferred Stock Risk: Different Durations

There is no question that a given amount of debt imposes more risk on the stockholders of a corporation than an equal amount of preferred stock at a particular moment in time (time of issue). Preferred stock dividends may be passed over by a corporation with much less severe consequences than the passing over of bond interest. Despite this fact, the question of whether preferred stock or bonds impose more risk on stockholders of the issuing corporation is not clear-cut. A complicating factor arises because the two securities issued at the same time may not be outstanding for the same period of time. Let us assume in an attempt to compare the relative desirability of issuing debt and preferred stock that the difference between the bond interest and preferred stock dividends (both on an after-tax basis) are used to retire the bonds. In this situation, assuming the yields required by investors of the two securities are reasonably close, and that the after-tax interest cost is less than the after-tax preferred stock dividend cost, in a finite number of years the bond can be completely retired using only these savings to accomplish the retirements.

EXAMPLE: A company is considering issuing $10,000,000 of 40-year bonds or preferred stock. The bonds can be issued to yield .10 and the preferred stock to yield .12. The corporate tax rate is .46. We want to compute the numbers of years it would take for the tax savings to be used to retire the bonds (the tax savings are adjusted for any difference in yields).

	Preferred Stock	Bonds
Dividends (or interest)	1,200,000	1,000,000
Tax saving	0	460,000
Net cost	1,200,000	540,000

The net savings using bonds compared to preferred stock are $660,000 per year. We can set the present value of these savings to be equal to the present value of the $10,000,000 of debt (or equivalently we can equate the future value of the savings to the terminal values). Using the after-tax borrowing rate of .054 as the discount rate, we find by trial and error, or by solving directly for the number of years, that it takes a little over 11 years to retire the debt. In 11-plus years the bonds will be retired, and this will take no more of a cash outlay than if preferred stock were issued and not retired. The bonds can be retired as the savings are realized or at the end of 11 years (assuming the savings can be reinvested to earn .054). The timing of retirement does not affect the calculation of 11-plus years.

We can solve analytically for the length of time required for the annual savings from the use of debt to be sufficient to retire the otherwise outstanding preferred stock. As long as the dividend payment of the preferred stock is larger than the after-tax cost of the debt, the savings can be used to retire the debt.

The important advantage of preferred stock compared with debt in a risk comparison is that if a preferred stock dividend is passed over, the company is not in default as it would be if an interest payment were passed.

While bonds have a clear-cut tax advantage over preferred stock, it can be argued that if the corporation has reached its limit of debt issuance, preferred stock may be the only feasible alternative. But if preferred stock is issued, the corporation wants to have the right to call the preferred.

The comparison of debt versus preferred stock is similar to the comparison of debt and common stock. Since the present tax laws allow interest as a deduction and do not allow the deduction of dividends on stock, debt tends to have an economic advantage over common stock at the corporate level.

Preferred Stock versus Common Stock

In comparing the issuance of preferred stock and the issuance of common stock, it is easy to confound the question being studied by comparing preferred stock and the retention of earnings. When this is done, there are two decisions being considered, one whether or not to pay dividends or retain, and the other whether it is more desirable to finance the investments with common stock or preferred stock.

Let us initially assume that shares of preferred stock and common stock are selling at the same price and are both paying cash dividends (with the preferred stock dividend being the larger). The common stockholder has better prospects of capital gains than the holders of preferred stock. The primary advantage to an investor holding preferred stock compared with common stock is that the preferred stock return is somewhat more predictable since the maximum preferred stock dividend is defined by the contract. Unless the stock is participating preferred (sharing in higher earnings), the dividend rate will be specified on the certificate and the company will generally make a real effort to try to avoid defaulting on that dividend. Since the return to preferred stock is reasonably well defined and since the preferred stockholders precede the common stockholders (the preferred dividends are paid before the common dividends), preferred stock is a popular type of security for mergers and acquisitions where the sellers want a well defined return each year.

The seller of a firm wants to avoid the taxes that are imposed if cash or debt is received as payment but wants more safety than is offered by common stock. Dividends of both common and preferred stock are taxed as ordinary income, but since the common stock offers better likelihood of capital gains, there are tax advantages associated with the common stock not available to the preferred stock. This advantage can be exploited even more by shifting to earnings retention for common stock rather than cash dividends. The prospect of the capital gains treatment adds to the relative advantage of common stock compared to preferred stock for high-tax-paying investors.

Why Issue?

Why and when should a firm consider issuing preferred stock?

In the first place, preferred stock is a form of raising capital, and in a situation where the firm is bumping up against debt capacity, preferred stock should be considered. It can be said that the issuance of the equity capital protects the current bond rating of the company.

A second time for considering preferred stock is when the company is in a zero tax status and is likely to continue in that status in the foreseeable future. The tax shield of debt interest has little or no value. The cost gap between preferred and debt is closed considerably when the corporation's tax rate is zero.

In 1976 Pacific Gas and Electric Company issued $110,000,000 of redeemable preferred stock (the price to Pacific was $27.50, and the proceeds to the company were $26.55). The stock was redeemable at $30 at any time prior to April 30, 1981, and at decreasing prices after that date. The issue reduced the proportion of mortgage bonds in the capital structure from 50.4% to 49.6% and increased its proportion of preferred stock from 12.9% to 14.3%. These numbers are more or less typical of public utility capital structures.

The annual dividend requirement on the new preferred stock would be $10,180,000 and the total preferred stock dividend requirement for all outstanding preferred stock would be $66,540,000. Assuming a .48 tax rate for the time period in question, this would require before-tax earnings of 66,540,000 / (1 − .48) = $128,-000,000. The loss of tax shield by Pacific is partially made up of the fact that an insurance company buying the shares has a .85 dividend-received credit. Thus the insurance companies holding the securities pay less on the $66,540,000 of dividends than would be paid on an identical amount of debt interest. While not compensating for the loss of interest tax shield, the dividend received credit does close the gap. It is at least a ball game. If we found that Pacific did not have a .48 tax rate, but rather was paying little or no taxes, preferred stock would go up on the choice scale. In fact, an inspection of Pacific's 1975 income statement reveals that income tax expense for the year was negative. An additional tax shield from more interest was not needed in 1975 to reduce the taxes of that year.

A third reason for issuing preferred stock has to do with acquisitions. The sellers of a firm frequently like the quasi-contractual nature of the preferred stock dividend compared with the common stock dividend. They feel they have somewhat more protection than with common stock. Debt would be even better, but the acquiring firm might not want to issue more debt in order to avoid weakening its capital structure.

A fourth reason for issuing preferred stock is that it might appear to have a lower cost than common stock. Consider a situation where the common stock is selling at a P/E of 6 and preferred stock can be issued to yield .10. There are managers who will take the reciprocal of the P/E and conclude that the cost of stock equity is .167. Since preferred stock can be issued to yield .10, it would appear that preferred stock is cheaper than common stock. It should be remembered that issuance of preferred stock at .10 will result in a higher cost to the common stock, since there will be another party having claims ahead of the common stockholders on payday. This "cost" is implicit and thus difficult to measure exactly, but it does exist. Secondly, if the .167 is the result of the market expecting a decline in earnings to the common stock, the discount rate required by the stockholders (the cost of stock equity) may actually be less than the ratio of earnings to price.

Public utilities find it useful to issue preferred stock for two reasons. First, insurance companies, given the 85% dividend-received credit, like to buy it. Secondly, since the dividend cost is explicit, state regulatory commissions find it easy to accept the preferred stock cost measure. With common stock there are no objective measures of the cost of common stock equity, and thus the cost estimate of common stock equity is apt to be affected downward by the biases of a consumer-oriented commission.

Another argument in favor of preferred stock as against common stock arises when the common stock is selling below its book value. The issuance of more common stock would "dilute" the book value per share. It is difficult to give much weight to this reason.

A minor reason sometimes perceived to be important is that the firm holding preferred stock as an investment can carry its investment at cost rather than market value for accounting purposes. Investment managers who want to avoid fluctuations in value and resulting income effects find preferred stock a relatively attractive investment outlet.

From the point of view of an issuing corporation's common stockholders, preferred stock offers the opportunity to introduce a form of leverage (the preferred stockholders receive a maximum dividend return) that can benefit the common stockholders if the corporation does well in the future. The preferred stockholders do not participate in any bonanza that might occur, since their dividend rate is fixed.

However, the fixed dividend can be a disadvantage as well as an advantage to a corporation. If money rates go down, a corporation can be stuck with a high-yielding preferred stock outstanding. In recent years many preferred stock issues have been redeemable at the option of the issuing corporation. This means that if preferred stock is issued to yield 9.5% and money rates go down so that price goes up for non-callable preferred stock and the yield of such stock falls to 5%, the corporation can call the current issue and replace it with securities paying a smaller amount of dividends (or interest).

It is not at all obvious that a firm's common stockholders benefit from the issuance of preferred stock (this is not to imply that they are harmed). It is obvious that the holders of common stock have a different risk situation than the holders of common stock. However, by the buying of mixtures of different types of stock and by the use of personal borrowing, the same types of risks and returns can generally be obtained as are obtained by the purchase of preferred stock. Market forces will tend to limit severely the advantages of capital structure manipulation unless there are tax advantages for one type of capital compared with another.

If the types of risks offered by the common stock and preferred stock purchased individually (not a mixture) are what the market desires and if the risks and returns cannot be exactly duplicated in any other way, then it is possible for a firm issuing preferred stock to sell at a premium. On a theoretical basis, it is unlikely that investors need the preferred stock to accomplish their investment objectives, but the existence of preferred stock in the capital structures of many firms suggests that the theoretical model is incomplete. Investors find having a broad spectrum of securities useful.

When we compare preferred stock with common stock, we find that preferred stock offers a type of leverage but that the investors by purchasing a mixture of securities can wipe out the leverage effect if they wish. If they desire the leverage and if the leverage of this type cannot be obtained in any other way, then at worst the preferred stock is akin to common stock and at best it might enhance somewhat the total value of the firm by offering the investors the form of investment that is desired.

Preferred Stock and Corporations

Corporations have an incentive to invest in preferred stock. With a .46 tax rate a $100 of bond interest earned will shrink to $54 after tax. Because of the .85 dividend-received credit, only $15 of a $100 preferred stock dividend will be subject to tax, resulting in $6.90 of tax. The corporate investor in preferred stock nets $93.10. Aside from risk considerations, a corporation could borrow at .10, invest in .10 preferred stock and make a profit if it had other taxable income. For example, assume a situation where a firm has taxable income of $1,000 and has $540 after tax. If the firm borrowed $8,000 at a cost of .10 and invested the $8,000 in a .10 preferred stock, it would now have:

Tax Calculation		Income Calculation		
Basic income	1,000	Basic income		1,000
Preferred dividends, 800 × .15	+120	Preferred dividends		+800
				1,800
	1,120			
Interest expense	−800	Interest	800	
Taxable income	320			
		Tax	147.20	−947.20
Tax rate	× .46			
Tax	147.10	Net		852.80

The net was increased from $540 to $852.80 as a result of receiving $800 dividends and paying $800 interest. Of course, the risk to the firm following this strategy has been increased.

This example implies that short-lived preferred stock could be an interesting investment for a corporation with idle cash (or the opportunity to borrow) and taxable income to protect.

Preferred Stock and People

Is preferred stock a good investment for people? A zero-tax or low-tax investor might find a high-yielding preferred stock to be attractive compared with low-yielding common stock, but probably the investor would be better off with an equally high-yielding corporate bond.

While straight preferred stock is useful to corporate investors, it is difficult to see its advantages for people type investors. Corporations should not expect to sell large amounts of preferred stock to people. A few investors might be attracted by high yields, but the primary market for preferred stock is likely to be corporate investors.

Preferred Stock and Accounting Policy

Prior to APB 16 (effective 1970), pooling of interest accounting could be used with preferred stock. Imagine a situation where a firm's stock equity can be acquired for $800,000,000. The book value of the stock equity is $7,000,000.

If $800,000,000 of debt is used, the acquiring firm will have that amount of debt on its balance sheet after acquisition. With pooling of interest, if $300,000,000 of preferred stock and $500,000,000 of common were used, the 10% preferred stock would be shown at less than $7,000,000. The preferred stock would be paying $30,000,000 per year of dividends.

While strange, the above type of situation can be found on balance sheets of major corporations. While the use of pooling has been tightened by the public accounting profession, the residual from past misuses still exists.

Amerada Hess Corporation's balance sheet in its 1971 annual report showed preferred stock at $7,606,956. The remainder of the stockholders' equity accounts either implicitly or explicitly referred to common stock. A footnote following the financial statements indicated that the aggregate involuntary liquidation value applicable to the shares exceeded the par value (the reported value) by $753,088,644. The market value of the preferred stock (using $110 per share) was $837,000,000. The income statement presented "net income" and "net income per share" but did not identify preferred stock dividends; however, the statement of consolidated retained earnings did contain this information. We find that the preferred stock dividend was $30,527,311 compared with the net income of $133,249,241 and the amount of $7,606,956 preferred stock shown on the balance sheet.

The Sun Oil Company's 1971 annual report shows preferred stock of $17,072,000 on the statement of financial position and indicates that this stock has involuntary liquidation value of $887,-738,000. Based on a market value of $36 per share, this stock had a market value of $615,000,000 and paid a cash dividend of $40,994,000.

It is not clear exactly what purpose the amount "preferred stock" shown on a balance sheet is supposed to serve. Currently the measure alerts the reader to the fact that some preferred stock is outstanding. The number shown—for example, par—is likely to be of no use to an analyst.

If the present practice is the best that can be done, it would be better not to show any amount for preferred stock and to indicate in a footnote that there is preferred stock outstanding but that no attempt has been made to account for it. This would be consistent with the accounting practice for stock options issued to management, but obviously it is not a desirable practice.

There are several other possibilities that would be improvements over present practice. These include using:

1. market value (either at time of issue or the current market price)
2. The present value of the preferred stock dividends, using an independently determined rate of discount
3. Liquidation value of stock
4. Call price of the stock

Any of the above would be an improvement over present practice. But gaining acceptance of a change by industry is not apt to be easy. Preferred stock frequently was issued in conjunction with mergers and acquisitions. The advantage to management of the understated preferred stock was that assets were also understated and thus future expenses will also be understated and incomes overstated. A proper statement of preferred stock showing its economic value would frequently have as by-product a depressing effect on earnings. From management's point of view this result would be undesirable, but the independent accountant's task is to measure economic events, not attempt to manipulate income or please management.

Finite-lived Preferred Stock

Preferred stock with a definite maturity has an interesting set of pros and cons.

The two primary objections are that a finite-lived preferred stock is enough like debt that some accountants (and the SEC; see ASR 268) think it should be classified as debt (at least, above common stock). Secondly, the fact that it has a maturity means there will be cash outlays. A treasurer of a growing firm does not like to see cash needed for other uses disbursed to retire preferred stock.

An argument in favor of a finite-lived preferred stock is the fact that the security becomes a much more desirable investment for a corporate treasurer who wants a high return but not as much interest rate change risk as accompanies an infinite-lived preferred stock security. From the viewpoint of an investor with short-term funds to invest, such a stock would be a very popular security, especially as the years until maturity decrease. The default risk would remain, but judicious investments in a wide range of low-risk firms could reduce this risk to manageable proportions.

Frequency of Dividends

How often should preferred stock pay dividends?

Let us assume that a $100 preferred stock purchased at $100 is paying $10 a year dividend. On the day before the dividend payment the stock will sell for $110, assuming that it will sell for $100 ex dividend and assuming one group of the investors wanting dividends are zero tax. Now assume a second group of investors who pay .7 tax on ordinary income and .3 on capital gains presently hold the stock. The investor holding the security and receiving the dividend will have the security worth $100 plus $3 after tax on the $10 dividend. The investor selling the day before the dividend will have $107 of cash. With zero transaction costs this investor can then buy a preferred share of a comparable firm after dividend payment for $100 and have $7 of cash left over. This is $4 more than the $3 that would result from receiving the cash dividend.

To justify a $110 price the day before the dividend, we have to assume the presence of investors with a zero tax rate. The high-tax investor described above will only pay something like $103 for the shares the day before the dividend. A zero-tax investor would be willing to pay close to $110 for the share immediately before the dividend.

The conclusion is that there is advantage to the investing community in having a preferred stock that pays a cash dividend relatively infrequently. Imagine a preferred stock that paid cash dividends annually or biannually or even every fifth year. This stock would facilitate interesting investment strategies for investors wanting capital gains. The plan requires tax rate differentials among the investors.

Preference Shares

Preference shares are similar to preferred stock except that they are likely to be junior to preferred stock (they will generally be rated one letter grade below preferred stock).

A Swap for Common

In the 1970s American Financial Corporation offered its common stockholders the right to swap shares of common stock for shares of preferred. The swap was on a one-for-one basis. At the time the common was paying $.04 per year, and the preferred would pay $1.80.

While the company was not obligated to retire the issue, it had the right to retire the shares starting in 1987 at $20 per share plus accrued dividends.

The stated objective of the offering was to give the stockholders the choice between a relatively certain cash flow from the dividends and the relatively risky capital appreciation from the common stock. An implicit objective was to decrease the number of shares of common stock and increase the earnings per share and the future growth in earnings per share.

One can ask why preferred stock was used and not debt. The transaction as structured would probably be considered to be nontaxable. A swap for bonds would be considered to be taxable. This is a strong argument against a bond–common stock swap. Bonds would also have the disadvantage of adding significantly to the risk of the stockholders' position. On the other hand, to pay $1.80 of bond interest, the firm would have to earn $1.80. To pay $1.80 of preferred stock dividend with a corporate tax rate of .46, the firm will have to earn $1.80/(1 - .46) = \$3.33$. Losing the tax shield of the interest is a major negative factor in deciding on the use of preferred stock. Assuming that low-tax or zero-tax investors will choose the switch, the use of a very subordinated debt would seem to be more desirable than the use of preferred stock. A higher interest could be paid with a lower after-tax cost to the firm.

Conclusions

Preferred stock should be part of all financial strategies in the sense of being considered, but should only be used in special situations. Until the tax laws are changed, preferred stock tends to be inferior to debt. However if a firm does not need the tax shield of the interest, the gap between the issuance of preferred stock and common stock is greatly narrowed, especially when the preferred stock is viewed as strengthening the capital structure. Also, preferred stock is a popular vehicle for achieving acquisitions. Finally, with the .85 dividend-received credit we can expect preferred stock to be considered an attractive investment by insurance companies, and by public utilities that want to fill the desires of insurance companies for this type of security.

Chapter 6

The Hybrid: Convertible Debt

Be alert to what is impending
When money to hybrids you're lending.
The danger here lies
Should the stock fail to rise
By the time that the "no call" is ending.

FMK

Finance officers are constantly seeking cheaper sources of capital. Convertible debt and convertible preferred stock are types of securities that receive attention because they offer a considerable amount of flexibility. Because of the difficulty of valuing these securities, they are extremely useful in situations where there is not agreement as to the appropriate cost of debt for a firm or when the appropriate cost, given a large amount of risk, cannot legally be charged (because of usury laws).

We will refer to convertible debt in this chapter, but an analogous analysis could be prepared for convertible preferred stock, or debt with detachable warrants.

Motivation for Issuing

There are several valid reasons for issuing convertible bonds. The primary reason is that it is an indirect means of issuing equity, though it might take some time for the debt to be converted into common stock. It is useful where the firm wants permanent rather than finite-lived capital.

In a situation where it is perceived that the common stock price is depressed, a firm might prefer to issue the convertible bond rather than issue common stock at a low price. However, it can properly be argued that there is more risk to the firm with the issuance of the convertible bond than with the direct issue of common stock. If the firm's fortunes were to tumble, there would be debt outstanding with resulting bankruptcy implications if payments were not made on time. This threat is not present if common stock is issued.

A primary attraction of convertible bonds is that a relatively low coupon rate can be set compared with a straight debt. This is a saving of cash paid out as interest as well as a reduction in the recorded expenses of the period. The accountant records the explicit cost of the capital (interest) but not the implicit cost of the dilution associated with the stock equity portion of the capital raised. Thus if straight debt costs .10 and convertible debt costs .04, $1,000,000 of straight debt would have a recorded interest cost of $100,000 and the convertible would have an interest cost of $40,000. Remember these are accounting measures of cost and not the economic cost that should be the basis of the decision when one is choosing between convertible and straight debt. The change in the number of shares committed is ignored in computing the explicit cost.

In some situations a firm cannot issue straight debt. Because of the high risk, a straight debt bearing the necessary high interest rate would likely force bankruptcy. The addition of a conversion feature allows the charging of a lower interest rate while at the same time giving the investor an equity kicker which will have value if the firm is successful.

In a situation where there is considerable risk, an investor might be able to evaluate exactly the acceptability of the rewards offered by straight debt. The payments are explicit and contractual. The rewards have an upper limit. With convertible debt, confusion as to the exact value of the debt is introduced. The immediate value of the conversion feature is difficult to determine. Setting the conversion price (the conversion premium) and the period of no-call (as well as the call price) will greatly affect the value of the conversion feature. Bringing these factors together to determine value is difficult. There is apt to be disagreement as to value among investors. A security does not have to appear to be attractive to all investors to be successful. The fact that a conversion feature disperses the judgments of the investing community is likely to make the inclusion of a conversion feature a good strategy when there is considerable risk in a firm's operations.

Why Not Issue?

The primary valid argument against the issuance of convertible debt is that it does result in a dilution in the stockholder's equity position. The holder of a convertible security can share in the winnings if the events turn out to be desirable. This is real dilution.

If events do not go well, with the result that the stock price does not increase, then an overhang of potential dilution is created, and there is still debt outstanding.

An important consideration is that financial analysts tend to consider convertible bonds as common stock equivalents in evaluating the common stock, and bond rating agencies tend to consider convertibles as debt in arriving at bond ratings. This is looked at by financial officers as a double penalty, and is considered as a negative factor arguing against the issuance of convertible debt. We will return to this point later in this chapter.

What Is Convertible Debt?

Assume a situation where a one-period $1,000 convertible bond paying .066 is convertible into four shares of common stock. Straight debt would have to yield .10.

The common stock of the company can either be $259.44 (with .9 probability) or $90 (with .1 probability). The possibility of only two events is chosen for simplicity. Assume the interest is received and then the bond is redeemed or converted. Figure 6.1 shows one interpretation of a convertible bond.

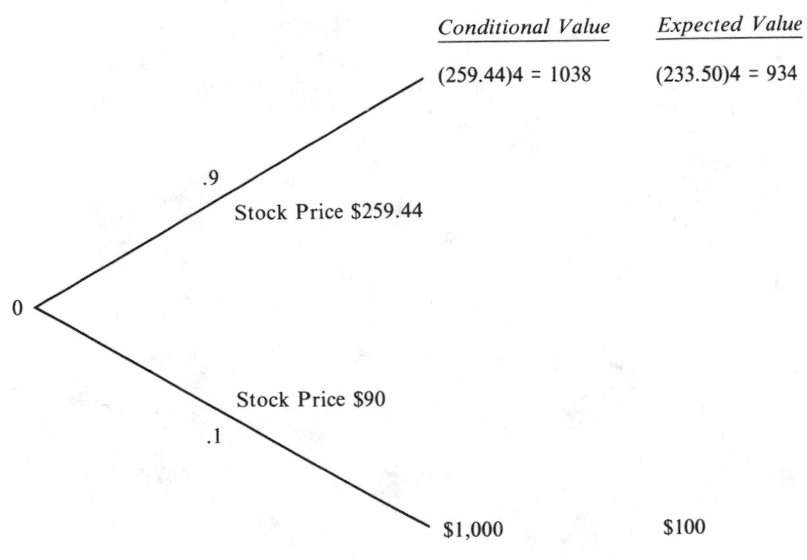

FIGURE 6.1
One Interpretation of a Convertible Bond

At time 1 the investor will either convert into four shares if the stock price is $259.44 or take the $1,000 if the stock price is $90. The value including the present value of the interest is:

$$\begin{aligned} \text{Value of bond} &= [4(233.50) + 100]\,(1.10)^{-1} + 66(1.10)^{-1} \\ &= (934 + 100)\,(1.10)^{-1} + 60 = 940 + 60 \\ &= \$1{,}000 \end{aligned}$$

Thus the value of the bond is equal to the present value of the interest plus the sum of the expected value of the converted bonds and the bond redemption price times the probability of no conversion.

A second interpretation is to define the bond as the sum of its value as debt plus an option to buy four shares of stock.

The value of the bond as debt is equal to its contractual flows as debt discounted at the cost of straight debt:

$$\frac{1{,}066}{1.10} = \$969$$

The option has value if the conversion takes place and the investor receives the value of the common stock, or 259.44 × 4 = $1,038. This has an expected value of 1,038 × .9 = $934. But the investor gives up the $1,000 redemption value with .9 probability. The net value of the option at time 1 is:

$$934 - 900 = \$34$$

The present value of the option is:

$$\frac{34}{1.1} = \$31$$

The value of the convertible debt is equal to the sum of its value as debt plus the present value of the option to convert. This is:

$$\begin{aligned} \text{Value of bond} &= \text{value of debt} + \text{value of option} \\ &= 969 + 31 = \$1{,}000 \end{aligned}$$

The third and final interpretation is to define the convertible debt as common stock with downside protection or insurance.

The common stock has an expected value of $242.50.

$$\begin{aligned} 259.44 \times .9 &= 233.50 \\ 90.00 \times .1 &= \underline{9.00} \\ & 242.50 \end{aligned}$$

The expected value for four shares is \$970.

But if the stock price is low, conversion will not take place and the investor will receive \$1,000 (with .1 probability). This is an expected value of \$100. However, the \$90 per share, or \$360 for four shares, is then forsaken. This has a .1 probability, so the expected value is \$36. The value of the insurance is \$100 less 36, or \$64. We now have:

$$\begin{aligned}\text{Value of bond} &= \text{value of common stock} + \text{value of insurance} + \\ &\quad\ \text{interest} \\ &= (970 + 64 + 66)\,(1.10)^{-1} \\ &= (1{,}100)\,(1.10)^{-1} = \$1{,}000\end{aligned}$$

Three ways of interpreting a convertible bond have been described. All three ways stress the hybrid nature of convertible debt.

Conversion Premiums

There are many ways of computing conversion premiums. Basically all of the calculations try to measure the gap between where the stock price is now and where it has to go for the investor to start making something from the existence of the conversion feature. The conversion premium is set by determining the number of shares into which the bond is convertible.

Assume the bond is going to be issued for \$1,000 and is to be convertible into 40 shares of common stock. The conversion price is then 1,000/40 = \$25. If the current market price of the common stock at the time of issue is \$20, the conversion premium at the time of issue is:

$$\frac{25 - 20}{20} = \frac{5}{20} = .25, \text{ or equivalently } \frac{1{,}000 - 800}{800} = .25$$

The market will compare this .25 conversion premium with premiums of other convertible bonds. The smaller the conversion premium, all things equal, the more desirable the security.

The conversion value of the security is equal to 40 times the market price of \$20, or \$800, at the time of issue. We can expect the conversion value of the debt to change through time. For example, if the stock price were to increase to \$38, the conversion value would be 38 × 40 = \$1,520. The conversion value represents the value of the bond if it were immediately converted into common stock.

One of the more important decisions involving convertible securities is the setting of the initial conversion premium. To attract investors, a large conversion premium would necessitate a higher interest rate than with a smaller premium. Also, a smaller premium would increase the probability of conversion. Most corporations issuing convertible debt hope that the debt will be converted so that the debt overhang is eliminated.

Through time we would expect the price of the bond and the price of the common stock to change, and these changes will change the conversion premium being paid by the investor. Assume the bond price goes to $800 and the stock price to $17. The conversion value of the bond is now 17 × 40 = $680, and the conversion premium associated with the current bond price is now:

$$\frac{800 - 680}{680} = .176$$

What Decisions Are There?

The firm must first decide on the interest rate that it wants to pay on the debt and then put together a conversion feature that will lead to the bond being accepted by the market with that interest rate.

As stated earlier, the conversion premium factor is to be decided by management. Other factors greatly impinging on value are the period of no-call, the call premium, and the maturity of the debt. The difference between the time of maturity and when the bond can first be called is of particular significance to the investor.

Why Should an Investor Convert Voluntarily?

There is a basic incentive for an investor *not* to convert. Holding the bond supplies protection, while at the same time the investor has upside potential because of the ability to convert into common shares if such a conversion is desirable.

If the common stock cash dividends become larger than the payments on the debt, the investor has a decision. The choice is between more cash with risk associated with common stock dividends and a safer but smaller amount of cash. If the investor converts, there is an assumption that the present value of cash dividends is larger than the present value of the interest payments. In addition, it is expected that the price of the common stock will remain sufficiently high so that one does not lose in the future by giving up the maturity payment of the debt. If all these conditions are satisfied, the investor has a conversion decision, but because of the risk it is not obvious that the investor should convert voluntarily. Except in rare situations where there are high safe cash dividends, the investor is better off holding the convertible bonds than converting.

Why Should a Firm Force Conversion?

The opportunity for a firm to force conversion arises when the price of the common stock is larger than the conversion price and the conversion value of the bond is larger than the call price. There are several reasons why a firm might want to force its investors to convert into common stock. It might be a way to strengthen the capital structure so that new debt can be issued.

Another reason for the firm to force conversion is that the cash flows of outstanding common stock are less than with debt. For example, a growth stock may be paying zero dividends; thus the after-tax interest payments are saved if conversion is forced.

Assume a $1,000 bond paying .10 interest is convertible into 40 shares of common stock. The common stock pays $1 per year dividend and is selling at a price of $50. The call price of the bond is $1,080. Should the company call? The corporate tax rate is .46.

The company can call, since the conversion value, 50 × 40 = $2,000, is larger than the call price. If the bonds are called, the investors must convert rather than accept the call price ($2,000 is larger than $1,080). The bonds converted into common stock will require $40 per bond of cash outlays for dividends. The bonds now require $100 of interest outlays, which are $54 after tax. The $40 is less than $54. The bonds should be called so that they will be converted into common stock. The investors will receive $40 of dividends instead of $100 of interest; thus they do not have their position improved by the call. The position of the present stockholders is improved by the call, since the cash flow out is reduced.

Earnings per share will also be affected by the conversion. Interest costs will be reduced, and the number of shares outstanding will be affected (the exact effect will depend on whether we are computing earnings per share with and without dilution and the nature of the conversion feature).

In some situations the amount of debt not yet converted has become very small and calling the debt is a reasonable way of eliminating an unnecessary financial complexity.

There is a theory that convertible bonds should be called as soon as the market price of the bond is high enough above the call price to insure conversion. If called at lower prices there would be cash outlays and retirement of the debt. Just as an investor prefers to hold the convertible bond rather than convert because of the downside protection offered by the bond, the corporation wants to force conversion so that the legal obligation to pay interest and principal are replaced by the more flexible commitments to common stock.

Maximum Bond Price and Call

With straight debt that is callable, the maximum price of the debt is set by the call price of the bond. The market cannot pay more than the call price if the bond is callable, since the corporation has the right to only pay the call price and retire the debt.

With a convertible debt the price of the bond can go above the call price, since the holder of the bond can convert the bond when it is called rather than submit it for cash redemption.

Despite the fact that a convertible bond can rise above the call price, before the event occurs we have to assume that as soon as the bond rises marginally above the call price, after the no-call period has ended, the bond will be called. Thus the call price sets an effective maximum expected price if the bond is callable. Before the bond value increases, the investor should not place a value on a convertible bond based on the hope that management will allow the bond price to rise above the call price without calling the bond.

The Overhang

If the common stock price does not increase sufficiently so that the firm can force conversion, it is said that the bonds "overhang" the firm. Frequently the threat of a bond overhang is offered as a reason for not issuing convertible debt. Let us consider the arguments. Assume a straight debt of 20 years maturity can be issued to yield .10 and a convertible debt of the same maturity is issued to yield .04.

Unfortunately the common stock price does not go up, and

after 20 years the debt is retired. Should the company be happy or sad with its decision to use convertible debt?

For 20 years the company paid .04 interest rather than .10. At maturity the same amount was paid as would have been paid with straight debt. At the end of 20 years the company is better off because of the 20 years of lower interest rates.

It is true that the company is sad that the common stock did not go high enough to justify conversion. But that is a separate question and should not be confused with the basic strategy question as to whether to use straight debt or convertible debt. If the price of the common shares does not increase, the firm may be sad that the convertible debt was not converted, but should be happy that the convertible debt was issued compared with the issuance of straight debt (it might have been even better to have issued common stock).

The First Call Date

Setting the first call date for a convertible bond is extremely important. After the first call date, if the bond market price goes above the call price it is likely that the bonds will be called. Since the bondholder has been receiving low interest payments from the date of issue until the call date, and since the call premium is likely to be a small percentage of the issue price, the actual yield to call will likely be less than could have been earned on straight debt (that is, the cost to the corporation is likely to be less than the cost that would have been incurred on straight debt).

If the common stock price increases rapidly during the period before the company can call, then the investor can earn a relatively high return. The value of the bond can raise high above the purchase price, and the return can be much larger than could have been earned on straight debt. This is assuming that the increase takes place before many years of low interest payments have taken place.

Thus the cost of convertible bonds may be high or low to corporations (ex post), depending on how rapidly the common stock price increases as well as how long the no-call period is. The longer the no-call period, the more valuable is the bond. The initial conversion premium is important, since it sets how high the common stock must go before forced conversion is feasible, and it also helps determine the profitability (cost to the firm) of any given stock price increase.

The Power of the Call Feature

The call features of a convertible bond are extremely important factors in determining a bond's value.

Assume a situation where a $1,000 convertible bond is paying .06 interest and a straight bond would be paying .10. The call premium is $80 and the bond is callable anytime after time 2.

The opportunity cost of buying the convertible bond is $40 per year. If the bond is called at time 2, the investor earns an extra $80. The cash flows arising because of the conversion feature are:

Time	Interest Opportunity Cost	Call Premium	Total
0			
1	−40		−40
2	−40	+80	+40

If the bond is called at time 2, the investor earns a zero return from investing in the convertible bond rather than investing in straight debt yielding .10.

If the bond is not called at time 2, but rather the corporation calls as soon as the bond reaches a price slightly above $1,080, the return to the investor can never be positive using the .10 discount rate.

The only way the investor in the convertible debt can win in this situation is for the common stock to increase rapidly enough so that the increase in stock price occurs prior to time 2 (when the debt can be called). The holder of the debt has to hope that the stock price increases rapidly enough to drive the price of the bond above $1,080 before time 2.

We can actually solve for the maximum number of periods that can pass without conversion for the investor to earn a .10 compound interest return (the same return that could be earned by investing in the straight debt). Remember, once the bond is callable, the holder cannot expect to receive more than the call price. It is only during the no-call period that the investor has hopes of making a large return on investment. The longer the period of no-call, the better is the probability of a large gain by the investor, since the common stock has a long period of time to increase above the conversion period.

Each period without conversion the investor is losing $40 of interest that could be earned. If the stock price does not increase rapidly (before the bond can be called), then the best that the investor can hope for is to receive the call premium.

Now let us assume the same facts but say the call premium is $120 instead of $80. Now if the bond is again called at time 2, the investor earns 100% incrementally on the convertible debt compared with straight debt:

TIME	CASH FLOW
1	−40
2	+80

The problem is that if the stock price does not go up rapidly and the debt is not called until time 3, the investor earns a zero return incrementally (compared to straight debt) on the convertible debt:

TIME	CASH FLOW
1	−40
2	−40
3	+80

If the bond is not called at time 3, even a lower return will be earned. These conclusions are all based on an assumption that the corporation acts rationally and calls the debt as soon as theory dictates that it do so.

Solving for the maximum delay time in calling, we find that with the given facts (including the two year no-call period and the $120 call premium) the debt must be called on or before time 2.75 years or the investor will not earn the .10 return available on other comparable investments. If the period of no-call was five years, then the investor would have five years in which to have the opportunity of large gains. With call being possible at time 2, the investor only has 2.75 years. The number would change with a change in the call premium or the difference between the interest rate on convertible debt and straight debt.

If bonds with short periods of no-call and low call premiums result in low returns for investors, they will also result in a low cost for corporations. We can expect the market to insist on reasonable periods of no-call, high call premiums, and appropriate interest rate differentials.

Other Conversions

We have been discussing the conversion of long-term debt into common stock. There is no reason why other possible types of conversions could not exist. For example, short-term debt could be convertible into long-term debt or long-term debt into short-term debt (this latter conversion would be dangerous to the firm, but in a sense it exists when a creditor can call a loan if a covenant is not fulfilled).

Warrants

Instead of issuing convertible debt, some firms choose to issue bonds with detachable warrants. The advantages of this security are that the debt remains outstanding (this may also be a disadvantage depending on the capital structure objective) and that new capital is brought into the firm on exercise of the warrants. There are also minor differences in the accounting for convertible debt and debt with warrants, but not enough differences to affect the choice materially.

Dilution

Anytime a convertible security or a security with warrants is issued, the present common stock ownership is being diluted. The amount of effective dilution will depend on the numbers of shares being introduced by the securities, the number of shares outstanding, and the terms of the conversion feature or the warrant. A warrant that offers the right to exercise at a price of $50 anytime in the next year when the stock price is currently $20 dilutes the present stockholders' position very little. On the other hand, the issuance of 1,000,000 warrants with an exercise price of $0 dilutes the ownership represented by 1,800,000 outstanding shares a large amount. This example is *not* fictitious. If you concluded that the above warrants are effectively issued common stock, you are correct.

Double Jeopardy

There are many business corporations which would not issue convertible bonds. One reason for this strategy is that bond rating agencies consider convertible bonds as debt and the bonds enter all calculations as debt. The accountant records the convertible bonds as debt. Thus convertible debt, dollar for dollar, has the same negative effect on bond ratings as straight debt.

While bond rating agencies consider a convertible to be debt, it is perceived by many financial managers that common stock financial analysts consider convertibles to be effectively common stock and compute fully diluted per share earnings.

Even if the securities are not always considered debt and common stock simultaneously, certainly the potential for the position does exist. It exists because convertible debt is part debt and part an option to acquire common stock. Thus the security is part debt and part common stock. The split can be made reasonably objectively (an estimate of the value of the debt component is not difficult to compute), but still the calculation of an equivalent number of implicitly outstanding shares of common stock that is represented by the conversion feature of the convertible is not easy. There is apt to be considerable difference of opinion. But in a situation where a \$1,000 bond is convertible into 40 shares of common stock, there is not likely to be an argument against the position that the number of shares implicitly outstanding ranges from zero to 40 depending on the price of the common stock. If the conversion price is \$25 and the common stock price is currently \$89, there are effectively 40 more shares outstanding. If the common stock price is \$1, the number of shares resulting from the conversion feature is closer to being zero than 40.

Earnings per Share

The issuance of convertible debt affects the earnings per share of a firm.

APB—Opinion 15 of the Accounting Principles Board of the

AICPA, issued in 1969—defined primary earnings per share and fully diluted earnings per share. A convertible bond will affect the primary earnings per share if at the time of issue the cash yield of the debt is less than two-thirds of the prime rate.

Assume the prime rate is .08, so that two-thirds of the rate is .0533. A .05 convertible bond issued at par will have a cash yield of .05, and since .05 is less than .0533, the bond would be considered to be a common stock equivalent. Since it is a common stock equivalent, the conversion feature would affect the primary earnings per share.

If the convertible bond now has a .08 coupon but still yields .05, it will sell at $1,374. Using a .05 discount rate:

Interest,	80 × 12.462	997
Principle,	1,000 × .377	377
		1,374

Now the cash yield is 80/1,374 = .058, and the bond is not a common stock equivalent even though the internal rate of return (yield) of the bond is unchanged.

This criterion of APB 15 has several faults. It compares a cash yield with the prime borrowing rate, which is a discounted cash flow rate of return. Also the two percentages being used reflect different risks and maturities. But most importantly, the measures reflect initial conditions only and fail to consider the changing economic conditions. We can assume the objective is to distinguish between securities that are more like debt than common stock, or alternatively more like common stock than debt. We can expect the changing conditions (e.g., a rising stock price) to affect that evaluation.

It is likely that corporations issuing convertible bonds will make sure that the cash yield at the time of issue is greater than two-thirds of the prime rate so that the primary earnings are not adversely affected by the existence of the conversion feature of the debt.

But even if the primary earnings per share are not affected by the presence of the conversion feature, the fully diluted earnings will always be adjusted. Sometimes the adjustment results in zero change. In some situations the dilution taking place is so severe that there are incentives to replace the convertible debt with straight debt to improve the fully diluted earnings per share.

Assume there are 100 bonds outstanding of $1,000 denomination convertible into 4,000 shares. The bonds are not common stock equivalents. There are 6,000 shares of common stock currently outstanding. The bonds pay .06 per year, and the firm is earning $20,000 before interest but after tax. The tax rate is .4.

The primary earnings are currently 20,000 − 3,600 = $16,400. The $3,600 is the after-tax interest cost. The primary earnings per share are $2.73.

$$\frac{16{,}400}{6{,}000} = \$2.73$$

For the fully diluted earnings per share we use the earnings before interest divided by the sum of the shares outstanding plus the converted shares:

$$\frac{20{,}000}{10{,}000} = \$2$$

It is possible to improve the fully diluted earnings per share by issuing straight debt at a cost of .10. Assume the bonds can be bought at a price of $100,000. The new earnings after the new after-tax interest cost of $6,000 are $14,000. After retirement of the convertible debt the earnings per share will be:

$$\frac{14{,}000}{6{,}000} = \$2.33$$

The fully diluted earnings are increased from $2, and the primary earnings are decreased. If management thinks the market is looking at the fully diluted earnings (or if we change the example so that the primary earnings are also $2), then there is apparent benefit in replacing the convertible debt. The replacement would be based on the cosmetic effect on earnings per share, not pure economic analysis.

If the bonds were convertible into 1,000 shares instead of 4,000 shares, there would not be the same incentive to replace the convertible debt. The fully diluted earnings per share would now be:

$$\frac{20{,}000}{7{,}000} = \$2.86$$

which is larger than the primary earnings of $2.73. The accountant would state that there was no dilution arising from the conversion feature and would only use the $2.73 primary earnings measure. In this situation the conversion feature would not affect the fully diluted earnings per share.

There are also interesting earnings per share effects arising from the issuance of stock options and warrants. The accountant attempts to give effect to their existence but does so in a clumsy fashion. With the so-called treasury stock method, the options and warrants outstanding will not affect the earnings per share as long as the stock price remains equal to or below the exercise price (there are complexities, but this is the essence). Only when the stock price is above the exercise price are the dilution effects of having options and warrants outstanding effectively included in the earnings per share calculation. We can expect sophisticated analysts to make different calculations of earnings per share than are offered on the formal accounting statements if the number of warrants and options is significant.

Other Equity Kickers

The president of the R Company said that it could profitably increase sales if only it had working capital. The loan officer of the bank said it would like to make a loan but the R Company had a lot of risk and a conventional interest-bearing loan was not adequate compensation.

How can we bring these two parties together? If the profit prospects are dim, there might not be any way of achieving a loan. But let us assume the president's optimism is justified and the banker believes it to be justified.

The first step is to make the debt convertible into common stock or to add warrants to the debt instrument. This gives the bank an opportunity to share in the good events if they occur. Unlike the fixed claim of interest, the bank now has an equity kicker that has no limit on the upside.

But both the conversion feature and the warrants depend on the market value of the common stock for their value. The bank may be optimistic about the firm's future, but is not willing to bet on the whims of the stock market. A way around this bind is to add a provision that ties the bank's receipts to the after-tax income measures of the firm. The banker has to be satisfied that the bank can live with the income measures resulting from generally accepted accounting principles. If it cannot, the exceptions must be carefully defined.

Again the objective is for the bank to share in the profitable years by a larger amount than the fixed interest payments allow.

This is not meant to imply that banks should always lend funds to risky firms. It does mean that if truly profitable opportunities exist, it should be possible for the firm needing the capital to obtain it from a lending institution.

It is true that a lending institution can structure the loan so that it only receives interest and the equity kicker is omitted. But this type of debt instrument can jeopardize the existence of the firm, and management might not be willing to accept the magnitude of the probability of bankruptcy that very high interest rates impose on the firm. The equity kicker arrangement with the bank is a way of spreading somewhat more risk to the bank but at the same time allowing the bank to have the protection of the basic loan agreement. In many senses the bank is still first in line.

Conclusions

There will always be situations where a firm cannot raise capital using straight debt because the interest rate would be excessively high (''excessive'' refers here to a comparison of what the borrower would be willing to make a commitment to pay and the rate needed to attract debt capital). An equity kicker can be used to reduce the contractual interest rate. One type of equity kicker is to make the debt convertible into common stock.

There is an implication in the above that only high-risk firms should follow a strategy of issuing convertible debt. A conclusion of this sort would be too strong; on the other hand, there is no question that the addition of a conversion possibility adds to the likelihood of a risky firm being able to issue debt. It is a way of reducing the contractual interest payments and at the same time offering the investor more protection than would be given by an investment in newly issued common stock of a risky business entity.

Chapter 7
The Distributions: Dividends and Other Things

"You buy the stock, you own the store."
Free enterprisers laud it.
But no one listens when I say
More dividends, and by the way
Now that my son's a C.P.A.
Let's have him do our audit.

FMK

Dividend policy is only a problem for those firms with positive earnings. It is both a problem and an opportunity for such firms. They have the resources (cash) with which to pay dividends, as well as the legal right (the presence of retained earnings). They do not have a legal obligation to pay dividends. Dividends are the result of a discretionary decision made by the board of directors of a firm.

In this chapter we will investigate different dividend strategies and suggest that the policy actually chosen must be heavily influenced by institutional factors such as the tax law and other rules of government.

The question of how a firm's dividend policy can be expected to influence the value of its shares is of interest to businessmen, investors, and economists. And yet until quite recently there existed no well-developed theory (or theories) of the relationship between dividend policy and share evaluation. In the past several decades, however, the work of Modigliani and Miller, Gordon, Lintner, and others has reduced this deficiency.[1]

Miller and Modigliani argued that with no income taxes and with other well-defined assumptions (such as perfect knowledge and certainty) a dollar retained is equal in value to a dollar distributed, so that dividend policy is not a relevant factor in determining the value of a corporation. However, when these assumptions are dropped, dividend policy increases in importance.

All Dividend Policies Are Equally Desirable. Or Are They?

It has been suggested that all dividend policies are equally desirable, since individuals by actions of their own can correct the dividend policy of a corporation. For example, a high-tax investor receiving $1,000 per year of dividends (in excess of the $100 dividend exclusion) could borrow $10,000 at a cost of .10. This would result in $1,000 of interest cost to balance the $1,000 of dividends. The $10,000 could then be invested in something akin to a nontaxable (immediately) single-payment deferred annuity, which would be used as backing for the $10,000 loan. It is not clear that the IRS would accept the transaction (one cannot borrow to finance such an annuity if the annuity is used as backing for the borrowing). Also, if one also holds tax-exempt securities, there is a question about the borrowing of the funds affecting the tax exemptness of the interest on the tax exempts.

Despite these objections, there is no question that tax shelter schemes of one type or another do relieve somewhat the impact of current dividend policies which do not seem to be optimum.

The Value of a Firm

Let us define the price (and value) of a share of common stock as equal to the present value of the next dividend (assumed to be declared and paid one period from now) and the price of the share at the time the dividend is paid.

If we keep repeating the substitution process, we find that the value of the firm is equal to the present value of all future dividends, where the word "dividend" is used to include all cash distributions made from the firm to its investors. We replace the price at each moment in time by the dividends that cause the stock to have value.

The fact that the value of a firm depends on future dividends does not mean the firm has to pay dividends now. The cash dividend may be a liquidation payment on termination of activities. It is only necessary that there be an expectation that someday there be a dividend.

In the absence of personal taxes and transaction costs the funds necessary to achieve growth targets may be obtained from retained earnings (thus no dividends) or as a result of new investment from the stockholders after a dividend (the funds are flowing in a circle from the firm to investors and back to the firm). Thus with a given investment policy, in the absence of taxes and transaction costs, logically dividend policy should not affect the value of a firm. Since taxes are necessary for dividend policy to matter, we shall focus on the interrelationship of dividend policy and tax regulations.

Two Situations without Taxes

Let us consider the two basic situations without taxes that lead to two different dividend decisions.

1. A firm only has earning opportunities that are inferior to the external opportunities available to its stockholders.
2. A firm has more desirable earning opportunities than it has cash.

In the first situation the firm should return the money to the stockholders. The external earning opportunities of the stockholders set a minimum cost that must be earned internally if the funds are to be retained. If the corporation can only earn a lower return than the stockholders can earn elsewhere, the funds should be distributed to the stockholders.

The second situation is more complex. Every dollar of dividends must be replaced by a dollar of external capital. If the funds are obtained from the present stockholders, there are transaction costs. If the money is obtained from new stockholders, the ownership of the present stockholders is diluted. If the funds are obtained using debt, the risk characteristics of the stock are being changed. There is no clear-cut guide for decision here. If the present stockholders want cash (and want effectively to reduce their investment compared with what it would be if the funds were retained), then a cash distribution is in order. However, the firm could retain the earnings and stockholders who want cash could obtain cash by selling a portion of their holdings (they would incur transaction costs).

Reasons for Dividends

Above we established one reason for dividends: the firm has inferior investment opportunities. A second reason is that dividends were paid in the past and a change in policy could harm investors. A third reason is that the stockholders deserve payment in return for the use of their capital, and that giving them cash reduces their transaction costs (they do not have to sell shares to get cash). Another objective reason for paying dividends is that trust departments are required to choose investments from a trust legal list, and the dividend record of a firm affects whether or not a firm is eligible for the list. It is desirable that a firm's common stock be on the list, since it broadens the market for the common stock.

There is a final factor to be considered once we introduce personal investors. It is not a reason for a dividend, but it is a desirable condition leading to the decision to pay dividends. It is desirable that the stockholders be zero-tax (or low-tax) investors. If the dividends are taxed at a high rate, we shall conclude that the firm's dividend strategy should be affected by the tax status of the firm's investors.

A firm paying dividends must have excess cash (compared with investment opportunities) and should have zero- or low-tax investors. If either of these two conditions is not satisfied, then we move from a policy of paying dividends to a policy where the situation has to be carefully analyzed. In the latter situation it is very likely that dividends should not be increased from their current level and in fact perhaps should not be paid.

We now make explicit reasons for retention of earnings. The three primary reasons are the personal tax effects (both tax deferral and a reduction in the tax rate from that of ordinary income to the capital gains rate), saving of transaction costs, and the fact that the firm has better investments than are available to the investors.

Paying Dividends and Raising Capital

When firms concurrently pay dividends and raise capital through security issues to stockholders, there are reasons to believe that a reduction in dividend payments could lead to an increase in share values. The importance of the problem is highlighted by the fact that a significant number of major corporations have continued to pay dividends while floating preemptive security offerings. Among the firms which have followed this policy in the past are Boeing, Celanese, Chrysler, IBM, Union Electric, and United Airlines.

Consider a situation where a firm has \$100 of investment opportunities. It has earned \$100 and can either return the \$100 or pay it out as a dividend. The personal tax rate is .65. If the \$100 is retained, only those investors wanting cash incur a transaction cost (they sell a percentage of their holdings). There are zero taxes to the investors who do not sell.

Assume the $100 is paid as a dividend and the stockholders pay $65 to the government. If they want to keep their percentage ownership unchanged, they must find an additional $65 to add to the $35 left from the dividend to return to the corporation so that the $100 investment can be undertaken. In this situation the $100 dividend is costly to the investors.

Note that we assumed a nonzero tax rate for investors and a competitive need for capital by the corporation. With these assumptions we can readily conclude that such a corporation should not pay a cash dividend.

We can model the effects of a policy of paying a dividend when capital is needed by the firm. We find that the dollar advantages of a retention policy compared to a dividend policy are large. For example, with a current dividend of $1 increasing at a rate of .10 per period and a personal tax rate of .7, there is an advantage of retention for four years of $1.93 of present value. This assumes the stock is sold at the book value after four years and the capital gain is taxed at a .25 rate. The calculations assume a .10 discount rate. Lengthening the planning horizon from four years increases the advantage of retention, since it increases the periods of saving tax as well as moving out the time of paying the capital gains tax.

We will consider the effect of retaining $100 for 20 years. Assume the firm can reinvest at .10 and then the gain is taxed at a rate of .25. A dividend now will be taxed at .7 and then reinvested by the individual to earn .03 after tax. We have:

Retained by the firm and then capital gain

$$100(1.10)^{20}(1 - .25) = 505$$

Dividend now and reinvested by the investor

$$30(1.03)^{20} = 54$$

Difference 451

You can change any of the assumptions and you will still arrive at significant differences in value after 20 years.

Dividends and Risk

In many discussions of dividend policy it is argued that under conditions of uncertainty an increase in a firm's dividend payout can be expected to increase the share price. This conclusion is reached by assuming (1) that stockholders have risk aversion, and (2) that the uncertainty of a firm's dividends increases as the time of payment lengthens into the future. It follows that investors discount expected future dividends using higher interest rates than dividends received in earlier time periods. It is then concluded that if shareholders are faced with the choice of a certain increase in current dividends or the possibility of a larger future dividend they will tend to choose the former, though the difference in amount will affect the choice.

In the situation we are discussing, the dividend policy affects the magnitude and timing of the tax payments. Decreases in present dividends tend to reduce the size of immediate tax payments. This permits one to make a strong case in favor of reducing a firm's payout ratio where funds are needed for investment. If not retained these funds would be obtained from the stockholders, after they have paid taxes on the distribution.

Some stockholders may not choose to purchase their allotted share of the firm's preemptive issues, preferring instead to pocket current dividends and sell the rights. However, we do not believe that the presence of dividend-preferring shareholders alters our basic conclusion that firms combining dividends with preemptive security issues ought to consider retaining a greater portion of earnings. There is little reason to believe that these shareholders will lose as a consequence of a decision to reduce dividend payments. To the contrary, they probably stand to gain. For a large portion of the firm's shareholders (those paying taxes at a high rate) who desire to have their earnings reinvested, as well as other investors not yet holding stock in the firm, there are good reasons to value shares more highly after dividends have been cut back. The dividend-preferring shareholders could quite likely sell their holdings at attractive prices, reinvesting the proceeds in firms that have a high payout ratio.

We are not arguing that all firms should discontinue dividend payments. There is a place for a variety of payout policies. We are suggesting, however, that there may be a high cost to investors if all firms cater to the dividend and reinvestment preferences of an average stockholder. The firm that combines dividend payments with the issuance of preemptive securities, for example, is causing some of its stockholders to pay unnecessary taxes. The firm can argue that it gives its investors a choice about whether or not they want to reinvest their earnings, but it does so at a high cost in terms of the additional taxes paid by a large number of its investors as well as the increased underwriting fees incurred by the firm.

There are stockholders who desire cash. A dividend supplies cash without the investor incurring brokerage expense. If the corporation, in its efforts to obtain additional capital, issues rights, the stockholder desiring cash will incur some transaction cost in selling the rights, but this cost will be smaller than that incurred with the retention of 100% of the earnings. If cash is retained by the corporation, the stockholders wanting liquidity will have to sell a fraction of their holdings to obtain cash, and this process will result in brokerage fees. Retired individuals living off their dividends and tax-free universities are apt to prefer dividend-paying corporations to corporations retaining income. While a 100% cash dividend has the advantage of giving cash to those investors who desire cash, the policy also results in cash being given to those investors who do not desire cash, and who must incur brokerage fees to reinvest the dividends. The retention of earnings gives the stockholders a form of optional dividend in that those desiring cash can sell their stock (incurring brokerage costs). Those wanting further investment merely hold their stock (with no transaction cost).

The arguments in favor of retention of earnings by some firms do not require that all investors prefer retention of earnings, but that some fraction of the market has this preference. There is a need for well defined securities that fit the investment preferences for a variety of investors.

Another advantage of paying dividends is that it helps avoid conflict with the Internal Revenue Code. The code provides for penalties if retained earnings are kept by a corporation for the purpose of avoiding personal income taxes. The primary purpose of the retention must be to advance the legitimate objectives of the firm, not to reduce the tax payments of the investors. We are recommending a dividend policy for firms that have a need for funds to carry out the normal appropriate investment policies of the firm. The result of our suggestion will be to reduce the tax bill of the investors, but this is not the primary purpose of the reinvestment. Nevertheless, it should be recognized that a clear-cut 100% payout of earnings is less likely to be questioned by the Internal Revenue Service than 100% retention of earnings.

A corporation using retained earnings bypasses the market forces, and this may not be desirable from the point of view of the economy. This assumes a more efficient allocation of resources will result from investors deciding what firms should receive additional investment capital instead of leaving this decision in the hands of the corporate managers. The method of taxing dividends and capital gains plus the presence of the costs of security transactions leads to a tendency for the corporation to retain the capital it needs, rather than for it to go to the market to obtain this capital.

Stock Dividends

With a stock dividend the holders of common stock receive additional shares equal to a given percentage of the shares currently held (the percentage must be small or the process is described as a stock split). One purpose of a stock dividend or a stock split is to reduce the market price per share to a level that is more attractive to the market.

Stock dividends are redescriptions of the holdings of the stockholders, but are not distributions of the firm's assets; thus they should not be considered to be the equivalent of a cash dividend. With a cash dividend the firm's cash and stockholders' equity are reduced by the amount of the dividend. With a stock dividend the stockholders' equity is not changed in total (individual components may be changed). If a stockholder holds 10% of the company before the stock dividend, the stockholder will hold 10% after the stock dividend. The number of shares involved would change, but not the basic proportion of ownership.

It is sometimes thought that a firm could issue a stock dividend without affecting the stock price. This is naive and incorrect. Whatever the total value of the firm before the stock dividend, it is going to be exactly the same after the dividend. Since the number of shares is increased, we can expect all per share calculations to be proportionally reduced.

The IRS recognizes the nothingness of a stock dividend and the dividend is not taxed as income. Even the tax collector recognizes that a stock dividend is not income.

Dividend Policy and Capital Structure

Because of the tax shield associated with interest, debt has a tax advantage at the corporate level. But bond interest is taxed as ordinary income at the personal tax level, and this is a disadvantage. Common stock has an advantage for the high-tax individual both because of tax deferral and because of the distinction between ordinary income and capital gains.

Consider a firm which earns \$100,000 before interest and taxes. The corporate tax rate is .4, the ordinary income personal tax rate is .7, and the personal capital gains rate is .25.

If debt is issued and \$100,000 is paid as interest, the *investors* will have after tax:

$$100{,}000(1-.7) = \$30{,}000$$

If common is issued, the *corporation* will have earned after tax:

$$100{,}000(1-.4) = \$60{,}000$$

The investor will net \$45,000, assuming the capital gains is equal to \$60,000 and that it is taxed:

$$60{,}000(1-.25) = \$45{,}000$$

Assuming a zero personal tax on ordinary income and a dividend of \$60,000 the investor will have \$60,000 which is still less than the net from bond interest. Assuming the gain of \$60,000 is taxed at the personal tax rate of .7, the investor nets:

$$(1-.7)60{,}000 = \$18{,}000$$

The example illustrates the fact that common stock may be better than debt from the point of view of a high-tax investor if the gain is taxed at a capital gains rate. In this example we are only considering the question of how the capital should be classified, as debt or common stock. Risk considerations are omitted from the example.

With a multiperiod case, the common stock alternative may be helped further by tax deferral.

This example brings together capital structure (debt versus common stock), dividend policy (the common stock alternative is enhanced by the retention of earnings), and investment policy (the retention implies a different investment strategy than if the cash were distributed to investors).

If we assume that different investors buy bonds than buy debt, then we can have the \$100,000 of bond interest taxed at a zero rate and bonds again appear to be sensible form of a capital. Thus the personal tax consideration does not eliminate the tax shield advantages of interest, but rather gives common stock a possible advantage associated with tax deferral and capital gains treatment.

The Acquisition of Common Stock

Major U.S. corporations have increasingly repurchased significant amounts of their own common shares. The reasons for this development and its implications for the theory of share valuation and for public policy, however, have been subject to numerous, and often conflicting, interpretations. In this section we will reach some fairly definite conclusions concerning the questions of share valuation. The growth of corporate share repurchasing has aroused considerable interest, and a number of explanations of the motivation behind this activity have been suggested. It has been argued, for example, that firms buy back their own shares to have them available to acquire other companies or to fulfill the obligations of stock option plans. Unquestionably, some repurchasing has been done for these reasons. Income tax considerations may make it possible for firms to acquire other companies more cheaply for stock than for cash, and use of stock options as a form of executive compensation has been widespread. However, it seems quite unlikely that the rapid growth of share repurchasing in recent years can be explained by merger and stock option plans. Most importantly, there is no essential reason why shares used for these purposes should be repurchased, rather than newly issued.

Corporations also repurchase shares with the intention of retiring them, or at least holding them indefinitely in the treasury. Several motives for such repurchasing activities have been suggested, virtually all relating the repurchase of the shares to the generation of liquid assets which cannot be profitably invested by the firm in the foreseeable future. In particular, it has been suggested that firms with excessive liquid assets have one or more of the following motives to repurchase shares:

1. Repurchasing shares is the best investment that can be made with these assets.
2. Repurchasing shares has beneficial leverage effects which cannot be obtained by distributing these assets to stockholders in another form, such as dividends.
3. Repurchasing shares, rather than paying dividends, has significant tax advantages for stockholders.

Is a firm's purchase of its own common stock an investment? Does a firm repurchase stock to produce leverage effects not otherwise attainable? What are the tax advantages associated with buying back shares?

The next two sections are devoted to a discussion of the investment and leverage questions. In brief, we shall argue that repurchasing is not an investment and does not produce "special" leverage effects. We then shall consider the argument that repurchasing shares can have beneficial tax effects for stockholders.

Share Repurchasing as an Investment

In this section we shall examine the logic underlying the argument that when a firm is generating more cash than it can profitably invest internally, share repurchasing is itself a good investment.

Share repurchasing does not possess the same general characteristics as other acts of investment, e.g., purchasing plant and equipment. Normal investments increase the size of the firm and do not decrease the stockholders' equity balance. A firm's acquisition of its own common stock, on the other hand, reduces the size of the enterprise. Specifically, the cash balance is decreased and the stockholders' equity balance is reduced. In short, repurchasing shares has few characteristics which identify it as a normal investment.

While share repurchasing is clearly not an investment by the firm, there is a change in the relative proportions of ownership if some stockholders sell their shares and some do not sell. The investors who do not sell are implicitly making an investment compared with the investors who do sell. Also, they make an investment compared with what would have happened if they had received a cash dividend.

Repurchasing and Leverage

It has been argued that the repurchase of shares increases the percentage of debt in the capital structure (by reducing the amount of common stock equity).

Even if we were to accept the argument that there is an optimal capital structure, we are still faced with the question, Why repurchase shares to change the debt/equity ratio, rather than pay dividends and accomplish the same objective? Buying back stock involves no changes in capital structure that could not also be obtained by combining a dividend payment with a reverse stock split. Both procedures have the effect of distributing cash to stockholders, reducing the firm's capitalization, and increasing its earnings per share, and thereby raising stock price per share (compared with what would have been if the number of shares had not been reduced).

Taxes and Share Repurchasing

The current tax laws provide powerful incentives for firms with excess liquid assets to repurchase shares, rather than pay dividends. Under the present tax structure many persons prefer capital gains to ordinary income. The reason for their preference is that the marginal rate of taxation on ordinary income is much higher than the rate on capital gains.

Consider now a corporation with excess cash that it desires to pay out to stockholders in the form most attractive from its shareholders' point of view. If it distributes the assets as dividends, they will represent ordinary income to shareholders, and will be taxed accordingly. If, on the other hand, the corporation buys back shares, a portion of its distribution will be regarded as a return to the shareholders' capital and will not be taxed at all, while that portion of the return which is taxed, i.e., the capital gain, will be subject to a lower rate than ordinary income. In addition, the investor who merely wants to reinvest is not taxed at all.

Given these incentives for returning cash to stockholders by repurchasing shares, a relevant question would seem to be, Why do firms ever pay dividends? One important answer is that many stockholders do not pay tax on the dividends they receive (e.g., Cornell University and low-income retirees). A second reason (related to the first) is that the receipt of cash dividends to low-tax investors reduces the transaction costs for those investors who need cash. But even if one were to accept the above explanations, the basic question still remains. Why do firms pay dividends to investors who are taxed at high ordinary income tax rates?

EXAMPLE: A firm has 100,000 shares outstanding and $100,000 available for distribution. Should it pay a dividend or reacquire shares? Assume the personal tax rate is .70 and the capital gains tax rate is .30. The initial stock price is $20. Initially assume the tax basis is also $20. There is an investor who owns 1,000 shares. With a cash dividend we have:

Dividend	
Cash received	1,000
Tax (.70)	700
Net	300

If the company acquires 100,000/20 = 5,000 shares and the investor tenders .01 of the shares held, we have:

Stock acquisition	
Cash received	1,000
Tax	0
Net	1,000

Even with a zero tax basis the investor would receive $700:

Stock acquisition	
Cash received	1,000
Tax (.30)	300
Net	700

But with a zero-tax basis the investor might decide not to sell. Not selling, the investor's percentage ownership goes up from .01 to .0105 (that is, 1,000/95,000). The investor has a choice of receiving cash (selling some stock) or increasing the relative investment in the firm.

In a world in which capital gains and ordinary income are accorded different tax treatment, the value of the firm's stock is influenced by the form of its cash distribution. In addition, with stock acquisition and a positive-tax basis, part of the cash distribution is not taxed at all. There are two factors at work that cause buying back shares to be more profitable than dividend payments (from the stockholders' point of view) under any reasonable set of assumptions that includes taxation of income. For one thing, part of the distribution under the share-repurchasing arrangement is considered a return of capital and is not taxed at all. Secondly, that part of the distribution subject to tax (i.e., the capital gain) is generally taxed at a lower rate than ordinary income.

Stock Acquisitions: A Flexible Dividend

One real advantage of stock acquisitions in lieu of cash dividends is that investors who do not want to convert their investments into cash do not sell their stock back to the corporation. By not selling, they avoid realization of the capital gain and do not have any taxation on the increment to the value of their wealth (they also avoid transaction costs).

The investors who want to receive cash sell a portion of their holdings, and even though they pay tax on the gain, it is apt to be less than if the cash distribution were taxed as ordinary income. By using stock acquisition as the means of the cash distribution, the company tends to direct the cash to those investors who want the cash and bypass the investors who do not need cash at the present time.

Dividend Reinvestment Plans: With a Discount

As of 1979 over 75 major U.S. corporations gave their stockholders the opportunity to have their dividends invested in the common stock of the firm. The transaction costs and discount from market price vary from firm to firm. We will assume the firm pays the transaction costs and in addition gives the investor the opportunity to purchase the stock at a 5% discount from the market price.

The advantage to the investor is a saving of transaction costs and a possible saving in purchase price (this latter saving will depend on whether or not all investors participate).

We will consider three different alternatives for a firm which is considering raising common stock capital:

1. Implement a reinvestment plan with a 5% price discount.
2. Do nothing.
3. Issue securities to the market and incur a 5% cost (or issue at a 5% price reduction).

Assume there are 100,000 shares outstanding and an investor owns 1,000 shares. The market price is $50 per share.

The investors can subscribe at a cost of $47.50 for .1% of their holdings. For holdings of 1,000 shares this is one share.

The total market value of the firm is now $5,000,000. After issuance of 99 shares at a price of $47.50, it will be $5,004,702.50 (assuming everyone does not invest).

If the holder of 1,000 shares does not reinvest, the value of the holdings decreases from $50,000 to:

$$5{,}004{,}702.50 \times \frac{1{,}000}{100{,}099} = \$49{,}997.53$$

To protect their holdings and maintain value the stockholders must reinvest.

Now assume that as a result of cash received the value of the firm increases to $5,004,950. The investors value now is:

$$5{,}004{,}950 \times \frac{1{,}000}{100{,}099} = \$50{,}000$$

the same as before. The investors who reinvest have their investment increase from $4,950,000 to:

$$5{,}004{,}950 \times \frac{99{,}099}{100{,}099} = \$4{,}954{,}950$$

Thus if the value of the cash obtained is higher than the amount of actual cash received, it is possible for all the stockholders to be benefited by the dividend reinvestment plan, but those who reinvest benefit more.

The value of the stock will remain at $50 but the investor only paid $47.50.

If new shares are issued at a price of $50 and the firm realizes $47.50 from each new share (a 5% cost of issue), then the $47.50 of cash must have a value of at least $50 or the value of the present stockholders' holdings will be reduced from $50.

We do not know whether dividend reinvestment plans benefit all investors. In a situation where a dollar of cash received is only worth a dollar, the investors who reinvest are not harmed. The investors who do not reinvest do have their holdings diluted. But these holdings would also be diluted if new capital were obtained at a net price of $47.50. If the value of the cash received is larger than a dollar per dollar received, then it is possible for all holders of common stock to benefit. If all investors participate in the dividend reinvestment plan, the value of the discount is neutralized. It is as if all the stockholders were receiving a stock dividend. Since all the stockholders receive the same discount, they all (collectively) have received nothing. However, the company has avoided the dilution that would have taken place (or the cost) associated with a new issue of common stock at a net price of $47.50. If the amount of the discount is taxed as ordinary income, the stockholders are actually worse off than without the discount. If all investors reinvest, they all have the same proportion of ownership and have gained nothing, but they pay tax on the discount.

Conclusions

The present tax law allows deferral of tax payment (or complete avoidance) on capital gains, and recognized gains may be taxed at different rates than ordinary income.

Dividend policies of firms have relevance for public policy in the areas of taxation of both corporations and individuals. As corporate managers adjust their decision making to include the tax law considerations, the makers of public policy must decide whether the results are beneficial to society. This question is not considered in this chapter.

A board of directors acting in the interests of the stockholders of a corporation must set the dividend policy of the firm. The distinction between ordinary income and capital gains for purpose of income taxation by the federal government accentuates the importance of investors knowing the dividend policy of the firms whose stock they are considering purchasing or have already purchased. In turn, this means the corporation has a responsibility to announce its dividend policy.

In the particular situation where a firm is expanding its investments rapidly and is financing this expansion by issuing securities to its stockholders, the payment of cash dividends is especially vulnerable to criticism.

Two public policy questions concerning corporate share repurchasing become apparent. First, should firms be allowed to buy back their own shares? If so, should they be required to give stockholders advance notice of their intentions for the future?

We have shown that repurchasing shares can have a significant impact on the after-tax returns of stockholders. Should the form of the firm's distribution, rather than its substance, influence the amount of taxes paid by stockholders? It seems clear that as more and more firms become aware of the advantages of repurchasing shares compared with paying dividends, this issue will have to be faced.

Should corporations that decide to repurchase shares be required to notify stockholders of their intentions? The value of the firm's stock is a function of the form of its cash distributions. Thus it seems reasonable that shareholders should be advised of a company's distribution policy and of changes in that policy. The corporation that repurchases shares without giving its stockholders advance notice is implicitly, if not explicitly, penalizing those who sell their shares without this information.

Chapter 8
The Allocation: Capital Budgeting Strategy

Capital budgeting is a mixed-up alphabet
With R.O.I.'s and I.R.R.'s and D.C.F.'s beset.
Such a potpourri of letters demands a master chef
*Who knows the secret: N.V.P. is really M.V.F.**

FMK

After a firm has completed its planning exercises, the resulting long-range plan has to be translated into a specific plan of action which actually allocates available cash among different projects. This specific plan may be called the capital budget, and the process of arriving at the plan may be called capital budgeting.

The finance literature has offered well-defined and reasonably exact decision rules for allocating capital among investment projects as long as we assume certainty. If we drop the certainty assumption, then strategy considerations become increasingly relevant. Strategy is a way of dealing with uncertainty.

The Mechanics

It is useful to divide all investments into two general classifications. First we group all investment opportunities that are economically independent of each other. Undertaking an investment that is independent does not affect the cash flows of other independent investments. An oil company can open a retail clothing store without affecting the cash flows of an investment in an oil field pump. Investments may be independent in this sense even when they are competing for scarce capital.

* M.V.F. equals Most Valuable Formula.

The second group of investments consists of sets of mutually exclusive investments. Only one investment from each set will be accepted, since the investments are mutually exclusive. A set may consist of all investments which perform the same economic function. For example, all possible formats for a production line or all possible uses for a unique economic resource such as a piece of land, are mutually exclusive alternatives. The land can be used for a parking lot, a tennis court, a motel, or an office building, or any combination, but we cannot use the land for all of the above (that is, only for a tennis court, and only for a parking lot). Of all the alternatives (and their combinations) only one can be chosen.

The discounted cash flow procedures are well known (present value and internal rate of return being the most widely used and most theoretically sound), and arguments in their favor will not be repeated here.[1] These discounted cash flow procedures should be the foundation of the formal corporate capital budgeting evaluation procedures.

If there are accept-or-reject decisions involving independent investments, both the net present value and the rate of return procedures lead to consistent and theoretically correct decisions. Choosing the best of a set of mutually exclusive investments adds some complexities in that the internal rate of return method has to be used carefully, but the pitfalls in its use are well known and there are ways of avoiding them.

The mathematics of capital budgeting without uncertainty are straightforward, and there is general agreement as to the effectiveness of the discounted cash flow evaluation techniques.

There are, however, several complexities that remain and that deserve consideration in a financial strategy book. Before proceeding, you might want to refer to Bierman and Smidt's *The Capital Budgeting Decision* to refresh your mind on the fundamentals of capital budgeting.

Getting the Ideas

The first step in reviewing a firm's capital budgeting policy is to make sure that the ideas for investments are being generated by all levels of management and are being submitted for consideration by higher levels of management.

Many firms have policies that lead to situations where good ideas are killed by lower levels of managers who perceive that the proposals would not survive the criteria being used to screen alternatives. A second reason for killing proposals is the perception that if the project were accepted, the performance measures being used would result in less than satisfactory performance evaluations, even if the forecasts were perfect and even if the investment satisfied the investment criteria.

Excessively stringent investment criteria and performance measures that are not congruent with the investment criteria are the two primary reasons why higher levels of management do not get to see many investment proposals that are economically desirable.

Difference in methods of performance evaluation and investment decision-making leads to very distinct biases in terms of the types of prospects that are seen by top management. For example, if the firm uses very high discount rates, there will be a tendency to submit for top management consideration only projects whose projected cash flows are difficult to verify. Normal safe investments with known cash flows will tend not to earn enough to satisfy the required high return.

A second type of investment tending to be rejected with high discount rates is one where the benefits start out slowly and build up through time. Conventional performance measures make it difficult to accept such projects.

Establishing procedures that lead to the generation and submission of ideas should be a major concern of planning groups. Grass-roots ideas should be encouraged, and even where the ideas are not accepted, it should be made clear that it is desired that such ideas be reviewed. It does not improve the competitive position of a firm if a foreman rejects a labor-saving or an energy-saving device because it only earns 15% and thus is below the firm's target return of 20%, when stockholders would be happy with a 12% return. The objectives of the capital budgeting process must be consistent with the goals of the stockholders.

The Objectives of the Firm

The objective of the capital budgeting process is to make accept-or-reject decisions involving independent investments (we should undertake all of the investments if they satisfy the criteria) and "best of the set" decisions involving mutually exclusive investments (we want to undertake only one of these investments). In making capital budgeting decisions, there is implied some known and agreed-upon objective for the firm. All methods of capital budgeting implicitly assume some objective.

As a first step we should understand what objectives should not affect the capital budgeting process. We are not attempting to maximize total sales or the firm's percentage share of market. Growth is not the goal (though it might occur if the correct decisions are made), nor are earnings per share and total earnings being maximized. The goal of the investment policy is not to maximize the return on investment (ROI), though at any given moment in time (with a given stock of capital investment), the higher the ROI, the better the situation.

It is interesting that we desire all of the above (increased sales, larger share of market, higher ROI, etc.) but they cannot be used to describe the goal of the firm that is the basis of the capital budgeting process. This is confusing, and frequently we will find projects accepted or rejected because of their effect on one of the above measures. The tendency to use these measures is understandable, but it is also regrettable.

There is only one theoretically correct goal for a business corporation that we can use to evaluate investments. This goal is to maximize the net present value of the stockholders' position, and we assume that in doing so we are maximizing the well-being of the stockholders. The investment decisions are being made from the point of view of the stockholders, and it is assumed that their interests are best served by a procedure that systematically assigns a cost to the capital that is utilized in the production process.

The capital budgeting process that is recommended must take into consideration a cost on the capital that is being utilized, or more generally we can say that the process must take into consideration the time value of money and the risk of the project. The investment evaluation process must recognize the amount of uncertainty and adjust the required return for the risk of the project being considered. If both time value of money and the risk are taken into consideration correctly (this is more easily stated than implemented), the goal of maximizing the well-being of the stockholders will tend to be attained.

Capital Rationing

Business managers have consistently argued over long periods of time that they have more investment opportunities than they have dollars to invest. Academic authors argue that if a firm has desirable investments (where the term "desirable" considers time value and risk), then the firm can go to the capital market and raise the funds. On one hand we have a situation seen by managers to be of great importance, and on the other hand we have a wide range of academic authors defining away the problem. Let us assume initially that the problem does exist. Can we give management a foolproof method of ranking independent investments so that capital can be rationed?

The so-called capital rationing problem (there are more investment opportunities than there is cash available) has been solved in the theoretical literature, which offers a variety of programming solutions, but these calculations have very demanding informational requirements and are complex.

Rankings can be obtained using a variety of techniques. For example, the index of present value (present value of benefits divided by present value of outlays) is attractive, since it leads to a number that seems to lend itself to ranking. However, counterexamples can be prepared that reveal that the rankings that are obtained are not reliable. One of the major problems is the fact that there is no reason to assume that the interest rate (cut-off rate) is constant through time.

In some very well-defined situations investments can be ranked, but these situations are not likely to be frequently encountered in the real world. While investments can be ranked subjectively in the same manner that one can rank the 10 best books of the year, there is no reliable objective way to rank investments. This conclusion is generally disappointing to managers, who like to rank investments objectively in order of relative desirability and accept the investments in sequence until all investable funds are committed.

Once we allow uncertainty to exist, so that even accept-or-reject decisions become much less definite, a ranking using one of several discounted cash flow procedures (such as index of present value or internal rate of return) can be used. The ranking cannot be defended on a theoretical basis, but given the unreliability of the imputs with the admission of uncertainty, the technique used to accomplish the discounting and ranking is probably not going to be the main source of error. Thus if a manager wants to rank the acceptable investments using subjective or quasi-quantitative techniques, given the degree of uncertainty that exists relative to the determination of the cash flows, this practice is relatively harmless.

Uncertainty

We now know more about defining the relevant considerations when there is uncertainty than we used to know, but we are still unable to find easily computed feasible solutions to accept-or-reject-type investment decisions when there is uncertainty. Each of the suggested solutions (such as simulation, risk-adjusted discount rates, or the capital asset pricing model) have real difficulties that have precluded its use with any degree of reliability.

It is not correct to assume that it is appropriate to take the risk of an investment into account via the discounting (and compounding) procedure. There is no reason for assuming that risk is always compounded through time, and that $(1 + r)^{-n}$ gives us a risk-adjusted present value equivalent, if r includes a risk adjustment.

Assume an investment is available that costs $1,000,000 and promises to return either $3,000,000 or $0, the events both having .5 probability. The payoff occurs in a time period shortly after the outlay. If the payoff were to occur in one year, the expected rate of return would be 50%. While this investment is acceptable using the criterion "Accept when the expected rate of return is greater than 10%," it is not all clear that investors who are currently expecting a return of 10% for a moderately risky investment would want this investment accepted. The .5 probability of losing $1,000,000 would scare off many investors. The opportunity to repeat the gamble many times might affect the willingness of a large corporation to accept the investment, as would a change in the size of the investment. Taking away six zeros would tend to make it easier to accept the investment. Adding three zeros would make it more difficult to accept (the prospect of losing $1,000,000,000 with .5 probability would be hard for any corporation to accept).

One important approach to risk management is diversification. This topic will be discussed in the chapter on mergers and acquisitions.

We shall next consider the allocation of investment funds among different divisions when there is uncertainty. The uncertainty is of two types. The cash flows imputed into the investment analysis may not actually occur, and secondly, different divisions may be using different estimation procedures. The investment proposals of different divisions may not be comparable.

The Strategy Element of Capital Budgeting

If there were no uncertainty, there would be no need for strategic capital budgeting. A firm would merely accept all independent investments yielding more than the cost of obtaining capital. Uncertainty creates the need to allocate limited resources to different divisions. We will assume the total resources to be allocated are less than the amount requested by the division.

In a sense the strategic capital budgeting problems that firms face are identical to the several capital budgeting problems that we are familiar with and know how to suggest solutions for. However, when there are several different components of the firm operating in several different industries and geographical areas, as is frequently the case, this adds to the complexity of the decision process. Given that there is distrust of the numbers contained in the capital budgeting proposals, top management looks to other bases than conventional analysis to allocate scarce resources.

Let us consider the manager who understands the theoretical capital budgeting literature but still has a problem of allocating limited capital among several different operating divisions in several different countries. Before the advent of the complex multinational firm that deals in many different industries and different countries, the capital market solved the problem of resource allocation. The market test was real to the executive who wanted to expand beyond the capabilities of internally generated funds. If the capital market decided the past performance did not warrant more capital, the refusal was firm and appeal was difficult.

Now a conglomerate can raise capital in the market, but that is not going to solve the problem of how much each division should be allocated to invest. That allocation is a managerial decision that is apt to be made on a subjective basis.

Allocating Resources to Divisions

One easy answer to the allocation problem is to say that it does not make any difference which division submits the project, but rather the relevant consideration is the desirability of the project itself. A division making zero income may have the best project in the firm, while the divisions making the most profit may not have any additional desirable projects. In a world of complete certainty and unbiased investment project analysis, the information as to which division originated the project could be ignored, and the profitability of the project itself could be the sole consideration. Ignoring the origin of the investment and considering only the cash flows of the investment is theoretically sound if we ignore the fact that cash flow projections and investment analyses are prepared by people, and they can be highly subjective.

Let us consider a situation where divisional managers are competing for scarce funds, there is uncertainty, and there is a past history of performance for the divisions of the firm. Assume the division making zero profits has had a long history of submitting projects that are expected to be highly profitable, but unfortunately some unforeseen event always happens that makes the forecasts bad predictors of the future. The actual results of the division inevitably are less than the forecast results. Thus the division has historically earned less than the required return even though a sensible capital budgeting procedure has been in existence. Consistent bad operating results tend to indicate that excessive optimism was contained in the capital budgeting requests in the past, or at least there was poor ability to forecast the future. Assume a highly profitable division has tended to more than meet the capital budgeting forecasts of the past. In fact, there is reason to think that this highly profitable division is not submitting enough capital budgeting requests (only the super projects are being submitted; marginally desirable projects are not being submitted).

The top managers could allocate capital by looking at the present capital budgeting requests and ignoring the past history of the divisions. But it can be argued that systematic biases in the capital budgeting analysis of the past should not be ignored, but rather should affect the way in which the present proposals are evaluated.

In allocating capital, should management attempt to evaluate the reasons why past profitable projects (at the time of submission) have turned out to be nonprofitable? The easy answer is yes. But then the more difficult question is, Does one use this information in allocating resources among the divisions?

The problem is that the evaluation of explanations leads to subjective judgments of past performance based on evidence that is going to be difficult to accumulate. Managers who are confident of their abilities to identify causal factors and are pleased to have the opportunity to explain unpleasant and difficult decisions to peers and subordinates would welcome this procedure. An attempt would be made to identify systematic biases that were introduced into the past investment analyses and to adjust new investment proposals for these biases. The inputs would be improved by the elimination of the observed biases.

The one drawback of a procedure that seeks out explanations is that it substitutes judgment for objective historical evidence. Assume a situation where the historical performance of one division has been a disaster, but now reasons for this unfortunate circumstance are being offered and it is being said that new investments will be profitable even though past investments were not. Should the hard objective evidence be used or the subjective evaluation of what is going to happen in the future?

Consider the following information contained in the 1977 annual report of a Fortune 500 firm. Division A contributed $98,000,000 of operating profit during the year and spent $157,000,000 on capital expenditures. Division B contributed $32,000,000 of operating profit and spent 3,600,000 on capital expenditures. The operating results were not unique to 1977, but reflected typical operations. How would you feel if you were the general manager in charge of Division B and received 11% of your profits to invest, while Division A received 160% of its profits to invest?

Obviously, the firm is using subjective evaluations in allocating resources between the two divisions. It is using strategy.

Capital Allocations Based on Strategy

In recent years a school of thought has arisen that recommends that capital allocations be made not on the basis of the desirability of specific projects and not on the basis of inaccurate measures of past performance, but rather on broad forward-looking strategy considerations.

The Boston Consulting Group has been a leading proponent of

this approach. It recommends that the capital allocation decision be heavily influenced by two primary factors, share of market and expected growth of market. The primary objective of the strategy is for the firm to attain a dominant position in a rapidly growing market. Thus the capital allocation procedure would first identify growing markets and then determine how funds should be spent in maintaining or attaining a dominant position.

If one could be sure that spending a given amount of capital in a growing market would lead to a dominant market position, decision making would be greatly simplified. However, one can never be sure of the effect of spending on customers, nor can one be sure of the reactions of competitors to one's spending. Consider a situation where Firm A is considering two different advertising strategies. Both firms are currently earning $5,000,000. The payoffs projected for A are:

Profit Payoffs for Advertising Strategies of Firm A

Competition	Spend 1,000,000	Spend 4,000,000
Reacts weakly	8,000,000	10,000,000
Reacts strongly	1,000,000	3,000,000

The competitors can react weakly or strongly. The profit payoffs for advertising at the spending level of $4,000,000 are both better than the profit levels at the spending level of $1,000,000. Independent of the reactions of the competitor, spending $4,000,000 is better than spending $1,000,000.

Now let us consider the decision from the point of view of the competitor:

Profit Payoffs for Advertising Strategies of the Competitor

Firm A	React Weakly	React Strongly
Spends 1,000,000	6,000,000	9,000,000
Spends 4,000,000	2,000,000	4,000,000

Inspection of the table indicates that the competitor should take strong action. "React strongly" is better than "React weakly" independent of what strategy Firm A employs.

We now have Firm A spending $4,000,000 and the competitor

reacting strongly. Firm A's profits will be $3,000,000, and the competitor will earn $4,000,000. Both firms, in trying to dominate the market, have reduced their profits. If both firms had acted differently (Firm A spends $1,000,000, the competitor reacts weakly), Firm A would have earned $8,000,000 and the competitor would have earned $6,000,000. This is a total profit for the two firms of $14,000,000. This is the optimum joint position. This is seen most clearly by combining the above two payoff tables. The number on the left is A's payoff. All numbers are in millions. The competition's profits are on the right.

Profit Payoffs

	Advertising Strategies for Firm A	
Competition	Spend $1	Spend $4
Reacts weakly	8/6	10/2
Reacts strongly	1/9	3/4

If the firms both try a strategy of being the dominant firm, they arrive at an inferior position. In the literature of game theory this situation is called the "prisoner's dilemma." Both parties following what appears to be an optimum strategy end up in inferior positions.

If collusion were feasible, the firms would arrive at an improved total profit position. For purposes of this section it is important to note that all firms following a strategy of attaining a dominant position will not necessarily lead to optimum positions for all firms. In fact, quite the opposite is likely to occur. If all firms in an industry follow an aggressive policy of investment to become the dominant firm in the industry, this is likely to lead to overcapacity and large losses for most of the firms.

Unfortunately we do not have simple reliable answers to the questions of strategy-type investment decisions. Any simplistic approach will give rise to counterexamples that illustrate the difficulties of using the given approach.

An Objective Method

An alternative to the use of subjective evaluations is to substitute the objective evidence for the explanations, and to use the cold hard numbers representing performance instead of the explanations of why the goals were not met. This alternative is obviously less "intelligent" in that it ignores evidence (all the explanations of why the past goals were not met). On the other hand, it can be well defined, predictable, and fair.

A manager would know how to get new investment funds. Good performance would lead to additional funds being allocated to the division. Bad performance would lead to a situation where it was extremely difficult to obtain additional resources.

One solution would be to allocate funds based on operating income. Thus Division A of our Fortune 500 firm would receive:

$$\frac{98}{98 + 32} = \frac{98}{130} = .75$$

of the investable funds and Division B would receive .25. An improvement in the allocation results when the operating incomes are charged with a cost for the capital utilized. Applying a capital cost of .05 to the assets utilized we obtain:

Dollar Amounts in Millions

	Assets	Capital Cost (.05)	Income after Interest
Division A	2,460	123	−25
Division B	208	10	22

The above table clearly indicates that Division A would have a very difficult time defending its request for capital funds. Given its past performance, it is in a position inferior to that of Division B in the competition for funds.

We might not want to use past performance as the sole basis of resource allocation, but rather as an important input into the allocation process. A high level of performance would be a desirable condition for getting extra funds, but it would not be a sufficient condition. In addition to performance, the high performance division would have to have projects that merited investment.

Also, not all the funds would be allocated based on performance. An automatic allocation scheme could lead to a situation where projects meriting attention were ignored because they were housed in a poorly performing division. Thus there could be a two-tiered system of strategic allocation. Some of the funds would be allocated based on performance, but there would also be a review to insure that projects that were desirable from a corporate point of view were also undertaken.

One interesting allocation procedure would be to allocate the funds based on income but give each division the opportunity of investing in one of the other divisions. Thus if Division A had better investment opportunities than Division B, the funds could be invested by B in Division A.

Capital Budgeting and Growth

Good capital budgeting techniques may encourage growth or discourage it. The direction of the influence will depend on the type of error (if any) currently being made. The objective is not growth but rather profitability.

If good investments are currently being rejected for wrong reasons (say, the payback period is too long), then growth is being stifled and a shift to net present value might result in an increased growth rate.

But now assume that a firm properly has a minimum required return of .10 and the following two investment strategies are available:

	Strategy 1	Strategy 2
Reinvestment rate (b)	.3	.8
Average return on new investments (r)	.15	.10
Growth rate (rb)	.045	.08
Marginal return on new investments	.10	.05

Strategy 2 leads to the larger growth rate, but some of the investments being undertaken have returns as low as .05. Strategy 1 has a lower growth rate but properly cuts off investments that yield less than the required return (assuming no uncertainty). Investors wanting a return of .10 are not going to be pleased with investments that yield .05, even if the growth rate is increased by the strategy.

Let us consider an investment now of $1,000 that will pay $1,050 one year from now (a .05 return). The investor with a .10 time value factor will value the $1,050 at $955 and would prefer receiving the $1,000 rather than having the firm reinvest it to earn .05. In this case the higher dividend (less retention) is more desirable than the lower dividend (and more investment). The tax situation of the investors is assumed away by assuming they want the firm to earn a minimum return of .10.

The distinction between the average return and the marginal return should be noted. If the investors state they want to have a minimum return of .10, this is a directive to the company not to accept investments with returns less than .10 (this is a marginal return). By acceptance only of investments with returns larger than .10, the average return earned by the firm and by the investors will be larger than .10. This assumes that there is no uncertainty and that at least one investment has a return better than .10.

Thus if a firm uses a weighted average cost of capital of .10 as a minimum acceptable return (or hurdle rate) and if its forecasts are perfect, it will earn an average return that is greater than its weighted average cost of capital. This assumes there are no necessary investments that have returns less than .05.

Looking at History

In setting a minimum required return, firms will sometimes look at the return they are currently earning. Past profitability should not affect the investment criteria being used to evaluate future alternatives. For example, a firm earning a zero return should not use a zero rate of discount to evaluate investments.

But should a firm that is earning a .25 return use that as the minimum required return? In the first place, a .25 return implies some investments earning more than .25 and some investments earning less than .25. Secondly, if new capital costs .10 and if it can be obtained at that cost, there is no logic in using a .25 minimum return just because that is the return currently being earned.

The Limit to Growth

Management will frequently specify unrealistic growth targets. For example, if a firm is currently earning .10 on both old and new investments, can it grow at .20 per year using only retained earnings? If a firm earns .10 and reinvests b portion of its earnings, it can expect to grow at rb, or .10b. If $b = 1$ and all earnings are retained, the growth rate will be .10, not .20. It is true that in the short run a firm can grow by being more efficient, by using resources more intensively, and by using debt, or be lucky (e.g., achieve a windfall price increase). But in the long run, without inflation growth can only come from profitable investments. Long-run growth of .20 without adding debt implies that investments earning at least .20 are available.

Conclusions

Capital budgeting decisions involve outlays and benefits that are spread out through time. In some cases the benefits or outlays may be deferred for many years. The primary problem facing management responsible for making capital budgeting decisions is to incorporate time value and risk considerations in such a manner that the well-being of the stockholders is maximized.

Because of the presence of intentional and unintentional biases in preparing capital budgeting requests, investment analyses cannot be accepted without review. In multi-divisional firms, one easy way of adjusting for bias and introducing an objective basis of allocation is to use past profit performance of the divisions as the basis for the allocation of at least some of the investment funds. Past performance gives some indication of how reliable past capital budgeting requests have been. Past performance, properly measured, is a reasonable indication of the amount of the bias present in the capital budgeting requests in the past. The use of past performance as the basis of allocation of at least part of the capital budget is apt to be perceived by managers as fairer than an allocation entirely based on subjective evaluations of the future.

Capital budgeting is too extensive a subject to be covered in one chapter. While the discounted cash flow calculations are powerful tools for evaluating investments, considerations of uncertainty move us from very absolute conclusions concerning acceptability of investments to a position of being willing to incorporate strategy considerations. Despite this disclaimer, the operating business person should realize that the basic discounted cash flow calculations are still the most reliable ways of evaluating specific investments, and are an important tool in deciding whether or not an investment is acceptable. An investment strategy that did not correctly incorporate the time value of money in the calculations would be a very unreliable navigation device.

Chapter 9

The Marriage: Mergers and Acquisitions

Matchmaker, Matchmaker, list me your terms.
Buy me some businesses. Catch me some firms.
Matchmaker, Matchmaker, do it up right
And marry me off tonight.
Matchmaker, Matchmaker, do as I urge
Find me some companies. Merge me a merge.
Matchmaker, Matchmaker though I'm no gold digger
I must marry to make my firm bigger.

FMK

Assume a firm has a mature product but has a new idea for a product that requires different production facilities and techniques and is to be sold in a different market. It can start from ground zero and build both new facilities and a new organization for the product, or it can seek out an established firm which it can acquire. Any firm interested in increasing its rate of growth must consider the strategy of mergers and acquisitions.

In the spring of 1979 Exxon offered $1,170,000,000 (cash) for the Reliance Electric Company. Reliance was a manufacturer of electric motors and controls. Exxon offered the explanation that it needed Reliance to accelerate the marketing of a device it had developed for controlling the speed of electric motors. The device would lead to saving of energy. The week before the tender offer Reliance was selling for $36. Exxon bid $72 a share for all the 15,000,000 shares outstanding. But the acquisition did not go smoothly. A federal judge ruled that Exxon would have to separate Reliance's motor division (thus eliminating Exxon's stated reason for the merger). Usually there is a clause in tender offers that states that in case of litigation the bidder, at its discretion, can withdraw the offer. In this acquisition Exxon did not include such a clause. It was an embarrassing omission. Exxon proceeded with the acquisition and hoped that the Federal Trade Commission would be more flexible. Most importantly, from a strategy point of view, Exxon decided that it was more desirable to acquire Reliance than build its own plants and organization (the FTC claimed that one consideration was the elimination of a major potential competitor).

There are a wide range of reasons for one firm to acquire a second firm. Growth deserves mention as does elimination of a potential competitor (this second reason correctly draws disapproval from the government and courts). Another major reason is the expectation of higher profits arising from a fortuitous purchase (a bargain) or from the opportunity to change a method of operation (including financial decisions) that the firm being acquired is currently employing.

An important reason for acquisition is that the firm being considered is desirable from a vertical or horizontal integration viewpoint. The term "synergy" is frequently used to encompass all possibilities of increased profits arising from the combined operations of two firms.

A neglected but widespread reason for acquisition is that the acquisition of a firm may be the best use of excess cash currently held by the acquiring firm.

A reason for an acquisition that is frequently stated but is not obviously valid is that the acquisition is a form of diversification resulting in a reduction of risk.

A final reason is that the acquired firm has something that the acquiring firm wants. This can be cash (as when a steel company acquires a bank), managerial talent, or a patent.

In 1979 RCA Corporation acquired C.I.T. Financial Corporation for $1,350,000,000. The objective seemed to be the cash generation of C.I.T. plus the stability of that firm's earnings. RCA already owned the Hertz Corporation (auto rentals) and the National Broadcasting Company.

Valuation of an Acquisition

Find a set of financial statements for a corporation where you do not know the market price of the common stock. After studying the financial information, estimate the stock price. How close were you to the actual price? Even more important, what factors did you consider in making your evaluation?

There is a tendency to consider the book value per share. But book value reflects sunk costs and accounting conventions, and at any given moment of time may be a bad estimator of economic value. Thus in 1979 the common stock of steel companies sold at a small percentage of book value and an even smaller percentage of replacement cost. One frequently finds reference to book value in the evaluation of a firm's common stock, but it is not obvious that the accounting measure of book value can be used in the setting of an offer price for a firm's common stock. An obsolete steel plant needing large expenditures for pollution control equipment may have value only as scrap; its book value is not relevant.

The Magic of Leverage

Let us assume that a firm completely financed with common stock is currently earning $1,000,000 before tax and $540,000 after tax per year (the corporate tax rate is .46). If it is felt that the $1,000,000 will stay constant, investors with a discount rate of .10 would value the firm at:

$$\frac{540{,}000}{.10} = \$5{,}400{,}000$$

Now assume that the firm can borrow at a cost of .10. Assume a prospective purchaser can also borrow at .10 and borrows $7,000,000 to offer $6,000,000 for the firm. The current stockholders are happy, since they receive $6,000,000 in return for $5,400,000 of present value. Once the firm is acquired, it issues $7,000,000 of long-term debt to repay the initial short-term loan used to finance the purchase. The $7,000,000 of debt requires $700,000 of interest payment, leaving $300,000 before tax and $162,000 of earnings after tax for the stockholders. The stockholders made a zero investment and receive $162,000 of earnings per year. In addition, since the acquisition only cost $6,000,000 and the loan was $7,000,000, there is an extra $1,000,000 of cash available for other purposes. The value of the levered firm is equal to:

$$\begin{aligned}\text{Value of levered firm} &= \text{value of the unlevered firm} \\ &\quad + (\text{debt} \times \text{tax rate}) \\ &= 5{,}400{,}000 + 7{,}000{,}000(.46) = \$8{,}620{,}000\end{aligned}$$

The $162,000 of earnings to stockholders has a present value of $1,620,000 using .10, which when added to the $7,000,000 of debt gives a value to the firm of $8,620,000.

According to the above analysis it would seem that all firms should be financed with 100% debt. This would be valid if there were zero personal taxes and no costs of going bankrupt.

While we should be careful of extreme conclusions, there is a generalization that we can make. Where we are using someone else's money (the capital source is called debt), it is possible to have a situation as above where the stockholders make little or no investment and end up with a great deal of value. We can call this situation one where "unfriendly" debt is being used.

Is the above fact or fiction? In 1978 the United Technology Corporation acquired the common stock of the Carrier Corporation. In January 1979 United Technology issued $300 million of 10-year notes yielding 9.45% to pay for the 17,000,000 shares of the Carrier Corporation that it had just purchased.

Leveraged Buyouts

Leveraged buyouts became very popular in the late 1970s. While more or less the same process had been going on for many years, during the seventies several new twists were utilized.

With a leveraged buyout, debt funds are obtained from insurance companies and banks (or other entities willing to accept a fixed return). The debt is layered with the degree of protection ranging from mortgage bonds to highly subordinated debt. Some of the debt will have equity kickers in the form of either warrants or conversion features. Preferred stock may also be used, but it is less widely used than debt.

The promoters get the common stock. It is not uncommon for 90% of the new capital to be in the form of debt. In the early years of the new firm essentially all the cash flow is committed to debt service.

One interesting twist is that the managers of the corporation may be given a significant portion of the new equity at a reasonable price. Thus they are apt to be friendly to the takeover.

The acquisition of Houdaille Industries, Inc., could well be termed a leveraged buyout. Approximately $356,000,000 was paid the owners. The sources of the capital were:

307,000,000	debt with some equity kickers from banks and well over a dozen insurance companies and other institutions
24,000,000	preferred stock from insurance companies
25,000,000	common stock from institutions, promoters, and management
356,000,000	

Not only was the debt capacity of the firm used to acquire it, but in addition there was $20,000,000 of excess cash in the assets that could be used to reduce the debt used in the acquisition.

Valuation: Earnings or Cash Flows?

Assume the analyst wants to compute the value of an acquisition. Should the earnings or the cash flow be used?

The easy and safe answer is to use the net cash flows available to the investors. This is theoretically correct and a reliable calculation if the cash flows include those capital expenditures necessary to maintain or expand the flow.

The use of earnings is also theoretically correct if the capital expenditures necessary to maintain the earnings are exactly equal to the depreciation expense that is being deducted. Also, it would be best to exclude interest deductions so that possible errors are not introduced.

In the normal situation the use of earnings (unadjusted) would be an unreliable input. For example, assume a firm that can be acquired for $7,000 has one asset with a book value of $8,000 and a life of one year. The forecasted income statement for the next year is:

Revenues	9,000
Depreciation	8,000
Income	1,000

With a .10 time value factor the income has a present value of $909. However, the $9,000 of revenue at time 1 has a present value of

$8,182. The firm with its one asset is clearly worth $8,182 rather than the present value of the earnings ($909).

To illustrate the situation where earnings can be used, assume that at the end of each year another asset costing $8,000 is purchased so that for each year the following income statement is projected:

Revenues	9,000
Depreciation	8,000
Income	1,000

Now the income and the net cash flow are equal, and we have for both calculations a net present value of 1,000/.10 = $10,000.

The first example (where earnings could not be used) is analogous to the acquisition of a firm that owns one major hotel that is depreciating. Cash flow, not earnings, should be used to evaluate the acquisition.

The second example (where both earnings and cash flows can be used) is analogous to the acquisition of a firm that owns 10 lathes and each year one of the lathes wears out and is replaced. Each year $8,000 is spent to maintain the cash flow.

It is general practice to assume that the lathe example applies rather than the hotel and that earnings can be used as an excellent proxy for the cash flow stream. The cash flow stream should include necessary reinvestment.

Real Investments and Acquisitions

A subtle complexity arises in the evaluation of an acquisition of a firm. This complexity does not exist when we are considering real investments. A real investment is defined here as the expenditure for plant and equipment that is not part of a corporate acquisition. With a corporate acquisition one acquires debt as well as assets.

Assume a firm has the following capital structure and weighted average cost of capital:

	Proportion	Cost	Weighted Cost
Debt	.50	.12	.06
Common stock	.50	.22	.11
			.17

There are zero taxes. The firm has $400 of cash.

The firm has considered and rejected the following real investment (the investment is a perpetuity, that is the benefits of $150 continue forever):

0	1	2		Rate of Return
−1,000	+150	+150	. . .	.15

Secondly, the company has the opportunity to invest in another corporation which has the following balance sheet:

Asset	900
Liability	600
Common stock	300

The common stock can be acquired at a cost of $400. The debt is paying .12 interest, or $72 per year. The company is earning $150 per year before interest and $78 after interest. The return on the investment of $400 in the common stock would be:

$$\frac{78}{400} = .195$$

The investment in the firm has a higher yield (.195) than the weighted average cost of capital (.17), and thus seems to be acceptable.

With the real investment the cash flows were defined to be:

−1,000	+150	+150	. . .

If we subtract the cash flows associated with $600 of debt paying .12 interest, from the investment flows we obtain:

Investment	−1,000	+150	+150	. . .
Debt	+ 600	− 72	− 72	. . .
Net	− 400	+ 78	+ 78	. . .

This cash flow is identical to the cash flow associated with the acquisition of the entire firm (which is the same real asset). The method of analysis should not suggest different decisions for two alternatives which have the same basic data. They both should be accepted or both be rejected. An analysis that accepts one and rejects the other is faulty. The acceptance of the investment in the common stock is not consistent with the rejection of the real investment. Both investments have a cost of $1,000 and will generate benefits before interest of $150 per year. Assuming identical risk characteristics, they should be treated in an identical manner.

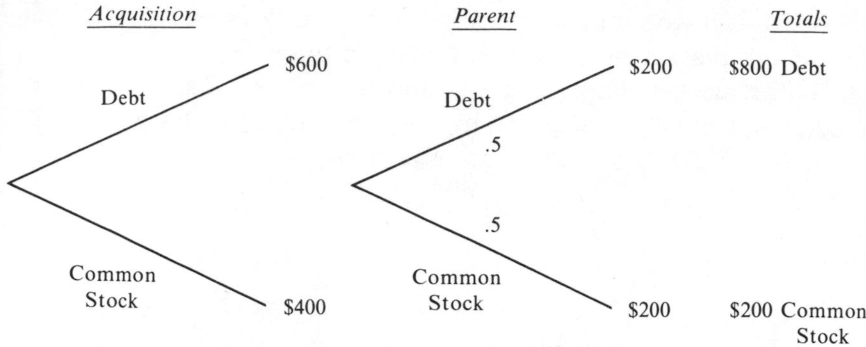

Figure 9.1 Acquisition of Firm

The reason that one alternative is rejected and the other is accepted is that different amounts of debt capital are implicitly being used. The real investment is being financed with .5 debt. The debt associated with the acquisition is shown in Figure 9.1 to be $800, or .8 of the total capital of $1,000. The larger amount of debt with no change in the cost of common stock and cost of debt leads to a bias in favor of the acquisition of the firm compared to the acquisition of the real asset. Remember both alternatives have identical basic (non-financial) risk characteristics.

The problem is one of "double leverage." There is the debt of the subsidiary, and there is the debt of the parent. The two investments should be placed on an equivalent basis. This can be done by evaluating both alternatives using the outlay of $1,000 and the benefits of $150 per year.

The Tender Trap

The investor receiving a tender offer associated with an acquisition has to make a decision whether or not to tender shares. What are the consequences to investors when a raiding company makes a tender offer? Should such maneuvers be encouraged or discouraged by government action? The tender price is invariably set at a premium above current market price. The premium is sometimes in excess of 100% over the market price before the acquisition activity started.

Let us assume that the price of a share now, the price after the tender is completed, and the price if the tender offer is rejected are equal to each other. This assumes that the market looks at the tender offer just as it would look at any other offer to buy shares, and that the current market price is an equilibrium price.

If the market thinks that a proportion of the shares outstanding, g, will actually be acquired by the tendering firm at a price of T, and if (1 − g) shares are not acquired, then:

$$P_o = gT + (1 - g)P$$

where

P = the equilibrium market price (before the tender offer is announced and after the tender is completed)
T = the tender price
P_o = the current market price after the tender offer is made

For example, if the Big Oil Company offers to buy 52% of the shares of the March Company for $35 and the stock is selling for $20 before the offer is announced, then the price after the offer is announced and before the tender offer expires can be expected to be approximately:

$$P_o = .52(35) + .48(20) = 18.2 + 9.6 = \$27.80$$

We assume shares acquired are awarded to investors tendering on a pro rata basis. The price after the tender offer is made will be $27.80. Some of the shares will turn out to be worth $35, and some will be worth $20 after the tendering process is completed.

The investor with 100 shares worth $2,000 before the tender offer can retain the shares and have shares worth $2,000 after the tender is completed. Alternatively, a tendering of the 100 shares can result in $1,820 of cash and 48 shares worth $960 ($20 each) or total assets of $2,780.

If the assumptions are accepted, the investor must tender the shares. Obviously, investors do not always tender their shares; thus the real-world model must be more complex than the simplified version illustrated in the above example.

For example, it may be that the stock price after the completion of the tender offer is expected to be higher than $35. This expectation might lead to a strategy of not tendering by the investor. Competitive bids that are higher than $35, or for a larger percentage of the shares at a price of $35, would also be more attractive.

Thus the tender trap arises in the mind of the investor when the current bid is the only bid that is expected and the price increase that occurs is expected to be a temporary departure from the equilibrium price (the $20 in the numerical example).

If the tender price is larger than the current market price (and the expected market price after the tender transaction is completed), the investor must logically tender the shares. Implicitly this includes an assumption that there will not be more attractive competitive bids.

If it is really believed that the stock price after the tender will return to $20, there is nothing to prevent the investor from tendering 100 shares, having 52 shares accepted at a price of $35, then repurchasing 52 shares at $20 after the tender is completed. More likely the stock will reach a new equilibrium that is above the old price of $20 and in fact may be above $35 (at least one major purchaser thinks the value is equal to or in excess of $35). If the price is expected to increase, the willingness of an investor to hold rather than tender is increased. But in the normal situation the price after the tender offer (but before the tender has expired) is between the old price (the price before the offer) and the tender price. While it is possible that one can base a "no sell" decision on expectations that are more optimistic than those of the market, this is a risky basis on which to make the decision. A bird in hand is attractive. However, not tendering because a bid from a competitive suitor is likely to occur is a reasonable strategy.

In many senses the tendering-of-stock decision is analogous to the classical secretary problem. A manager has a pool of applicants and wants to hire one secretary. There is no knowledge about the skills of the applicants, and there is a cost of screening an applicant. A decision must be made at the end of each interview, and once you reject an applicant, you cannot go back to that applicant. How many applicants do you see? When do you say yes to a tender offer? Should the first offer always be rejected? If the answer is yes, a corporation bidding for the stock should try to avoid being the first company to bid.

One further complication must be considered. In some situations the future price of the common stock is expected to be adversely affected by the successful completion of the tender offer. It may be thought that the raiding company will consciously or accidently depress the common stock price and then acquire the remaining shares at low prices. Fortunately, this type of situation is not widespread, though the possibility does exist. To protect investors from being seduced by a larger tender price for a fraction of the outstanding shares and then being offered less attractive prices for the remainder of the shares, there could be legislation that required that the raiding firm pay a price for future shares at least equal to the price paid for the tendered shares. This type of legislation would remove the possibility of there being a "tender trap" of the type described.

Recommendations

Tender offers give investors a choice and thus are likely to be beneficial to investors. They act as a defense for the small stockholder against self-serving management. Bad management of a firm will lead to a depressed common stock price and the possibility of a raid. The tender offer for the stock at a price higher than the market price is going to enable the investors to improve their financial position compared with the current market price resulting from current management.

There is no reason for government to establish rules that protect the status quo. The interests of investors are best advanced by encouraging a situation where the management that has the best ideas for administering the assets has the possibilities of gaining control of the assets.

Bear Hugs

The acquiring firm has a wide range of strategies available to it. It can offer a low tender bid (say 20% over market value) and hope that no one enters the competition or alternatively if necessary that it can increase its bid price in steps.

The "bear hug" is an alternative strategy. The company offers the firm a substantial amount over market price (say 100%) in the hope the competition is preempted from entering the bidding. The tender offer is conditional on receiving the support of the board of directors of the firm being acquired.

The Saturday Night Special

There was a day in the past when a stockholder could receive a tender offer in the mail where the tender offer would have a very short fuse, such as 72 hours. If not accepted in 72 hours, the firm tendering did not have to accept the shares (also if enough shares were not tendered, it did not have to accept). There have been several steps taken by government to limit the amount of time pressure that can be exerted on the stockholders. The ability of a firm to use the time pressure technique is now relatively limited.

Rejected Suitors and White Knights

In September 1978 Kaiser Cement Corporation offered $32.50 per share for the Florida Mining and Materials Corporation and purchased over 500,000 shares. Florida Mining retained Merrill Lynch, White Weld Capital Markets Group to find an alternative purchaser (a "white knight"). Moore McCormack Resources was interested, bid $40 a share, and received the support of Florida's board of directors. Kaiser made a tidy profit on the shares it held (it had purchased a block of 32% of the outstanding shares at a price of $32.50).

In 1979 both Pan Am and Texas International Airlines tried to gain control of National Airlines. Texas "lost" and agreed to sell its 7,099,370 shares of National stock for $50 a share. In addition, Texas was paid $3,000,000 by Pan Am for the privilege of buying the shares. Texas had paid much less than $50 per share, so it made a nice profit of approximately $50,000,000 on its merger attempt.

Having been successful in not gaining control of National, Texas next bought stock of the Trans World Corporation (parent corporation of TWA) and announced that there was a possibility of acquiring TWA. The market value of TWA at the time was about $400,000,000, while that of Texas was less than $50,000,000.

In August 1979 Mattel Inc., the toy company (Barbie Dolls), reached an understanding regarding a merger with Macmillan, Inc. Two weeks later the American Broadcasting Company bid $335,000,000 (compared with Mattel's $329,000,000) and replaced Mattel as the leading suitor. Later ABC withdrew its offer.

Price/Earnings Ratios

Manager concerned with acquisitions tend to be concerned with the effect of the acquisition on earnings per share. The effect of a merger on the immediate earnings per share is one of the first numbers computed, and will heavily influence the willingness of an acquiring firm to proceed with the merger.

The earnings per share will be increased by an acquisition if the price/earnings ratio of the acquirer is larger than the ratio of common stock price to be paid to the common stock earnings of the firm being acquired. This conclusion assumes common stock is being used to finance the acquisition.

While we can make a generalization, we cannot use the relative size of the price/earnings ratios of the firms as the sole basis of making the acquisition. It may be that an acquisition that decreases the earnings per share now is a good acquisition (the earnings per share in the future will be increased sufficiently to compensate for the current decrease).

The Amount of Premium

There are two sets of stockholders affected by a merger or acquisition, those of the firm being acquired and those of the firm doing the acquiring. We will primarily consider the effect of an acquisition on the well-being of the stockholders of the firm doing the acquiring. What is the perception of a common stockholder of an acquiring firm when a large premium over market price is offered? Consider a stockholder of a company which offers $30 a share for a company which is currently selling at $25 per share. This is a 20% premium over market price and well within reasonable bounds established by other acquisitions. Assume the offer of $25 per share is rejected because of the possibility of a competitive offer and the new tender price shoots up to $50 per share. This is a 100% premium over market and the average investor of the acquiring firm may start wondering whether the acquisition is being made in the interests of the stockholders or for the interests of management. We shall see that large premiums can be justified under given circumstances.

Returning to the situation where the stock price is $25, let us consider the situation where the acquiring corporation has excess cash and the acquisition will be accomplished by the use of this cash. Assume the firm's stockholders are in the 70% tax bracket and the choice to the corporation is an acquisition of a firm worth $30 per share to the investors of the acquiring corporation or to give the funds to the shareholders in the form of a cash dividend. If capital gains were not taxed, the company could afford to pay as much as $100 per share for the firm which is only worth $30 per share. Of course, a better alternative may be to find another firm where the gap between value and price per share is smaller than for the firm being considered. To keep the analysis simple, we will assume there is only one firm to be considered.

Why can the firm pay $100 for a stock that is worth only $30? If the $100 is distributed as a dividend, the stockholders being taxed at a 70% rate would pay $70 of tax and would net out $30. If the firm bought the stock worth $30 at a price of $100, the stockholders would again have $30 of value. If the stock could be purchased for less than $100, the stockholders would actually be better off with the acquisition than with a cash dividend. The assumption of a zero capital gains tax is necessary for the acquisition of the firm at a cost of $100 to be as valuable as the $100 dividend. Without a zero capital gains tax, the different tax bases under the two plans would be of importance.

It could be argued that the company should only pay $83 for the stock because the individual shareholder receiving $83 could pay the 70% tax and still have $25, which is enough to buy one share on the market of the firm being acquired. The $100 maximum price is correct if the firm acquiring the shares can enhance the value of the acquired firm to a level of $30 per share. The $83 is correct if there is no value enhancement arising from the acquisition.

The amount that the firm could afford to pay would be somewhat reduced by the fact that the tax basis is increased with the cash dividend and then reinvestment. It has been convenient to assume the tax basis change is worthless (and thus we obtain an offer price of $100). However, we can also compute an indifference price if there is assumed to be value to the tax basis change. If we assume that capital gains will be taxed at .25 20 years from now and if a time value factor of .06 is used, we obtain a maximum value of $92.* Changing the time horizon or the rate of discount would change the maximum price to be offered in achieving the acquisition.

There are tax incentives (at the personal level) for a company to engage in acquisitions rather than pay large cash dividends. The above example illustrates one reason why a company such as Ken-

* Let X be the cash dividend or the stock price bid, t_p the personal tax rate, and t_g the capital gains rate.

$$(1 - t_p)X + t_g(30)(1 + r)^{-20} = 30$$

$$.3X + .25(30).3118 = 30$$

$$.3X = 27.6615$$

$$X = 92$$

necott Copper possessing large amounts of excess cash was willing to pay a premium of well over 100% of the market price of Carborundum's common stock to acquire the common stock of that company. If we add to tax considerations the synergy effect (the sum of the two firms as a joint operation is worth more than the sum of the individual firms), it is not difficult to justify offering prices that are more than 100% of the current market price of the stock of the firm being acquired.

If justifying the offering price, we have assumed that the choice is between the acquisition of the firm and a cash dividend to be taxed at ordinary rates. Consideration of other alternatives will modify the maximum price that can logically be offered for the common stock. Also stockholders with different tax rates will have different perceptions as to the reasonableness of the price that is offered. If the stockholders have a zero tax rate, they will tend not to be in favor of paying a premium over market price. They would prefer to receive a cash dividend to paying an amount in excess of the current market price of the common stock since on the receipt of the cash dividend they could use the cash to acquire the stock without the premium.

The Earnings per Share

We will consider the effect of an acquisition on the earnings per share of the acquirer. It is necessary to distinguish between the short- and long-run effects. The short-run effects are relatively easy to predict. For example, we can assume that the next period's earnings will be the same as this period's earnings. The earnings per share will be increased if common stock is used in the acquisition and the price/earnings multiplier of the acquiring firm is larger than the price/earnings multiplier of the firm being acquired, and if market price is paid for the firm.

Assume that Firm A is acquiring Firm S for 125,000 shares ($1,000,000 of value) and the facts presented in Table 9.1 apply:

TABLE 9.1

	A	S	A + S
Total earnings	$10,000,000	$2,000,000	$12,000,000
Number of shares	1,000,000	500,000	1,125,000
Earnings per share (EPS)	$10	$4	$10.67
Market price	$80	$20	$80
P/E ratio	8	5	7.5

Table 1 shows the price/earnings multiplier is larger for A than for Firm S, and we can predict that the acquisition of S by A will increase the earnings per share of the joint firm compared with the earnings per share of A ($10.67 compared with $10). To increase a firm's earnings per share, it is necessary to acquire another firm with a lower price/earnings ratio. The price to be used for the firm being acquired in this calculation is the price that has to be paid to accomplish the acquisition.

Now assume the earnings per share of S were $2 and total earnings of S were $1,000,000. Table 9.2 shows that the new price/earnings multiplier of A is smaller than for S. The acquisition will now reduce the earnings per share of the joint firm compared with the earnings per share of A (it will be $9.78, down from $10).

TABLE 9.2

	A	S	A + S
Total earnings	$10,000,000	$1,000,000	$11,000,000
Number of shares	1,000,000	500,000	1,125,000
EPS	$10	$2	$9.78
Market price	$80	$20	$80
P/E ratio	8	10	8.18

In a situation where an acquisition or a merger affects the earnings per share, analysts will frequently try to compute a pro forma earnings per share without the acquisition. A statement that "the acquisition contributed $.67 per share of the $10.67 total earnings per share" can then be made. The analyst wants to distinguish the change in earnings caused by improved operations and the change caused by financial types of transactions, including mergers and acquisitions. On the other hand, a merger that reduces the immediate earnings per share from $10 to $9.78 would be very hard to justify in the board room of Firm A. A decrease in earnings per share is a tough pill for a firm to swallow. It would be possible to avoid the decrease in earnings per share by using debt or preferred stock rather than common stock.

Dealing with Analysts: The Price/Earnings Ratio

In Table 9.1 we start with a P/E ratio of 8 for Firm A and 5 for Firm S. What will be the price/earnings ratio of the firm after the acquisition? It can be shown that if there are no special synergistic effects, the postacquisition P/E ratio is a weighted average of the P/E ratios of the component firms where the weights are the total earnings of the separate firms. For the situation described in Table 9.1, if we define E_A as the earnings of Firm A and E_S as the earnings of Firm S, we have (all numbers in millions):

$$\text{New P/E} = \frac{E_A}{E_A + E_S}(\text{P/E of A}) + \frac{E_S}{E_A + E_S}(\text{P/E of S}) =$$

$$\frac{10}{10 + 2}(8) + \frac{2}{10 + 2}(5) = 7.5$$

This would imply a market price of the common stock of \$80 after the acquisition (equal to 7.5 times \$10.67). This is unchanged from the \$80 market price before the acquisition.

For the situation of Table 9.2 we have:

$$\text{New P/E} = \frac{10}{10 + 1}(8) + \frac{1}{10 + 1}(10) = 8.18$$

This P/E would imply a market price of the common stock of \$80 after the acquisition (equal to 8.18 times \$9.78), which again is equal to the before-acquisition market price.

This model assumes that the market recognizes no gain or loss as a result of the acquisition transaction. Thus the stock price of A is the same before and after the acquisition. The P/E after acquisition is a weighted average of the P/E's before acquisition.

Returning to the situation of Table 9.1, why does A have a P/E of 8 and Firm S have a P/E of 5? We will explain the level of the price/earnings ratios with the aid of a popular valuation formula:

$$P = \frac{D}{k_e - g}$$

where

D = current dividend
k_e = cost of equity
g = growth rate of dividends and earnings
P = stock price

For example, assume Firm A is currently paying \$6 per share dividends so that the retention rate is .4. The stockholders want a return on investment of .15 and expect a growth rate of .075. We then have:

$$P = \frac{D}{k_e - g} = \frac{6.00}{.15 - .075} = \$80$$

Note that Firm A has a .075 growth rate and a P/E ratio of 8.

Firm S of Table 9.1 has a dividend of $2.80 per year and a growth rate of .01. We then have for price per share:

$$P = \frac{D}{k_e - g} = \frac{2.80}{.15 - .01} = \$20$$

S's growth rate is only .01, and the firm has a P/E of 5 (see Table 9.1).

Another way of explaining the P/E ratios of A and S of Table 9.1 is to determine the implied growth rates and the implied expected returns on investment of retained funds.

If we define D as (1 − b) E where (1 − b) is the dividend payout percentage and E is the earnings per share, then we have:

$$P = \frac{(1 - b)\,E}{k_e - g}$$

or, dividing both sides of the equation by E:

$$\frac{P}{E} = \frac{1 - b}{k_e - g}$$

This equation says that the price divided by earnings for a firm is equal to the dividend payout percentage divided by the difference between the cost of equity and the growth rate. Solving for the implied growth rate, we have:

$$g = k_e - \frac{E}{P}(1 - b).$$

Assume that the stockholders for both firms of Table 9.1 want a return of .15. The retention rate for S is .3 and the P/E ratio is 5. The implied growth rate for Firm S of Table 9.1 is:

$$g = .15 - \frac{1}{5}(1 - .3) = .01$$

It can be shown that with zero debt:

$$g = rb$$

where r is the return on new investment.

With S having a retention rate of .3, this implies a return (r) on new investment of .033:

$$\begin{aligned} g &= rb \\ .01 &= r(.3) \\ r &= .033 \end{aligned}$$

The low average return expected on new investment and the resulting low growth rate help explain the low price/earnings ratio being applied by the market to the stock of S. Assume Firm A has a retention rate of .4. It has a P/E of 8. The implied growth rate is:

$$g = .15 - \frac{1}{8}(1 - .4) = .075$$

This implies a return on new investment of .1875.

$$\begin{aligned} g &= rb \\ .075 &= .4r \\ r &= .1875 \end{aligned}$$

Firm A has more desirable investment opportunities than S, and this leads to a price/earnings multiplier of 8 for A compared with 5 for S. The P/E ratio of a firm reflects the market's perceptions of the earnings opportunities (growth) of the firm. When one firm has a P/E of 8 and a second firm has a P/E of 5, we can expect the new P/E of the joint firm to be between 8 and 5. The growth potential of the high-P/E firm will be diluted by the addition of the firm with less growth opportunities.

Analysts are aware of the above models. Thus when an electronics firm with a P/E of 20 merges with a steel company with a P/E of 6, the earnings of the steel company after acquisition will not be capitalized with a P/E of 20. We can expect the new P/E of the merged firms to be between 20 and 6.

In Table 9.2 the earnings of S were only \$1,000,000 (down from the \$2,000,000 of Table 9.1), but the stock price remained at \$20. Assume the retention rate is .30 and the dividends are \$1.40 per share and the growth rate is .08. We then have:

$$P = \frac{D}{k_e - g} = \frac{1.40}{.15 - .08} = \$20$$

A growth rate of .08 with a retention rate of .30 implies a return on investment of .267.

$$.30r = .08$$
$$r = .267$$

The new higher P/E ratio of 10 for Firm S of Table 9.2 is justified because the firm is now expected to earn .267 on new investment.

Let us consider why the merger presented in Table 9.2 may be desirable even though the new earnings per share are reduced to $9.78. Table 9.3 shows the earnings of A without the acquisition and with the acquisition of Firm S. Not until a passage of 43 years does Firm A + S have higher earnings per share than Firm A. It is very unlikely that the board of directors of Firm A would find Table 9.3 to be a persuasive argument in favor of the merger. There is too long a passage of time before the earnings per share of A + S catch up to A. If the switch had taken place in year 2 or 3, there could be room for persuasion. A period of 44.3 years is too long a period to wait. The stockholders of A cannot be expected to be enthusiastic about an acquisition where the benefits are so far in the future.

TABLE 9.3

Year	Without Merger EPS of A g = .075	With Merger EPS of A + S g = .07554
0	10	9.78
1	10.75	10.52
2	11.556	11.31
3	12.423	12.17
4	13.355	13.09
5	14.356	14.08
15	29.59	29.14
25	60.98	60.40
44.3	246.25	246.26
50	371.88	372.97

A Limitation of the Model

It has been shown that a low-P/E company will dilute its earnings per share in acquiring a high-P/E company. This does not mean that the acquisition may not be desirable, but it is a negative factor.

The dilution takes place if the purported facts are accurate and if there are no additional changes. One change that will modify the above conclusion is a change in the capital structure. If additional changes take place, the conclusion that the acquisition will dilute the earnings per share may not be valid. A shift to the utilization of more debt might cause the pro forma earnings per share to be larger with the acquisition than without it, despite the fact that the P/E of the firm being acquired is larger than the acquiring firm's P/E.

There is another complication in applying the model. If a price in excess of book value is paid for the firm, the earnings in future years will have to overcome larger expense charges arising from the upward-revised asset bases (or the presence of good will).

The Debt Level

Frequently an acquisition is accompanied by a significant change in the debt level of the firm after acquisition. Thus two changes are taking place, one in the basic asset composition of the firm and a second in the capital structure of the firm.

As illustrated above, the acquisition of a firm is likely to cause a change in the P/E ratio being applied to the earnings. A change in the capital structure is also likely to cause a change in the return required by the stockholders. The addition of the debt increases the risk to the common stockholders, which in return results in the stockholders requiring a higher return.

The use of debt in connection with acquisitions follows naturally from the application of the following model:

$$\text{Value of levered firm} = \text{value of unlevered firm} + \text{tax rate (amount of debt)}$$

Assume the market value of Firm A is $80,000,000, with a corporate tax rate of .46. If $50,000,000 of debt is substituted for common stock, the value of the firm increases to $103,000,000:

$$80{,}000{,}000 + .46(50{,}000{,}000) = \$103{,}000{,}000$$

If the firm can be acquired for $80,000,000, the acquiring firm could theoretically increase the value to $148,000,000 by the use of a maximum amount of debt.*

*That is, 80,000,000/(1 − .46) = $148,000,000.

Continuing the above example, assume that stockholders want a .10 return from investing in the firm, and that the firm is expected to earn a constant $14,815,000 before tax and $8,000,000 after tax. Thus the value to investors if the firm is only financed with common stock is $80,000,000:

$$\frac{14{,}815{,}000(1 - .46)}{.10} = \$80{,}000{,}000$$

Now assume $50,000,000 of debt can be issued to yield .10. The tax is now $4,515,000:

Earnings before interest	14,815,000
Interest	5,000,000
	9,815,000
	× .46
Tax	4,515,000

The net to stockholders after tax is:

$$14{,}815{,}000 - 4{,}515{,}000 = \$10{,}300{,}000$$

and the present value of this flow using .10 is again $103,000,000.

While the exactness of the above relationships may be objected to, there is no question that the tax deductibility of interest combined with the contractual nature of interest (setting a maximum cost) does make debt an attractive means of financing acquisitions. If the acquisition is financed entirely with debt and if the amount of interest to be paid is less than the earnings before interest and taxes, the earnings per share of the acquiring firm will increase. This does not mean that the acquisition is necessarily desirable, but an increase in earnings per share is a number that is likely to move management in the direction of the acquisition.

We can expect financial analysts to take careful note of the new level of debt and to attempt to identify the portion of the increase in earnings per share that is caused by the increase in debt.

Referring again to Table 9.2, where the acquisition of S using common stock results in a decrease in earnings per share, let us assume that $10,000,000 of debt paying .09 is used to finance the acquisition. The tax rate is .46 and the earnings of S before taxes were $1,852,000. With the $900,000 of interest tax shield, the new tax is $438,000 and the new earnings of A are:

Basic earnings of A		10,000,000
Earnings of S	1,852,000	
Interest	−900,000	
Taxes	−438,000	514,000
		10,514,000

The new earnings per share using debt are $10.51, an increase of $.51 compared with the $10.00 before the acquisition.

An intelligent analyst will look at the $10.51 and realize that there is now more risk. A careless analyst might conclude that Firm A is merely more profitable after the acquisition.

Diversification

An oil company (Mobil) acquires Marcor, which is a combined retail firm (Montgomery Ward) and packaging firm (Container Corporation). This is a dramatic example of diversification by acquisition. If previously Mobil was looked at as a rapidly growing energy company with a large number of profitable investments in the energy area, this evaluation should now be revised.

Is there any set of assumptions that would lead to great excitement about Mobil's eagerness to buy Marcor stock? If previously it was felt that energy was a bottomless pit for investment funds, with certain losses with "dry holes" and government regulation if oil was found, then the switch in investment direction might well be received with a sigh of relief, and more enthusiasm for Mobil stock. There is little advantage investing in the common stock of a company engaged in a series of gambles when the firm cannot win whatever the outcomes (this does not have to be an accurate description of the world, but merely an accurate description of the analysts' perceptions).

The merger that is least likely to attract attention is the merger that crosses over industry lines, and where the operations of the entities are highly independent. The acquisition of Mobil Oil Corporation of Marcor was obviously an attempt by a company in a beleaguered industry (officials of the United States government including several presidents have indicated a distrust of "big oil") to move from an industry rapidly heading for controls to industries not yet so fettered. If the federal government reduces the profitability of one industry, it can expect funds to flow from that industry to other more profitable activities. Mobil executives seemed to be betting that stockholders would welcome a shift from funds invested in a controlled industry. The talk of taxing excessive profits and breaking up vertically integrated companies is likely to have a multiplier effect in terms of discouraging investment in the industry being reviewed for such taxation and dismemberment.

Another industry that considers itself under siege is the steel industry. Many steel industry common stocks in 1980 were selling at one-half of book value and a much smaller percentage of replacement cost. Management considers this situation to be the result of bad governmental policies concerning foreign trade (allowing the dumping of foreign steel) and the implementation of excessive pollution control legislation. Thus in 1979 National Steel Corporation acquired the United Financial Corporation of California. While the stated objective of the acquisition was to provide a source of earnings that would counterbalance the swings in earnings of a steel company, the facts that a finance company does not have environmental controls and there is no "dumping" problem may have been considerations. A common stockholder in a steel company in 1979 is likely to have trouble being enthusiastic about further investment in the steel industry. A shift to an investment in a financial corporation at least opens up the possibility of normal profits that have been missing for 20 years in steel.

With most acquisitions for diversification one would not expect there to be a drastic improvement in the common stock price of the acquiring firm. The selling firm has at least as much information as the buyer, and there is no reason to think that the buyer rather than the seller will reap the surplus. Also, the individual investors could have achieved the same diversification by buying the stock directly.

Diversification and the Shareholders

For simplicity we generally assume the goal of a firm is profit maximization (in present value terms) in order to maximize the well-being of the common stockholders. Periodically we should question this assumption, since corporations are also in existence to serve other groups, for example, management.

When a firm diversifies by merging with or acquiring a firm in another industry, who benefits? Let us consider the position of the shareholder, and for purposes of focusing on diversification, let us assume zero personal tax rates.

The individual shareholder can diversify easily by buying stocks in different firms in different industries. When Marcor is selling at a price of $25, the holder of Mobil common stock does not need Mobil to bid $35 per share for Marcor stock to achieve diversification. The stockholder can easily achieve diversification by investing in mutual funds or buying stock in a variety of firms. The stockholder of a company does not need that company to incur costs to achieve diversification.

The objective of diversification is risk reduction. The advice not to put all one's eggs in one basket is good advice if the objective is to avoid a feast-or-famine situation.

If diversification can generally be achieved efficiently by investors, then why do firms diversify? In the first place there are many investors who are not well diversified and would like to have the corporation diversify on their behalf. But even more importantly there is a group which has its major asset invested in the firm, and this asset is difficult to diversify. The major assets of managers are their careers. If a company goes bankrupt or enters a period of financial difficulty, the middle-aged manager pays a heavy economic price. It is reasonable for such a manager to seek a higher level of security by trying to stabilize the income of the corporation.

Since the diversified stockholder does not benefit significantly from the diversification, why are there not more complaints from such shareholders? The shareholders may not seek diversification, but given an income tax schedule that reaches 70% for ordinary income, there are reasons for the shareholders to accept diversification.

Real Changes

The justification for many mergers and acquisitions is that they will lead to real changes in income. This is the synergy effect where one plus one equals three (or more). As stated earlier, in 1979 Exxon bid $72 per share for Reliance Electric Company common stock, which was selling for $36. The stated justification for offering over $1,170,000,000 for Reliance was that Exxon had developed an energy-saving electronic device for controlling the speed of electric motors. The acquisition of Reliance would accelerate the entry of

Exxon into the electric motor market, and thus there would be synergy.

The situation may be one where one firm is doing something wrong and the other firm's management thinks it can correct the situation. It might be a cigarette company (Philip Morris) acquiring a beer company (Miller's) and thinking it can supply marketing know-how. Or it could be a company that thinks it can supply production and engineering improvements (Emerson Electric has done this very successfully).

In situations where there is synergy both the stockholders of the selling firm and the stockholders of the buying firm can benefit. The market price of the stock may be $25; the sellers may think it is worth $30 and be pleased to sell at $35 at the same time that the buyers see an intrinsic value of $45 once they institute the planned changes.

For the stock of the acquiring firm to reflect immediately the above judgments, the information would have to be publicized. This publicity would not always be consistent with the best implementation of the corporate strategy. Philip Morris did not want to tell the world its plans for Miller's when it acquired the beer maker.

If a firm feels it is not desirable to reveal all its plans either because of strategy considerations or because of the risk of claiming too much and then being embarrassed, all is not lost. If the predictions turn out to be valid, the financial statements will reflect the fact that the acquisition was a wise one, and the stock price will now go up. If the belated nature of the increase is troublesome, then some of the plans should be revealed to gain some of the stock price increase earlier.

Be a Monopoly

One of the easiest bits of advice for a consultant to offer a corporation is "Be a monopoly." Preferably one wants to have a monopoly of a product where the demand is inelastic (that is, people cannot do without the product; if price is increased, there will be a very small decrease in the amount demanded). The organization of OPEC is an example of the formation of such a monopoly. The world has not learned how to do without oil in the short run; thus the price of oil can be increased at a rapid rate to relatively large amounts without greatly decreasing the amount of oil consumed.

The owners of the oil reap large profits. The corporate management which can find a product similar to oil, where the supply side can be legally organized in a manner similar to OPEC, has tremendous profit opportunities. Unfortunately for corporate managers but fortunately for consumers, these "star" products are difficult to find, since legislation makes it illegal to form monopolies by combining the operations of competing firms or by colluding on price. Thus mergers that tend to reduce competition are likely to attract governmental attention and are apt to be declared not in the common interest and to be disallowed. It may be possible to merge in an attempt to round out a product line where it can be argued that there is an increase in competition.

The Spin-off: Splitting the Corporation

If it is desirable for some corporations to merge, it may be desirable for other firms to divest.

There are several situations where divestment may logically be desirable. In the first place, the unit may be more valuable to another corporation because synergy of some type would result. In fact, all the reasons for mergers are, with slight adjustments, reasons for divestment.

There is another basic reason for divestment. Assume a corporation has a major unit that is not healthy. The financial difficulty of the major unit may overshadow the fact that other units of the corporation have excellent prospects.

In such a situation bond covenants might prevent the spinning off of profitable units, since these units are a major part of the debt security. However, there is no reason why a suitable split of the debt cannot be arranged so that the debtholders are approximately as well off (or better off). Adding warrants or conversion features is one method of accomplishing the acceptance of a corporate spin-off.

A third reason for divestment exists when the central core of the corporation adds overhead costs but little or no value. In fact, it can be that the large size of the corporation reduces managerial flexibility as well as preventing identification by employees with the well-being of the corporation. Smaller organizational units standing on their own bottoms might collectively be more valuable than an entire set of units operating as one corporation.

Low Growth and Divestment

Should a unit with low or zero growth be a leading candidate for divestment?

Growth possibilities should dictate whether or not investments in capacity should be made, but growth should not affect the spin-off decision except indirectly. If you forecast zero growth and a firm bidding for the business forecasts growth and thus bids high, the growth forecast will affect the willingness to accept the offer to buy.

Assume there are no growth opportunities and the forecast growth is zero. The book value of the unit is $20,000,000, and it is currently earning $2,000,000 of cash flows per year. The parent requires a return of .20. Since the unit is not growing and is not earning the required return, should the unit be divested?

One important fact has not yet been revealed. The best price that has been offered for the unit is $8,000,000. The firm is earning 2,000,000/8,000,000 = .25 on the opportunity cost; thus the firm is meeting the defined required return and the unit should not be divested.

The growth rate is not relevant except as an input into the cash flow forecast. The opportunity cost, the amount being earned, and the required return are relevant. A perpetuity (zero growth) may have large value, as may a decaying cash flow stream; the type of generalization that leads to divestment if there is no growth is not valid. Computations must be made to make the decision.

An Unsuccessful Tender Offer

A firm does not want to make an unsuccessful tender offer. If a small amount of the stock is acquired, various difficulties arise. If the percentage obtained is less than 20%, the equity method of accounting cannot be used. Also, unless 80% is obtained, the company cannot file a consolidated tax report. Finally, a given percentage is needed so that the firms may be merged (the old corporate legal entity may then be discarded). In some states the percentage needed is one share more than 50% and in other states it is two-thirds of the stock.

The desire to avoid being almost successful frequently leads to tender offers that can be withdrawn if the given number of shares are not obtained. But the conditional nature of the offer will affect the number of shares that are tendered (the investor does not like to have the shares tied up while the corporation decides what to do next). A second strategy is to offer a relatively high price compared with the current market price, with the tender offer having as short a fuse as is legal.

Defensive Maneuvers

A company will sometimes seek a merger or make an acquisition in order to move to a better defensive position relative to thwarting the advances of a firm which is trying to acquire it. This might be good strategy from the point of view of management, but is unnecessary from the stockholders' viewpoint. The stockholders can accept or reject the offers of raiders based on the merits of the offer. They do not need management to move the firm to a more defensible position. The move has no value to the stockholders as a collective group. They do not have to be saved from themselves.

Tax-free Exchange

For an acquisition to be tax free to the seller, it is necessary for the seller to receive stock. This is a strong incentive for the acquiring corporation to use common or preferred stock. It is not necessary that only stock be used. The acquiring firm can acquire less than 50% of the shares for cash and still have the transaction eligible for nontaxable classification.

Goodwill

If Firm A acquires Firm B at a price that is in excess of B's book value, goodwill is created if the purchase method of accounting is used. In the United States goodwill will be written off (expensed) over a period equal to or less than 40 years. Thus future incomes are decreased by the goodwill write-off.

The generally accepted accounting principles of other countries allow the recording of the goodwill but do not require that it be written off. This leads to the interesting situation where the reports of U.S. companies and foreign companies are not comparable without adjustment.

Assume a situation where a firm with zero tangible assets and earnings of $10,000,000 per year is being evaluated. The cost of the firm is $100,000,000. A U.S. firm doing the evaluation would look forward to an increase in income of $7,500,000 (that is, $10,000,000 minus $2,500,000), while an English firm if it paid exactly the same price for exactly the same firm would have its earnings increase by $10,000,000.

Theoretically the market sees through the sort of artificial difference being described and the method of accounting should not affect the decision. However, perceptions are also important. Some managers perceive the creation of goodwill (and its resulting effect on income) as a negative factor because of its effect on earnings per share. They view negative goodwill with its positive effect on income as a factor facilitating an acquisition.

Mergers: Negative Goodwill

The strangest things affect an acquisition decision. Consider a situation where Firm A is considering acquiring Firm B. The book value of B's stock equity is $30,000,000, and 100% of the common stock can be acquired at a cost of $20,000,000. If the acquisition is accounted for as a purchase, there will be $10,000,000 of negative goodwill. This negative goodwill, when written off, will have a favorable effect on income.

It can (and should) be argued that this type of effect is not real. In the first place, the accounting entries do not affect the cash flows. Secondly, the increase in the income of the period arising from the amortization of the negative good will would be more or less balanced by the write-off of the extra $10,000,000 of assets that were acquired.

A consideration such as the existence of negative goodwill should be so far down on the list of factors to be considered that it never can affect a decision.

Conclusions

There are many motivations that lead to mergers and acquisitions. The payment of a larger premium over market price does not necessarily indicate an unwise decision. Unfortunately, sometimes management might not be able to reveal all its reasons for offering the large premium. Thus stockholder unrest can arise where there would not be unrest if all the facts were known. But even worse, there can also be situations where management's analysis is faulty and the purchase price is excessive. Time will reveal which is the true situation. Looking back, any one of us can be wiser than the wisest manager.

Chapter 10
The Complexity: Financial Strategy and Inflation

Inflation is not all that bad,
In fact there are some outright "goods,"
For all now live without a move
*In more expensive neighborhoods.**

FMK

Inflation is frustrating to corporate managers. They feel strongly that they "should do something." The fact that there is inflation is beyond their immediate control, but a wide range of decisions are within their control. Unfortunately the adjustments made for inflation frequently are of an incorrect nature. Corporations too often mix and match the several possible adjustments and end up with calculations that are extremely misleading. We will first consider the use of debt to counterbalance the inflation and then discuss to what extent the investment decision process of a corporation (using present value or the internal rate of return method) should be affected by forecasts of inflation.

The Problem

If there currently is inflation, we suspect that prices will change dramatically in the future, and intuitively we conclude that an adjustment should be made. We need to define four terms for the analysis to follow:

"Current dollars": revenue and costs are measured as they will be measured when the cash is received and disbursed.

* Senator Alan Cranston. "Inflation is not all bad. After all, it has allowed every American to live in a more expensive neighborhood without moving." Reported by Robert D. Hershey, Jr. *The New York Times,* February 3, 1980.

"Constant dollars": revenue and costs in current dollars are adjusted to reflect changes in purchasing power. All dollars reflect the same purchasing power after adjustment.

"Nominal interest rates": the actual cost of money measured in current dollars.

"Real interest rate": the cost of money if constant dollars are used.

Combining the wrong dollars of an investment with the wrong interest rate gives rise to major errors in capital budgeting under inflationary conditions. Also, easy generalizations are generally inexact. For example, let us consider the conclusion that one should be in debt during an inflationary period.

Debt and Inflation

The chairman of the board said, "Given that we expect inflation, let us increase the amount of debt leverage we are using." It is well to consider the assumptions that are implicitly behind this statement.

First, let us assume a situation where with no inflation investors would be satisfied with a .04 return and it is expected that there will be a .12 inflation rate. New one-period debt of $1,000 can be issued to yield 16.48%. If these are the facts, then the investor in the debt will receive $1,164.80 at time 1. At time 1 the $1,164.80 is worth $1,040 (that is, 1,164.80/1.12 = $1,040) in purchasing power. The investor earns the required return of .04, and the real cost to the corporation is .04. There is no bargain. The debt is no cheaper than if there were no expected inflation and the debt were to cost .04 in terms of current dollars. There is no special advantage to issuing debt if the nominal rate on the debt is linked to the real rate (.04) and the inflation rate (.12) by the following relationship:

$$\begin{aligned}\text{Nominal rate} &= \text{real rate} + \text{inflation rate} + \text{product of the two}\\ &= .04 + .12 + (.04)\,(.12) = .1648\end{aligned}$$

The above is an equilibrium situation. The real cost of the debt is equal to the real return desired by investors.

Now assume debt can be issued at a cost of .1424. The real rate that the investors will earn and the cost to the borrower is now .02:

$$\begin{aligned}.1424 &= r + .12 + .12r\\ .0224 &= 1.12\,r\\ r &= .02\end{aligned}$$

The firm gets a bargain by issuing debt (the real return being paid is less than the real return desired by investors).

To balance the last example, if the firm can only borrow at a cost of .1872, then:

$$.1872 = r + .12 + .12r$$
$$.0672 = 1.12r$$
$$r = .06$$

Now the real cost of borrowing is greater than the equilibrium cost of .04. At a cost of .1872, even with .12 inflation, debt is not cheap. The real borrowing rate of .06 is larger than the cost of .04 with no inflation.

We have illustrated three different nominal interest rates where the real cost of borrowing was computed and compared with the real cost desired by investors. We have shown that the expectation of inflation does not necessarily mean that debt should be issued. Secondly, even if the nominal borrowing rate is .1424 and it seems that debt should be issued (the real cost of borrowing is only .02), if the best investment only yields .10 in current dollars, then it is not desirable that more debt should be issued (assuming zero taxes). The debt cost is larger than the investment's return.

Now assume there are investments that yield more than .1424 thus capital should be raised. It has not been proven that debt at .1424 is more desirable than common stock. For example, we could take away the tax shield characteristic of debt interest, and it is far from obvious that debt is more desirable than common stock even where the real cost of debt is only .02. The real cost of common stock may be equivalently low compared with the inflation rate.

While it would seem to be a desirable strategy to be heavily in debt during periods of rapid inflation, we cannot be sure. The decision should depend on the nominal interest cost, the rate of return available on investments, and the cost of alternative sources of capital. Certainly a firm should consider the use of debt when it expects inflation. Whether it actually uses debt will depend on detailed analysis, not solely on the existence of inflation.

Inflation and Capital Budgeting

It is natural and correct to want to take inflation into consideration when one evaluates investments. However, it is important that inflation be considered correctly. There are many ways of introducing errors into the analysis, and they all have been found by corporations. It is important that the correct time value factor be matched with the correct set of cash flows relative to the adjustment or non-adjustment for inflation.

EXAMPLE: Assume the following facts apply for an investment being considered by Firm A. The cash flows are the actual dollars to be spent or to be received based on the forecast economic conditions:

Period	Current Dollars: Cash Flows	Expected Price Index
0	−18,017	100
1	10,000	112
2	10,800	125.44

The firm can obtain funds at a cost of .09, and we assume for simplicity that there are zero taxes and all the capital being used is debt. Using the .09 rate as the discount rate, the investment has a net present value of $247 and the investment seems to be acceptable. The conclusion is consistent with the fact that the internal rate of return of the investment is .10, which is greater than the cost of money. This analysis and conclusion are correct.

Many firms do not use the above analysis. The estimate of the cash flows is in terms of current dollars, and these forecasts seem to fail to consider the change in purchasing power. Converting the cash flows to constant dollars, we obtain the following cash flows:

Period	Current Dollars: Cash Flows	Price Level Adjustment	Constant Dollars
0	−18,017	1	−18,017
1	10,000	100/112	8,929
2	10,800	100/125.44	8,610

Now the net present value using .09 is a negative $2,579. The investment is now not acceptable. But it is an error to convert the cash flows to constant dollars and then use the nominal interest rate of .09 to accomplish the discounting.

In this situation, the first solution given above is the correct solution. No adjustments have to be made! One can use the current dollar cash flows and the nominal interest rates and obtain a decision that is consistent with maximizing the well-being of the stockholders. For example, if $18,017 is borrowed at a cost of .09, we would have:

Time	Amount Owed	Cash Flow of Investment	Amount Left after Payment of Debt
0	18,017		
1	19,639	10,000	
2	10,506	10,800	294

After using the cash flows of the investment to pay the debt, there is $294 left over for the residual investors at time 2.

The current dollar cash flows of period 2 do reflect the forecast of a .08 increase in the benefits of period 2 compared with the benefits of period 1. This set of cash flows reflects the expected price changes as well as other considerations.

We reach two conclusions:

1. The use of current dollars and nominal interest rates is a correct procedure.
2. The use of constant dollars and nominal interest rates is an erroneous procedure.

The use of constant dollars and nominal interest rates is an erroneous procedure in the sense that it indicates the investment should be rejected even though stockholders benefit from undertaking the investment.

Better Off—Worse Off

It can be argued that the above investment should be rejected, since the investors will be worse off at the end of the period than at the beginning of the period. We will now assume that the investors start with $18,017 of capital at time 0 (the cost of the investment) and they can lend external to the firm and earn .09. The .09 is accepted as a reasonable measure of the opportunity cost of funds. If the investment is undertaken after two periods, the investor will have:

$$\text{Terminal value} = 10{,}000\ (1.09) + 10{,}800 = \$21{,}700$$

but adjusted for inflation this amount in terms of initial purchasing power will only be worth:

$$\frac{21{,}700}{1.2544} = \$17{,}299$$

The position of the investor at time 2 with the investment is worse than it was at time 0. However, this is the wrong comparison. Let us consider how the investor would have done without the investment. The amount of dollars at time 2 would be:

$$18{,}017(1.09)^2 = \$21{,}406$$

and with price level adjusted this is equivalent to initial purchasing power of:

$$\frac{21{,}406}{1.2544} = \$17{,}065$$

The investor is better off with the investment than without it! The fact that the financial position of the investor has deteriorated is interesting but does not help the investor make the decision. The .09 truly represents the return from the best alternatives to the investment. Even though the investor is worse off at the end of the period than at the beginning, the investor is better off with the investment than without it.

The Use of Constant Dollars

In the above example constant dollars were used incorrectly to evaluate the investment. In some situations the investor prefers not to forecast the cash flows in current dollars but is willing to forecast the constant dollar cash flows. This bypasses the necessity of forecasting the inflation rate (it can be argued that the bypassing is only approximate). If the cash flows are in constant dollars, the real interest rate should be used. Unfortunately, while the nominal borrowing rate can be observed in the capital markets, the real interest rate cannot be so observed. We do not know the value of the real interest rate.

It is difficult to state a given number for the real rate and defend that estimate. All the nominal observed rates are affected jointly by government action and the forces of economics. Isolating out the real interest rate is difficult. A number of the magnitude of .04 can be used, but it should not be thought that we know the real rate is .04. In equilibrium, we can hypothesize that:

Normal rate = real rate + inflation rate and the product of the two

Thus if the real rate were .04 and the inflation rate were .12, under equilibrium conditions we would expect the nominal rate to be:

$$\text{Nominal rate} = .04 + .12 + (.04)(.12) = .1648$$

Assume $100 is invested to earn .1648. After one year the investor will have $116.48. But $116.48 converted to constant dollars with an inflation rate of .12 is 116.48/1.12 = $104. Thus the investor earned a real return of .04 on the initial investment of $100.

Unfortunately, if there is not equilibrium, the above relationships do not hold. We can observe the nominal rate and the inflation rate and can compute the real return that is actually earned, but we cannot conclude that amount is the real return that investors want to use in evaluating future investments. For example, if the inflation rate is .15 per year and if an interest rate of .15 is observed, we might infer that the real interest rate is zero. The application of this faulty conclusion would result in erroneous decisions. The actual real return may be zero, but that does not mean that investors want a zero real return.

Changing Discount Rates

There may be times when one forecasts different inflation rates and, equally important, different interest rates in future time periods. Money may cost .25 in period 1 but we expect it to cost .20 in period 2 and .10 in period 3. We have the following present value factors for cash flows received in each of the three time periods:

Time 1:			$(1.25)^{-1}$	= .8000
Time 2:		$(1.25)^{-1}$	$(1.20)^{-1}$	= .6667
Time 3:	$(1.25)^{-1}$	$(1.20)^{-1}$	$(1.10)^{-1}$	= .6061

Consider the following two investments:

	0	1	2	3	Internal Rate of Return
Investment A	−1,000	1,200			.20
Investment B	−1,000	200	200	1,200	.20

The net present value of A is negative and it should be rejected:

$$
\begin{aligned}
-1{,}000 \times 1.0000 &= -1{,}000 \\
+1{,}200 \times .8000 &= 960 \\
\hline
& -40
\end{aligned}
$$

The net present value of B is positive and it should be accepted.

$$
\begin{aligned}
-1{,}000 \times 1.0000 &= -1{,}000 \\
200 \times .8000 &= 160 \\
200 \times .6667 &= 133 \\
1{,}200 \times .6061 &= 727 \\
\hline
& 20
\end{aligned}
$$

The two investments have the same internal rate of return but one is acceptable and the other is not. The high cost of money in period 1 dictates that A be rejected. B is able to overcome the high cost of money in early time periods by the receipt of high returns in a period of relatively low money cost (period 3).

If the period 1 cost of .25 were used for all three periods, B would also have been rejected. If the three interest rates reflect management's projections, the use of any one rate is incorrect.

Maintaining Real Income

It is difficult to maintain real income during periods of inflation. With taxes on income, it becomes doubly difficult.

First we will consider a zero-tax situation where there is a .10 inflation per year. Assume the investor wants to earn a .04 real return. To earn a .04 real return, the investor will have to earn .144. For example, assume a $100 investment will earn .144 and pay $114.40 in one year. The $144.40 is equivalent to 114.40/1.10 = $104 in terms of beginning of the period dollars. This is a real return of .04 on the initial investment. The .144 necessary nominal return is equal to the sum of the required real return, the rate of inflation, and the product of the two terms.

Now assume that interest income is taxed at a rate of .6. The after-tax real return available with no inflation is (1 − .6).04 = .016. What return before tax is necessary to earn .016 in real terms if there is .10 inflation?

Assume that a .294 nominal return is available. A $100 investment will return $129.40 one year hence. The tax on the taxable income of $29.40 is $17.64:

	129.40
	100.00
Taxable income	29.40
Tax rate	× .6
Tax	17.64

Subtracting the tax from $129.40, we net $111.76, but now we have to adjust for the inflation. The $111.76 adjusted for inflation is:

$$\frac{111.76}{1.10} = \$101.60$$

Thus a .016 after-tax real return is earned if a nominal before-tax return of .294 is earned (the .294 can be determined analytically). The necessity of the .294 interest return can be appreciated by recognizing that the interest must make up for the .10 erosion in the value of the $100 investment. In addition, this amount has to be large enough to survive a .6 rate of taxation.

High rates of taxation combined with the high rates of inflation make it very difficult for an investor to earn a positive after tax real return unless the value of the asset increases more or less in proportion to inflation, and the increase is not taxed. This helps explain the flight by investors to real assets (gold, silver, art, real estate) during periods when inflation is expected. It is very difficult to hold one's real after-tax position holding assets denominated in nominal dollars if the nominal income is taxed at high ordinary rates.

Depreciation and Taxes and Inflation

Given inflation, corporations would like to deduct as an expense price-level-adjusted depreciation in computing taxable income. For example, with price-level-adjusted depreciation and with a doubling of the price level $1,000,000 of depreciation becomes $2,000,000. With a .46 tax rate the additional depreciation saves $460,000 of taxes.

With 40 years of inflation behind us, price-level-adjusted depreciation is very attractive. Unfortunately (for the business community) its acceptance by Congress is very unlikely. More likely are other forms of liberalization of the methods of writing off capital assets. For example, if assets can be expensed when acquired, the price level adjustment question becomes irrelevant for those assets.

Conclusions

We have illustrated correct and incorrect methods of evaluating investments under conditions of inflation. We have not attempted to illustrate all the possible combinations of incorrect calculations. The discounted cash flow calculations are powerful tools of analysis, but if the inputs do not have a sound theoretical foundation, the output is not useful.

It is reasonable to want to adjust for inflation. The calculation of cash flows using current dollars does adjust for inflation in the sense that the current dollar forecast reflects the expected price changes. While the adjustment to constant dollars is useful in evaluating whether the investor is better or worse off at the end of the period than at the beginning, it is difficult to use constant dollars to make accept-or-reject investment decisions. The combination of constant dollars and the nominal interest rates is a major error.

Inflation should be taken into consideration by financial planners. The cash flow projections should reflect the forecasts of price level changes. Make sure the cash flow projections are consistent with the best economic forecasts and do good basic economic evaluations with no fancy adjustments that are not fully understood. Keep it simple.

Chapter 11
The Bottom Line: Earnings per Share

The only number for which they care
Is the bottom line—earnings per share.
This will indicate a loss or show that profits are mounting,
But can be altered by the method used for its accounting.

FMK

Several years ago a financial consultant wrote a paper that had the theme that earnings per share did not affect the value of a company's common stock. This extreme position is useful as a means of dramatizing the fact that one can be misled by focusing on earnings per share. The purpose of this chapter is to reaffirm the basic importance of earnings per share and at the same time suggest that improved earnings per share that are the result of good decisions are much more important than increases arising from accounting conventions.

A manager should not choose the strategy that leads to the maximum immediate earnings per share. Rather, the optimal decision will have the most desirable effects on earnings per share through time.

The strategy of maximizing the short-run earnings per share is rejected in favor of a strategy that is based on sound economic decision making. This does not mean that earnings per share are not important, but rather that long-run earnings per share are thought to be so important that the decisions should not be made on short-run considerations.

Accounting and Earnings per Share

Accounting conventions are of such a nature that real decisions that favorably affect the value of the firm may adversely affect short-run earnings.

Let us consider the class of accounting entries where the incurrence of an expenditure (or a liability) gives rise to an expense even though all parties would agree that the future revenues of the firm are benefited by the expenditure. Among the items giving rise to immediate expenses even though they benefit the future are advertising, research and development, maintenance, and training and education expenditures. All of these items can be reduced or eliminated and benefit immediate earnings. The value of the firm as an operating entity might not be increased by the reduction in spending, but the income of the period is increased.

If a firm financed by common stock has $10,000,000 in marketable securities, a deferral in starting construction of a new plant will have a desirable effect on income. Unspent cash invested in securities will earn interest revenue and income will be higher than if the cash was spent on construction. This occurs because the accountant does not record the opportunity cost of stock equity capital committed to construction. This omission gives rise to different firms having different incomes merely because of differences in capital structure and in construction timing.

Retirement of Bonds

Another opportunity for manipulation occurs when a company has low-interest-paying debt outstanding during a period of high interest rates. The bonds can be purchased at a discount from face value. This gives management an opportunity to buy its own bonds at a discount from the maturity amount and to report a gain from the transaction. The gain is of an accounting nature and is not real.

In one situation a corporation purchased $40,000,000 of .04 debt for $30,000,000 and reported a gain of $10,000,000. The financial vice president was proud of having earned .33 on the investment (that is, 10,000,000/30,000,000 = .33). According to the VP this was the best investment the firm had made in the past year.

The firm did not earn .33; in fact it earned nothing and incurred brokerage expenses. If the current yield to maturity is .10, the retired debt saved interest through time of .10 (that is, the retired debt was yielding .10 when it was purchased). The debt issued to accomplish the refinancing would also yield .10. Thus the firm was effectively substituting one .10 debt for a second .10 debt. The fact that the outstanding debt was paying a contractual rate of .04 does not change the fact that when it was purchased it was yielding .10.

The .33 alleged return is the result of dividing $10,000,000 of income by the outlay of $30,000,000. A true internal rate of return of .33 would accrue through time, not instantaneously. The $10,000,000 of income resulted from the increase in interest rates from .04 to .10, and this took place in past time periods. At the time of bond repurchase by the corporation the events leading to the possibility of gain had already taken place.

When the company buys the old debt and replaces it with more or less identical new debt, it has accomplished nothing real (except incurred some transaction costs). Nevertheless, the accounting income is affected. The analyst will want to adjust for gains arising from this type of transaction.

Depreciation and Earnings

The method of depreciation will affect the earnings and thus decisions. Imagine a situation where a market is expected to grow tremendously in the next 10 years. A firm is considering two alternatives. It can build a small plant that will be used at 100% capacity the day it is completed. The annual depreciation expense for this alternative is $10,000,000. The second alternative is to build a plant which has excess capacity initially but which will not be operating at capacity until year 5. The depreciation expense of the second plant is $18,000,000 per year. In addition, the larger plant requires the issuance of more shares of common stock.

Assume sound economic (present value) analysis indicates that the larger plant should be built, but that earnings per share will initially be depressed by the larger depreciation expense and the larger number of shares outstanding.

There are two choices available. One is to ignore the accounting measures and make the decision based on the economic criteria. The second choice is to improve the accounting measures so that they are consistent with the economic measures. A third alternative is to make a bad decision (do not build the larger plant) that appears to be good.

Stock Acquisition

In the chapter on dividend policy we discussed the real merits of stock reacquisition. We will consider the effect on earnings per share. First, stock acquisition in lieu of a cash dividend will have the effect of increasing the earnings per share. Secondly, this increase is not a real change.

Consider a firm earning $800,000 with 1,000,000 shares of common stock outstanding selling at a price of $8 per share. The current earnings per share are $.80. If the firm reacquires 100,000 shares at a cost of $800,000 and if there is no change in the earnings, we now have earnings per share of $.89, up from $.80.

If the stock continues to sell at 10 times earnings the market price is now $8.90. The total value of the stockholders' equity is $8,-000,000, that is, (800,000/900,000) × 900,000 × 10. This is unchanged from the stock equity of a year previously. The earnings per share increased because of the shrinkage in the number of shares, but there is no change in total value.

Mergers

Assume that the price/earnings ratio of an acquisition is defined in terms of the price to be paid in accomplishing the acquisition. The earnings per share of the acquiring firm will be increased as long as the P/E ratio of the acquiring firm is larger than the P/E ratio of the acquired firm, and common stock is used for the acquisition.

Consider the following two firms where A is acquiring B:

	A	B
Price per share	$20	$10
Earnings per share	$1	$2
P/E ratio	20	5
Shares outstanding	1,000,000	200,000
Total earnings	$1,000,000	$400,000
Total value	$20,000,000	2,000,000

If A acquires B, we would expect the earnings per share of A to increase.

Assume A gives 100,000 shares and acquires B. The new total earnings are $1,400,000, and there are 1,100,000 shares outstanding. The new earnings per share of A are $1.27, up from $1.00 per share.

If B were to acquire A in exchange for 2,000,000 shares, there would again be total earnings of $1,400,000, and there would now be

2,200,000 shares outstanding. The earnings per share of B would decrease from \$2 to \$.64.

We have not investigated whether an acquisition of B by A or A by B is desirable from an economic point of view. All we have determined is the effects of the acquisitions on the immediate earnings per share. Immediate earnings per share is not a reliable measure of desirability for the merger.

Debt and Earnings per Share

It is easy to move the question of debt versus common stock from the economic basis where we do not know the answer, to earnings per share effects where we can be reasonably definite about the consequences.

Assume a situation where the amount of capital is \$100,000,000 (2,500,000 shares of common stock outstanding) and debt can be borrowed at a cost of .12. The current price of a share of common stock is \$40, and the corporate tax rate is .46.

It can be shown that the issuance of debt will increase the earnings per share of the firm as long as the earnings before interest and taxes are greater than \$12,000,000 per year (that is, greater than .12 × 100,000,000). If earnings before interest and taxes are equal to \$12,000,000, the earnings per share at this earnings level will be \$2.592. This is equal to the earnings per share where the firm is indifferent as to capital structure (using this one measure). The indifferent earnings per share is equal to the after tax interest rate times the stock price.

$$(1 - .46)(.12)(40) = \$2.592$$

Assume \$50,000,000 of .12 debt is issued and 1,250,000 shares are retired. We now have:

Earnings	12,000,000
Interest	6,000,000
Earnings before tax	6,000,000
Tax	2,760,000
Earnings after tax	3,240,000

$$\frac{3,240,000}{1,250,000} = \$2.592 \text{ earnings per share}$$

If actual earnings before tax and interest are larger than $12,000,000, we will be happy that the debt was used. If the earnings are less than $12,000,000, the earnings per share will be depressed by the issuance of the debt. This is shown in Figure 11.1.

If we are willing to base the decision on maximization of earnings per share and assume that earnings before interest and taxes will be larger than $12,000,000, the issuance of the $50,000,000 debt is a correct decision. It is only when we recognize the probability that earnings could be less than $12,000,000 and incorporate this fact in the analysis that we find that the debt versus common stock decision is not resolved by inspection of the effect on earnings per share.

FIGURE 11.1

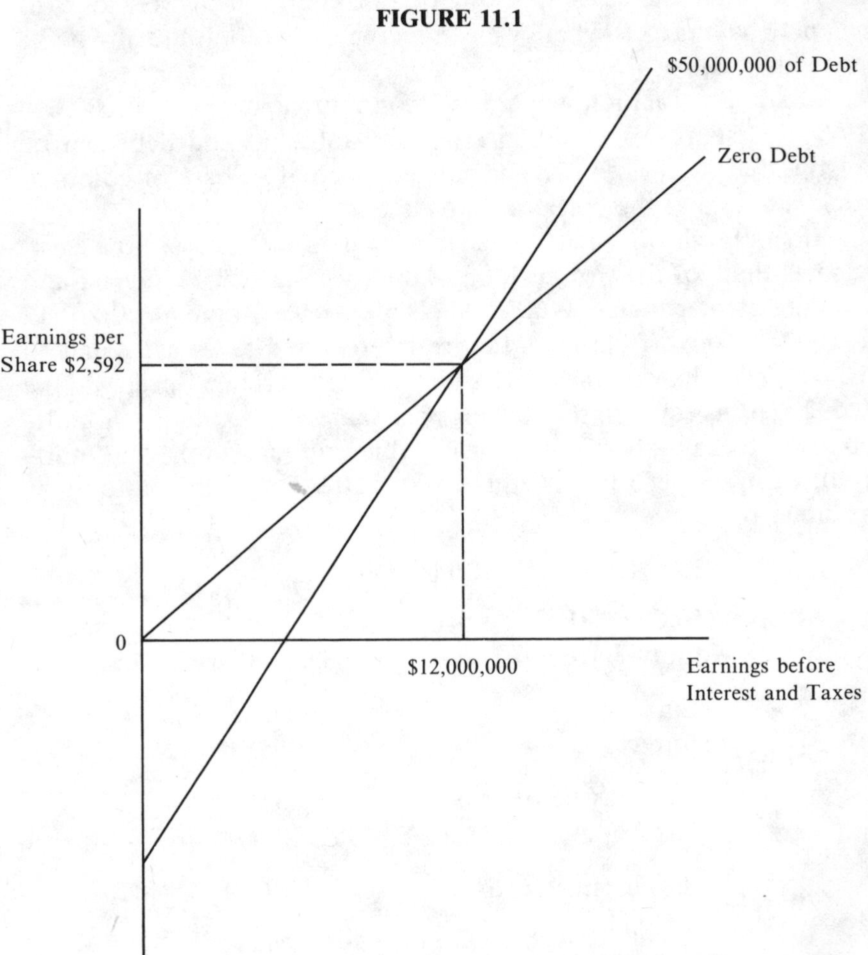

So far we have considered the effect of the substitution of debt for common stock on earnings per share. Now let us consider the undertaking of a new investment which can be financed by debt costing .12 before tax and .0648 after tax. An investment expected to yield an after-tax return in excess of .0648 will have a desirable effect on earnings per share. However, if there is risk (the possibility that lower returns may be earned), it is not obvious that the effect on earnings per share is sufficient to compensate for the increase on risk.

A financial manager will likely want to compute the effect on earnings per share of issuing debt. The fact that the earnings per share increase is not a sufficient reason to decide a decision is correct.

Growth and Earnings per Share

Stocks with relatively high P/E ratios have achieved these high ratios because the market perceives a high growth for dividends, which implies a high growth in earnings per share. We want to consider a model for estimating a firm's growth rate.

Assume that a company has achieved all the earnings improvements that are feasible as a result of increased efficiency and any other changes that do not require capital outlays. Now additional growth can only take place as a result of investment.

Without any debt the growth rate in dividends and earnings is equal to retention rate times return on new investments.

If the firm retains .6 of its earnings and expects to earn .20 on its investments, the expected growth rate is $.6 \times .2 = .12$.

Now assume that for every dollar of common stock equity there is two dollars of debt costing .12. The after-tax cost of debt is .0648. The growth contributed by the use of the debt leverage is equal to the difference between the return on investment and after-tax cost of debt times the product of the retention rate and leverage ratio (debt divided by common stock). For the example we have:

$$.6 \, \frac{2}{1} \, (.20 - .0648) = .16224$$

If we add .16224 to the basic growth rate of .12, we obtain .28224.

Note the large contribution that debt makes to the total growth rate. In the example this is caused by the large difference between the expected return to be earned on the new investments and the after-tax cost of debt.

Assume that the earnings are $100. The model says that the growth rate of .28224 will lead to earnings next period of $128.224. The $60 of retained earnings plus $120 of debt ($180 of investment) will earn $36. The $120 of debt will pay (after tax) $7.776 interest. The after-tax after-interest new earnings will be $28.224. Adding this amount to the $100 original earnings, we obtain the $128.224 which results from applying the .28224 growth rate.

From a strategy standpoint we find that expected growth in earnings is a function of:

The return that can be earned on new investment
The amount retained
The amount of debt
The after-tax cost of debt

It is important to recognize that a change in the retention rate or the amount of debt will cause a change in the average return expected to be earned on new investment (larger investments will cause the acceptance of less desirable investments).

Investors and Earnings per Share

Assume you can choose one conventional financial number to consider for each of 10 firms before you invest in one company's common stock. What number would you choose? Most investors would choose earnings per share for most companies. For some industries we might choose differently.

If we were allowed to ask questions about the earnings per share number, we would make inquiries concerning the quality of the earnings number. The method of accounting for such items as depreciation, interest, research, maintenance, oil exploration expenses, and unusual nonrecurring events would be checked as well as their impact on earnings. Other facts such as the impact on earnings resulting from acquisitions would also be of interest. The trend of earnings and the amount of leverage would also enter into the valuation.

If the restriction that we use a conventional financial number were removed, theoretically we should shift to the present value of all future dividends (risk adjusted). That would avoid the question of the relative importance of financial information since it would shift the analysis to a forecast of the future dividends.

Conclusions

We conclude that the investor is interested in the historical earnings per share, but a well-informed investor will not stop there. The only truly relevant earnings numbers are the earnings of the future. The current earnings are relevant only as the basis of the forecast of future earnings.

In answer to the question as to the most important single number, some investors would choose the book value per share. Since book value measures are the result of generally accepted accounting principles which are not aimed at presenting value measures, there is a general reluctance to use the book value measures as the primary basis of obtaining an intrinsic value for common stock. If a good value measure were available, it would give earnings per share more competition than book value does.

It is true that the theoretically correct input into a stock valuation calculation is future dividends. Instead of dividends we could use "cash flow to stockholders," since the numbers would be identical. But the relevant measures are *future* cash flows or dividends to stockholders which are not observable, so we come back to the use of earnings per share, which can be observed.

Chapter 12
The Soft Debt: Leases

Despite those managers disposed to say,
"Unlike debt, from a lease you can walk away,"
The advantages of leasing cannot clearly be known
Till the costs are computed and a profit is shown.

FMK

Children like to ask each other what would happen if one fell out of an airplane and landed in a pile of feathers, hay, etc. Business has the same type of question about what happens if you are leasing and the firm runs into financial difficulties. The answer to the children's question is that it depends on the size of the pile of feathers. If you fall from a mile above the earth into a mile-high pile of feathers, you might have not broken many bones. If you have a "soft" lease, you can run into financial difficulties and ease out of the lease. But before reaching the conclusion that a lease is soft debt, you had better read the contract carefully. Lessors can be every bit as mean as bank loan officers if you do not pay the lease payment when due.

Lenders will frequently lend funds to a lessor because of the credit rating of the lessee. The loan is not apt to take place if the lessor is in weak financial condition and the lease is of such a nature that the lessee can walk away from it without severe penalty.

If the lease is canceled only with a significant penalty, the lease becomes analogous to debt, and special treatment is needed for comparing buying and leasing of an asset.

The Strategy Implications of Leasing

There are two major aspects of the leasing decision from a strategy prospective. One is the economic characteristics of the lease contract compared with the economic characteristics of the buy decision. Secondly, there are accounting differences and these differences can lead to different income measures.

While there are easily a dozen reasons for either leasing or not leasing, we shall focus on the two major factors that tend to affect strategy choices. The calculations will become a bit messy, but if you wade through them, you will gain some useful insights into how lease and buy alternatives should be compared.

The Economic Decision

The three primary reasons why leasing arrangements tend to be economically desirable from the point of view of the lessee are tax rate and discount rate differences for the lessee and the lessor, different expectations as to the type of the asset or as to some other input into the calculation, and different methods of calculation.

In 1971 the Anaconda Company started to build a mill to process alumina into aluminum ingots. The cost of the plant was expected to be in excess of $100,000,000. While ordinarily Anaconda would have built and owned such a plant, in 1971 Anaconda was in a special situation. The government in Chile had expropriated the company's copper mines, resulting in a tax loss of over $300,000,000. The loss could be carried forward; thus with an expected zero tax rate for the next few years Anaconda could not use the investment tax credit or the accelerated depreciation expense associated with the new plant. A complex leveraged leasing arrangement was set up by U.S. Leasing International and by the First Boston Corporation where high-tax entities became the lessor owners by contributing over $30,000,000, and insurance companies with excess cash made $72,000,000 of loans. With this arrangement the tax benefits went where they could do the most good, to entities currently possessing taxable incomes. The tax rate differential between the equity holders and the Anaconda Company was the factor that enabled U.S. Leasing International to put together a deal where everyone expected to benefit (except for the tax collector). A zero tax firm cannot make use of an investment tax credit.

Note the word "expected" in the above sentence. If the tax rate of the equity holders were to decrease or the tax rate of Anaconda were to increase, the actual results of the lease might not be as beneficial as they originally seemed to be. It happens that in the situation being described Anaconda made an abrupt return to profitability and what seemed to be a brilliant maneuver at the time of signing the contract now seems to have been something less desirable. But the generalization is still valid. Tax rate differentials are an important factor behind the leasing industry, especially when they are combined with different discount rates for the different firms.

The second reason for leasing is different expectations. If the lessee thinks a computer will have a life of 3 years and the lessor bases the lease payments on a life of 10 years, the lease terms will look good to the lessee compared to buying. If the lessor's estimates are wrong the lessor normally stands to lose. Recently lessors insured themselves against these losses. However in 1979 Lloyd's of London was hit for tremendous claims. It had insured lessors against losses arising from their expectations of computer life being different from the actual economic life of the asset. The way the contract worked was that if the lessee terminated the lease after the noncancellation period had ended, Lloyd's would pay the party financing the lease any amount due on the purchase price of the computer. A bank would now lend to a lessor, since Lloyd's guaranteed the loan. Even if a lessor overestimated the life of the computer, the lessor would not be harmed. If the life of the computer turned out to be larger than the estimate on which the rentals were based, the lessor would win heavily.

Unfortunately, Lloyd's insured a large amount of lease contracts (more than $1,000,000,000), and in 1979 IBM announced a more powerful computer with a lower cost, and Lloyd's found itself paying very large sums to banks. In this situation Lloyd's had overestimated the life of the computers being leased, resulting in the lessee having a good deal, and the lessors not having losses.

As we will illustrate, a faulty method of calculation can also lead to leasing either being desirable or seeming to be desirable.

A Method of Calculation

Assume the Auto Corporation is thinking of leasing equipment rather than buying it. The equipment costs $3,000,000, or it can be leased at a cost of $1,000,000 per year. The life of the equipment is known to be five years and there is no salvage value. We will assume all the facts are known with certainty.

The corporate tax rate is .46. The company can borrow debt capital at a cost of .10. The lease would be noncancelable, so would be the equivalent of debt.

To evaluate investments, the company uses a hurdle rate of .20 (this can be considered to be a weighted average cost of capital).

Assume there is no investment tax credit and the firm uses five year straight line depreciation for tax purposes.

The first step in the evaluation of buying versus leasing is to compute the net cost of buying. We define the net cost of buying (with zero investment tax credit and zero residual value) as:

$$\text{Net cost of buying} = \text{cost of asset} - \text{present value of tax savings}$$

The annual depreciation expense using straight line depreciation is $600,000. With a tax rate of .46 the depreciation tax savings per year are $276,000. Using a rate of discount of .20, the present value of the depreciation tax savings is:

$$276{,}000 \times 2.9906 = \$825{,}000$$

where 2.9906 is the present value of a five-year annuity using .20 as the rate of discount. The cost of buying net of the depreciation tax savings is:

$$3{,}000{,}000 - 825{,}000 = \$2{,}175{,}000$$

Now let us consider the net cost of leasing. The annual after-tax cost of leasing is $(1 - .46)1{,}000{,}000 = \$540{,}000$. If it is desired to use .20 as the rate of discount, we obtain:

$$540{,}000 \times 2.9906 = \$1{,}615{,}000$$

This amount is less than the net cost of buying, and leasing would seem to be preferred. While seemingly correct, the above calculation is in error. It biases drastically in favor of leasing and is an unreliable indication of preference. To see that the calculation cannot be used, we will compute the cash flows for each year if we buy. We start with the debt amortization schedule assuming that $3,000,000 is borrowed and is paid off with equal payments of $791,390 per year (payments at end of each year):

Period	Amount Owed	Interest	Principal
1	3,000,000	300,000	491,390
2	2,508,610	250,861	540,529
3	1,968,081	196,808	594,582
4	1,373,499	137,750	654,040
5	719,459	71,946	719,444*

*There is a rounding error.

The cash flows of buying are:

Period	After-Tax interest	Principal	Tax Savings: Depreciation	Sum 1 + 2 −
1	.54(300,000) = 162,000	491,000	276,000	377,00
2	.54(250,861) = 135,000	540,000	276,000	400,00
3	.54(196,808) = 106,000	595,000	276,000	425,00
4	.54(137,350) = 74,000	654,000	276,000	452,00
5	.54(71,946) = 39,000	719,000	276,000	482,00
				2,076,00

With leasing the after-tax outlay is $540,000 per year. This is larger than the after-tax cash outlay of every year with buying! Leasing is clearly demonstrated to be inferior to the buy alternative in this example, but the present value of leasing is less than the present value of buying. What is the problem?

The leasing cash flows include debt flows, but the buy analysis as originally computed excludes them. The use of a relatively high discount rate causes the debt flow component to have a large positive net present value with leases. Since the debt flows were not incorporated in the original buy analysis, we have a definite bias in the calculations in favor of leasing.

It is sometimes argued that the buy analysis should include debt flows also. The difficulty with implementing this suggestion is that the net cost of buying would then be affected by the specific debt repayment schedule chosen. Figure 12.1 shows the net present value profile for two debt contracts paying the same interest rate of .10. It can be seen that except for the situation when .10 is used as the discount rate, the two contracts have different net present values.

For rates of discount larger than .10, debt d_1 has a larger net present value than debt d_2. We generally would prefer that the cost of buying not be affected by the exact schedule of debt repayment.

We will suggest two solutions to the paradox that the present value of costs of leasing is less than the net cost of buying even when the leasing outlays are larger than the buy-borrow after-tax outlays in every year.

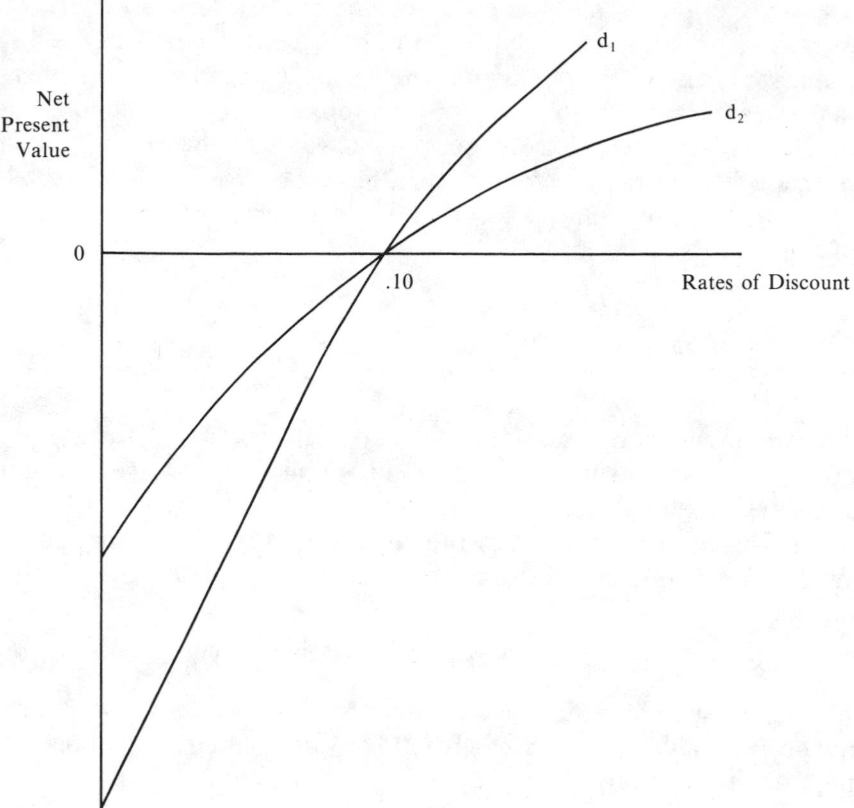

FIGURE 12.1. Two Different Debts, Same Interest Cost

A Method of Solution

The first method of solution is to use the after-tax borrowing rate of .054 rather than the hurdle rate of .20. We obtain the following:

Net cost of buying = 3,000,000 − 276,000 × 4.28202 = \$1,818,000

The net cost of leasing is now:

Net cost of leasing = 540,000 × 4.28202 = \$2,312,000

The net cost of leasing is now larger than the net cost of buying. This agrees with the cash flow analysis which indicated that in this situation leasing is inferior to buying.

The computation of the present value of the after-tax cash flows works here even though it did not work when .20 was used as the discount rate. The difference is that the use of the after-tax borrowing rate effectively eliminates the debt component of the lease alternative. It can be shown that the net present value of the after-tax cash flows of debt is equal to zero if the after-tax borrowing rate is used. Thus the debt flows (and tax shields) are being washed out by the use of the .054 discount rate.

An Alternative Solution

The previous section implicitly makes a strong case for the use of the after-tax borrowing rate to evaluate buy versus lease. But not everyone would agree.

Let us return to the use of the .20 discount rate to evaluate buy. We previously obtained a net cost of $1,818,000, the net cost of buying is now:

$$\text{Net cost of buying} = 3{,}000{,}000 - 2.9906(276{,}000) = \$2{,}175{,}000$$

To compute an equivalent number for leasing, we will start with the present value of the lease before tax using the before-tax borrowing rate. We obtain:

$$1{,}000{,}000 \times 3.7908 = \$3{,}791{,}000$$

where 3.7908 is the present value of a five-year annuity using a .10 discount rate. But the calculation must be adjusted for the present value of the tax savings associated with the noninterest component of the lease payment. This present value of tax savings must be deducted from the before-tax present value (debt equivalent) of the lease. Table 12.1 shows the separation of the $1,000,000 per year base payment into interest and principal components. The principal component is analogous to the depreciation deduction of the buy alternative. Table 12.1 also shows that tax savings associated with the principal component have a present value of $1,007,000. The net cost of leasing is equal to the before-tax present value of the lease payments minus this $1,007,000:

$$\text{Net cost of leasing} = 3{,}791{,}000 - 1{,}007{,}000 = \$2{,}784{,}000$$

For the same interest rate the net cost of buying is $2,175,000, and buying is again more desirable than leasing.

TABLE 12.1 Separation of Lease Payments into Interest and Principal

	Beginning Debt	Interest	Principal	Present Value Using .20
1.	3,790,800	379,080	620,920	517,000
2	3,169,880	316,988	683,012	474,000
3	2,486,868	248,687	751,313	435,000
4	1,735,555	173,556	826,445	399,000
5	909,110	90,911	909,089*	365,000
				2,190,000
				× .46
				1,007,000 present value of tax saving

*There is a rounding error

Figure 12.2 shows the types of graphs that can be obtained from the above calculations. In explanation of Figure 12.2, at a zero rate of discount:

Net cost of buying = 3,000,000 − .46(7,000,000) = $1,620,000
Net cost of leasing = 3,791,000 − .46(3,791,000) = $2,047,000

Figure 12.2 shows that leasing costs more than buying for any rate of discount applied to the tax saving. For both alternatives increasing the discount rate reduces the value of the tax savings. With the buy alternative the initial cost remains unchanged, and with the lease alternative the before-tax present value of the lease remains unchanged. Under some conditions the two curves will intersect.

The solution in this chapter is not very intuitively appealing. But while some objections may have merit, generally the objections offered are faulty. To try to illustrate the reasonableness of the leasing net cost calculation, we will return to the use of the after-tax borrowing rate. In the previous section using a .054 discount rate we determined the net cost of leasing to be:

Net cost of leasing = (1 − .46)1,000,000 × 4.28202 = $2,312,000

Applying the after-tax borrowing rate of .054 to the principal components of Table 12.1, we obtain tax savings of $2,312,000.

The net cost of leasing is again:

Net cost of leasing = 3,791,000 − 1,479,000 = $2,312,000

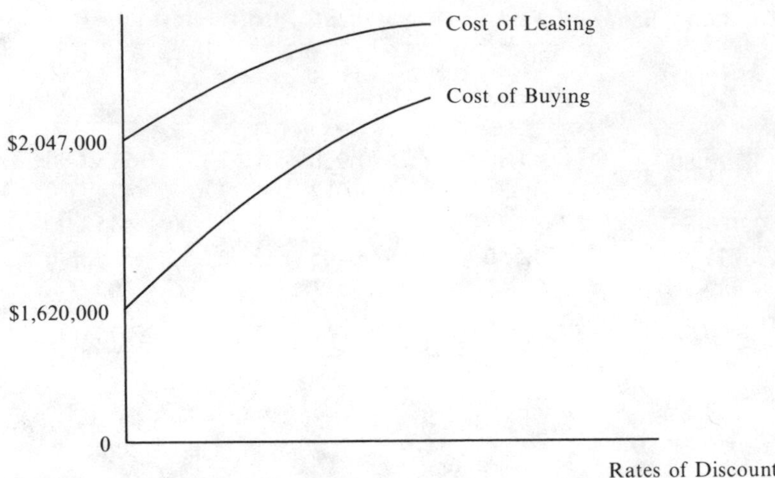

FIGURE 12.2. Net Costs of Buying and Leasing

Thus an interesting thing happens if the after-tax borrowing rate is used as the rate of discount. The present value of the after-tax cost of leasing is exactly equal to the before-tax cost of leasing (using the before-tax rate) minus the present value of the tax savings of the principal component of the lease payment. The first calculation of the $2,312,000 includes the entire tax shield of leases and discounts the after tax cost of leasing using the after-tax borrowing rate. This calculation is valid only if the after-tax borrowing rate is the discount rate. The second calculation is valid with any interest rate applied to the tax savings of the principal component, as long as the specific rate chosen has a valid economic justification.

Conclusions

Stripped of all complications, leasing is a type of financing. In fact, it is 100% debt financing. The use of a lease arrangement rather than straight debt is a major financial policy decision.

There are valid reasons why an entity should find it advantageous to lease and some logical reasons why leasing should not be advantageous. *But until the calculations are actually made we cannot generally guess as to whether or not leasing is advantageous.* Generalizations relative to leases are difficult to make.

This chapter has offered an approach to how the buy versus lease decision should be analyzed. In many financial decisions we do not know exactly the consequences of the alternatives. With the buy versus lease decision we know exactly a large percentage of the information. The residual value and future tax rates are not known with certainty, but aside from these measures the other inputs are objectively determined. The primary difficulty has been to determine the method of analysis. Beware of discounting the after-tax lease payments using a hurdle rate or a weighted average cost of capital. This calculation is not comparable to the conventionally computed net cost of the buy alternative.

Chapter 13
The Added Dimension: International Financial Strategy

When it comes to future exchange rates
We have only two ways we can go:
With those who admit that they don't know;
*Or with those who don't know they don't know.**

FMK

There are two primary dimensions of international financial strategy as seen from the viewpoint of the top-level financial manager. The first is the economic impact of the investment financial decisions that are being made. The second is the effect of the decisions on the reported accounting earnings. Some executives would place the impact on accounting earnings at the top of the list of relevant considerations.

In addition to the decision of the firm, we have decisions made at the government level. The governmental decisions and institutions heavily influence the balance of payment among countries and firms and thus affect the currency exchange rates. The changes in the currency exchange rates also affect corporate strategies.

Balance of Payments and Exchange Rates

In this era of the multinational corporation and dependency of countries on each other, it is necessary for all financial executives to have a basic understanding of international finance. While there are

* Secretary of Labor Ray Marshall "When it comes to forecasting, there are only two kinds of economists. There are those who don't know and those who don't know that they don't know." Reported by Edwin McDowell, *The New York Times,* February 3, 1980.

more similarities than differences between international and domestic finance, one should understand the differences that exist.

There are many different ways of measuring the balance of payments. For purposes of this section we will define the balance of payments as consisting of the sum of five subtotals:

1. Net investment (investment in foreign countries minus their investment in the United States)
2. Net consumption (total consumption exports minus consumption imports)
3. Net productive asset exchange (total capital exports minus capital imports)
4. Net investment income (investment earnings minus earnings on U.S. investments by foreign nationals)
5. Miscellaneous (e.g., government transactions)

Any country wants a positive balance of payments. But equally important as the balance of payments is the cause of any positive or negative balance. Let us consider the first four subtotals and their effect on the balance of payments.

1. A negative balance of payments caused by net investment is not a bad event. The investments are claims against the future, and the future benefits should more than balance out the initial outlays.
2. A negative balance of payments caused by net consumption is bad from the point of view of long range planning at a national level. An average individual cannot for a long period of time consume more than is earned, and neither can a country. Excessive consumption is apt to weaken the value of the currency, making it more expensive to import additional goods.
3. The effect of the net productive asset exchange is more difficult to evaluate, since the import of productive assets is a form of investment and is not the same as the importation of consumption goods. The export of productive assets at a profit increases the capability of consuming now.
4. The net investment income, if positive, helps finance the purchase of consumption goods, the purchase of capital imports, or the purchase of foreign investments. If negative, the country is paying for past investments or past consump-

tion. Since consumption does not generate future revenues, borrowing for consumption by a nation (or a state or a city) is not a wise strategy.

The balance of payments for the United States is an interesting problem. If the U.S. payments balance is large and positive, portions of the rest of the world are pushed into liquidity problems (it is said that if the U.S. sneezes, the rest of the world catches cold). If the U.S. balance of payments is negative because of excessive consumption, the value of the dollar weakens, creating a different set of problems.

If the balance of payments is negative, foreign nationals are given claims against the United States that are satisfied either by the sale of securities (to bring the balance back to zero) or by the sale of gold by U.S. entities. While the gold flow arising from transactions such as the investment in real assets overseas is not a negative event, the gold flow out arising from consumption is negative in the sense that sooner or later it must cease, or be balanced by another transaction.

There is a problem with comparing imports and exports without identification of their purpose. The importation of caviar and furs has different economic significance than the importation of machine tools or turbines. For one thing, the lives of the different products will differ. But the primary distinction is analogous to the difference between a developing country importing fishing equipment and importing fish. To evaluate the economic significance of a negative balance of payments, it is necessary to know what is being imported.

If the United States has a large negative balance of payments caused by importing consumption goods and if the rest of the world thinks the country is living beyond its means, sooner or later the country will use up its credit and will have to reduce consumption or increase the amount of its exports.

A persistently large negative balance of payments over long periods of time is apt to mean a shift in the ownership rights of the country's factors of production. The claims of external lenders may be in the form of government bonds, bank time deposits, corporate debt, ownership of real estate, or common stock, but these claims will tend to increase in a situation when a country is running large negative balances of payments over long periods of time.

The balance of payments of a country, especially the subtotals, will affect the rates at which the currency of the country is being exchanged.

Spot and Forward Rates

When a "spot" rate is quoted, we obtain the current rate at which two currencies may be exchanged immediately. A "forward" rate refers to the rate at which two currencies may be exchanged at a future moment in time, but the trade takes place now. Payment is made at the time of delivery, but the terms of exchange are specified now.

If a company is going to receive 100,000 yen in 12 months and would prefer to eliminate the exchange rate risk, the company can sell the 100,000 yen today for delivery in 12 months. The sale of yen today sets the price in terms of the amount of dollars that will be received now. The receipt of the 100,000 yen will be one year from today. This is a "forward contract" involving the delivery of 100,000 yen in one year.

In like manner, if the firm has to pay 100,000 yen one year from now for a piece of equipment and wants to eliminate exchange rate risk, it can purchase 100,000 yen now for delivery one year from now. This is a second type of forward contract.

The Use of Foreign Capital

Assume the ABC Company has a foreign subsidiary. If the subsidiary is building a plant in a foreign country, does the ABC Company use its own capital, or does it borrow locally? In concept the answer is easy. Use the type of capital that is cheapest. However, an additional complexity is the fact that if domestic funds are used, it might later be difficult to remove the funds from the country. This fear frequently leads to a desire to minimize the amount of parent equity capital that is placed at risk.

If there is zero probability of repatriating the capital and earnings on the capital, then there is no incentive to invest in the country. The prospect of being able to withdraw cash flow from the country must be present to entice foreign dollars into the country for investment.

Let us assume that institutional obstacles to money flows between countries do not exist so that we can concentrate on the economic factors.

Theoretically, the first step is to decide whether the firm's investment is desirable, and the second step is to decide on the nature of the financing. In actual practice the two steps are done interactively.

One of the first considerations in deciding the type of financing is to determine whether the nominal rate of interest is higher or lower than the rate that one would expect given the forecast exchange rate changes. The possibility of obtaining a relative bargain borrowing in a foreign country will depend on the expected future exchange rates.

Need for a decision arises when the finance officer of a firm observes the possibility of borrowing funds at a lower stated cost in a foreign country than it can borrow in its own country. For example, a United States firm might find local banks asking a 16% rate of interest at the same time that a German bank will lend funds at 10%. One explanation for this difference in nominal interest rates is that the 16% loan is payable in dollars and the 10% loan is payable in marks. The true effective cost of borrowing must take into consideration the exchange rate risks that accompany the interest rates. The interest rates reflect the expected inflation in each country, and the exchange rates can be expected to change in a manner more or less consistent with the rate of inflation.

Assume the dollar is expected to be devalued relative to the mark. If $1,000 is borrowed in the United States and used in the United States, then at the end of the year $1,160 must be paid.

Assume that the exchange rate is now 1.08 marks for $1 and at the end of the year the exchange rate is expected to be 1 for 1 (this is a .08 reduction). If 1,080 marks are borrowed, at the end of the year 1,080(1.10) = 1,188 marks are owed, and this translates to $1,188. Borrowing in marks at .10 costs $28 more than borrowing in dollars at a cost of .16 if the exchange rate forecast is accurate.

The indifference rate is .188 (.10 + .08 + .008). If borrowing in the U.S. cost .188, the borrower of dollars would have to pay $1,188 at the end of the year, which is the same as the borrower of the marks has to pay. If dollars can be borrowed at less than .188 it is better to borrow dollars than borrow marks.

The nominal cost of borrowing is not an adequate estimate of the cost. The expected exchange rate changes must also be considered.

If with the same exchange rates funds cost .188 in the United States but only .06 in Germany, there is a strong incentive to borrow in Germany. The firm will then be speculating that the devaluation will not be so large that the German mark becomes so expensive that the .06 debt denominated in marks is more costly than .188 in dollars.

Large corporations are becoming more and more willing to cross national boundaries to borrow funds. We have discussed the relative cost question and devaluation. Another important reason why firms like to borrow in foreign lands to finance local investment is that it offers protection against inflation in the country where the investment is taking place. Another reason for using foreign debt is that the debt of a foreign subsidiary frequently does not appear on the consolidated balance sheet of the parent company. Also, there may be restrictions on the importation (or exportation) of capital, and finally there are advantages in establishing good relations with local banking institutions by borrowing funds.

For simplicity we have assumed away exchange restrictions and tax differences. Tax considerations will very much affect both the type and sources of capital.

Investment Decisions

When a firm invests in a foreign country, the exchange rate risk is added to other risks. Using the assumptions of the example of the previous section, with .08 devaluation a German investor in the United States must earn .188 in the United States in order to earn the equivalent of .10 in Germany. To be acceptable, an investment would only have to earn .10 in Germany to be competitive with a .188 investment in the United States. A forecast of a change in the exchange rate relationships would change these numbers.

A problem arises when a foreign subsidiary uses debt as well as equity funds from a parent (the same problem can exist with a domestic subsidiary or even without a subsidiary). The amount of debt involved in the financing has to be taken into consideration.

Assume a situation where no exchange rate change is expected. A foreign subsidiary has requested a $1,000 investment from its parent, which requires a minimum 10% return on its real investments. The parent has a capital structure of $1 of debt for each $1 of common stock. The subsidiary promises a 20% return on the $1,000 investment. It appears to be an acceptable investment. Debt of the subsidiary costs 8%.

At the level of the subsidiary further analysis indicates the following details for the investment:

	Time 0	Time 1
Investment	− 10,000	+ 10,920
Debt (8%)	+ 9,000	− 9,720
Equity cash flows	− 1,000	+ 1,200

While the investment returns 20% to the parent on the $1,000 investment, we cannot compare the 20% expected return and the 10% required return described for real investments. The 20% return is the stock equity expected return on a highly levered investment. The basic investment (unlevered) has a 9.2% return. It is only by introducing the debt of $9,000 that the investment is made to seem to be acceptable. The 10% required return is for a normal investment, not the returns to an equity position.

It is not sufficient for a foreign subsidiary to "promise" an acceptable return on a parent's investment. The basic underlying characteristics of the investment and its capital structure must also be analyzed. This implies a more systematic method of risk analysis than is illustrated in the conclusion that 20% is larger than 10% so the project is acceptable.

Tax Considerations

The tax laws in the area of international trade change rapidly, and are apt to be aimed at accomplishing social and political objectives. For example, when the United States government wants to encourage investment in developing foreign countries, it offers insurance to cover the investments of the U.S. companies operating overseas. It also allows a wide range of foreign taxes to be deductible against U.S. taxes as a tax credit. (A tax credit is more powerful than a tax deduction, since $1 of foreign taxes reduces U.S. taxes by $1, rather than by a fraction of $1 as would be the case if the foreign tax expenses were a tax deduction rather than a tax credit.)

When the dollar was under pressure, Congress passed a provision that encouraged companies to increase exports. This provision allowed the setting up of separate corporations (Domestic International Sales Corporations or DISCs) to do the exporting. A portion of the income earned by engaging in foreign trade could then be protected from U.S. income taxes by a series of maneuvers, including not transmitting the income to the parent.

There are other provisions in the Federal Tax Code that offer special advantages (such as Western Hemisphere Trade Corporations), but the important thing to realize is that countries will frequently arrange their tax laws to facilitate international trade and to encourage the trade to go in a given direction. For example, the European Common Market countries have used the value-added tax (a type of sales tax) very adroitly to accomplish trade goals.

To make intelligent international finance decisions, companies must understand the tax laws of the countries concerned well; otherwise, faulty corporate decision making is going to take place.

FAS 8

In 1975 the Financial Accounting Standards Board (FASB) issued Financial Accounting Standards No. 8, titled "Accounting for the Translation of Foreign Currency Transactions and Foreign Currency Financial Statements." This standard accomplished two primary objectives:

1. It placed the accounting for foreign transactions on a "temporal" basis.
2. It required the recording of gains and losses as they occurred (instead of allowing their deferral).

The "temporal" refers to the use of two exchange rates, a current rate and a historical rate. The current rate is used for cash, accounts receivable, real assets carried at market values, and all payables (including long-term debt). The historical rate is used for real assets recorded at cost as well as prepayments (such as prepaid rent).

Assume the foreign subsidiary of a U.S. company acquires a plant in a foreign country at a cost of 20,000,000 yen when the exchange rate is $1 for 20 yen. The asset is recorded on the books of the foreign company at 20,000,000 yen and on the parent's books at 1,000,000 dollars. Assume the plant is financed by long-term debt payable in yen paying 10% interest, and that the life of the plant is infinite so that there is no depreciation. In the first year the plant earns just enough to pay the interest. At the end of the year the exchange rate has changed so that $1 is worth 15 yen. The balance sheets of the company for the beginning and end of the year are as follows:

	In Yen		In Dollars (Adjusted)	
	Beginning of Year	End of Year	Beginning of Year	End of Year
Plant	20,000,000	20,000,000	1,000,000	1,000,000
Long-term debt	20,000,000	20,000,000	1,000,000	1,333,333
Stock equity	0	0	0	–333,333

For the beginning and end of the year the plant is converted at the historical rate of 20 yen to $1. The end of the year debt is converted at the current rate of 15 yen to $1. The resulting increase in the debt leads to a loss of $333,333. The loss arises from the use of the current exchange rate in converting the long-term debt. The loss would affect the year's income.

The possibility of having a firm's income statement affected by the types of loss illustrated in the above example is causing much concern among the managers of international firms. The financing of plant assets with long-term debt denominated in foreign currencies can easily lead to large gains and losses affecting income from period to period. This risk of fluctuating incomes is said to have a depressing effect when firms are considering the undertaking of investments.

There are several obvious difficulties with FAS 8. It is possible that the above firm has entered into a long-term contract to supply product produced in the plant so that the payment obligations of the debt are essentially balanced by net revenues. It is also possible that the plant is actually worth $1,333,333 (in terms of dollars) at the end of the year, so that there was not actually a loss of $333,333. Following FAS 8, the loss would be recorded despite the existence of a contract that tended to provide the cash flows necessary to pay the debt, or despite a change in the dollar value of the asset.

In evaluating investment proposals, it is important for the decision maker to know that the existence of FAS 8 affects the willingness of management to undertake foreign investments. As long as quarter to quarter gains or losses associated with items such as long-term debt affect operating incomes (while long-term assets are not changed), management will be concerned with the magnitude of the accounting exposure that exists. Unfortunately, the accounting exposure and the economic exposure are not necessarily identical. A firm may be perfectly hedged economically and still have accounting exposure.

We can expect that FAS 8 will be modified. But whatever changes are made in FAS 8, there will still be gains and losses arising from exchange rate changes. This factor must be considered in evaluating foreign investments.

Conclusions

Very few major corporations operate solely within the boundaries of one country. We can expect the importance of international finance to grow as foreign trade and investments increase, but even today the area is of significant importance to operating financial managers. From a financial strategy point of view the primary consideration is to be aware of exchange rate risks and, where the level of the risk is not acceptable, to follow a "hedging" strategy that will reduce if not eliminate the risk. Unfortunately, buying and selling forward contracts in foreign currencies does have a cost, and the companies do have to balance the reduction in risk exposure against the cost of accomplishing the reduction.

There are no easy dollars to be earned in foreign exchange manipulation. Ex post, one might point to the wisdom of a specific strategy, and how a firm outsmarted the market by being long or short in a given currency. But the average business firm has sufficient risk in producing, selling, and collecting for the sales of the product, and does not need the additional risk of speculation in foreign currencies.

Chapter 14
The Fourth Dimension: Risk Management

When you've plugged in all the formulae,
But have no clear position,
Then that's the time you should rely
On gut felt intuition.

FMK

Appraisal of risk management is easiest with the assistance of 20/20 hindsight.

The United States government guaranteed a loan to the Lockheed Corporation. When the guarantee expired, the government had made over $30,000,000 of profit. Ex post the guarantee turned out to be profitable for the government, but before the final results were in there was considerable risk.

Frequently, ex post, one wonders how a company could have gotten itself into such a bad situation. Consider a computer leasing company which ordered $50,000,000 worth of computers (with no cancellation rights) right before IBM brought out a new faster a cheaper computer that made all $50,000,000 worth of computers obsolete before they were received.

In trying to sell atomic energy equipment, Westinghouse salespersons found it useful to guarantee uranium to fuel the reactors it was selling. At first Westinghouse actually owned enough uranium, but business was so good it soon guaranteed more uranium than it owned (or had the prospect of mining). When the price of uranium went through the ceiling in 1973–74, Westinghouse found itself with a liability for supplying uranium over a billion dollars in excess of that expected when the contracts were signed. Should the company have committed itself to supplying uranium at a fixed price when it did not have contracts at fixed prices to obtain the uranium? Ex post, it is clear the company should not have made the commitments to supply uranium unless it was willing to accept the large amount of risk. One suspects management did not consider the amount of risk exposure.

In a comparable situation the Rolls-Royce Corporation contracted to supply airplane engines by a specified date to Lockheed when the engine had not been designed. In fact, the metal necessary for the engine had not yet been produced. As might be expected, both companies moved into financial difficulties when the engines were not available at the due date.

Risk management is sometimes equated with the purchase of conventional insurance. While this is one aspect of risk management, we will broaden the definition to include any actions taken that will affect the risk characteristics of the firm. A firm may be "buying insurance" when it makes an investment that is not an insurance policy, but rather a desirable set of cash flows.

The Classic Hedging Model

The classic hedging model is directed at risk elimination. It applies exactly to the Westinghouse situation.

Assume that in June a wheat processor (a miller) wants to be able to sell flour to a bakery in November at a given price of $10 per unit. In order to do this, the miller must buy at $9 per unit. The bakery wants a fixed commitment in June, because it is signing contracts to supply bread at a fixed price and it does not want the risk of a rising flour price to jeopardize its profits.

In June a farmer is afraid there will be a glut of wheat in November and wants to make sure that he obtains $9 per unit for November wheat. In June the miller buys the wheat for $9, with delivery to take place in November. The farmer is insured the $9 selling price. The miller is insured against an increase in wheat prices, and the bakery is insured against an increase in flour prices.

The miller and the bakery are hedged. They have simultaneously sold and bought wheat. The buyers of the bread are speculating (they are long on bread).

The Westinghouse Corporation made commitments to supply uranium but did not buy "futures" in uranium. It had risk exposure.

A buyer of common stock has risk exposure. A holder of convertible bonds who sells the common stock short has a type of hedged position (there is not likely to be a perfect hedge). The same is true for a person who holds common stock and sells calls on the common stock. This is a type of risk hedging.

Utility Functions

It is common practice to write down a set of cash flows for an investment and make the decision using that one set of cash flows. The one set of flows is frequently implicitly assumed to have an expected monetary value, the result of summing the set of monetary outcomes each multiplied by its probability. That is, behind the one number may be many outcomes, each outcome measured in dollars with each outcome having a probability. For simplicity this will be illustrated by the flipping of a fair coin (the probability of each outcome is .5), with the outcome being $100,000 if there is a head and $20,000 if there is a tail. It costs $35,000 to play the game. Figure 14.1 shows the situation.

Figure 14.2 is a somewhat simplified version of the decision outcomes.

The gamble has an expected monetary value of $25,000 (.5 × 65,000 − .5 × 15,000); thus on an expected monetary value basis the investment is acceptable. Would you be willing to try the gamble? Could you accept the .5 probability of losing $15,000?

Most large corporations would accept the investment. If three zeros were added to the monetary outcomes so that there was a .5

FIGURE 14.1

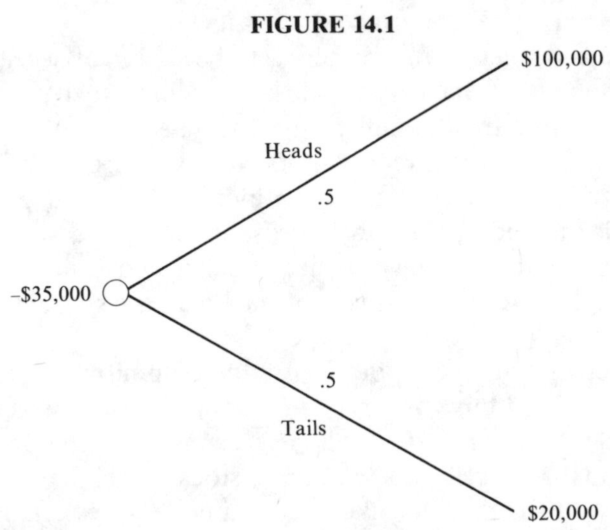

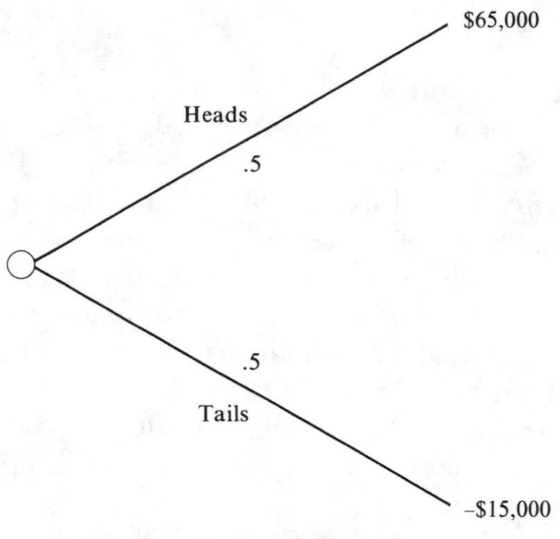

FIGURE 14.2

probability of losing $15,000,000, it would not be safe to predict what percentage of the firms would accept the investment. Even where the board of directors found it acceptable a division manager would be apt to find the investment excessively risky with the .5 probability of a $15,000,000 loss. Where a decision maker rejects the gamble with a positive expected monetary value, we have an illustration of risk aversion. The fact that people and organizations have risk aversion or risk preference attitudes is generally summarized by the statement that they have utility functions.

"Utility function" represents the value an individual places on different amounts of money or wealth. It reflects the wealth preferences and risk attitudes of a person. While we know how to determine the utility function of an individual, we do not know how to determine the utility function of a group of individuals (e.g., a corporation) or how to compare the utility measures of one person with the utility measures of another person. Thus formal utility analysis has severe limitations as a decision-making tool for a complex organization such as a corporation.

In the early 1960s a major breakthrough occurred which shifted the primary risk analysis from that of the individual investor's utility to a determination of the market's risk return preferences. The primary advantage of the theory is that actual returns may be observed and be used to determine the price the market is placing on risk. The model is called the capital asset pricing model (CAPM), and it is built on the portfolio theory of Harry M. Markowitz.[1]

Portfolio Considerations

Risk can be either magnified or decreased by mixing of investments. Even a set of identical investments, if they are not perfectly correlated, can be used to change the risk. Perfect correlation would require that an increase in one investment result in exactly predictable increase in the second investment. A decrease in one investment would have the same effect in the second.

To illustrate risk reduction, take a situation where an investor can make a $4,000 outlay and undertake an investment that promises to pay either $10,000 one period from now or $0. Both of the events have .5 probability. The expected cash flow is $5,000 at time 1, with an outlay of $4,000 at time 0. Normally the firm requires a .10 return.

While the expected cash flows of the investments have an internal rate of return of .25, which is a high return, this is an extremely risky investment, and we might be reluctant to undertake an investment where one of the two outcomes is a loss of $4,000 and this outcome has a .5 probability.

We need a second investment which will diversify our risk. Consider a second investment that also costs $4,000 and promises either to pay back $8,000 one period from now or $0. Both events have a .5 probability. The expected cash flows of this second investment have a zero internal rate of return, and this second investment taken by itself is not acceptable. Its expected present value is negative using any positive rate of interest. Thus we have two investments, one of which has a large internal rate of return but has a large amount of risk and the second of which has a zero rate of return. While we might accept the first investment, we would prefer a lower level of risk. Neither investment is obviously a great investment.

So far we do not know what events trigger the outcomes that have been defined for two investments. These are shown both in Figure 14.3 and in Table 14.1.

TABLE 14.1 Outcomes of Two Investments at Time 1

	Event	First Investment	Second Investment	Both Investments
Heads:	e_1	10,000	0	10,000
Tails:	e_2	0	8,000	8,000

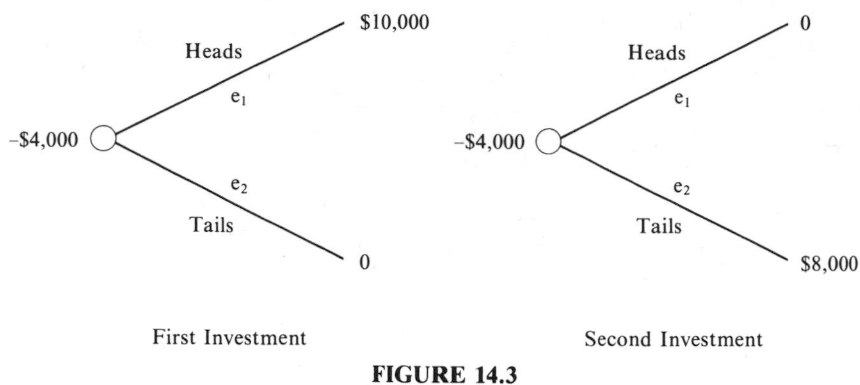

FIGURE 14.3

Table 14.1 shows the outcomes of the two investments for time 1. When the bad event occurs for the first investment (e_2), the good outcome occurs for the second investment. The result is that the outcomes of undertaking both investments are reasonably desirable for the two possible events. For an investment of $8,000 we get back either $10,000 or $8,000, and the internal rate of return of the expected cash flows is .125. The possibility of losing the $4,000 as with a single investment has been eliminated. If we consider only the individual investments, they are not very attractive because of their risk. When we consider the portfolio effects, the combined investment becomes attractive with no risk of a large loss. If event e_2 occurs, the investor is not happy, since a zero return is earned, but at least disaster has been avoided. The second investment, which taken by itself is clearly not acceptable, acts as insurance for the first investment.

This example can be used to illustrate another interesting point that is useful in this era in which there seems to be a necessity to explain and justify the level of profits that have been attained.

Assume that some higher authority has decided that .125 is a fair return and that anything above .125 is excessive and will be "returned to the people."

The investment (the portfolio) has an expected return of .125, so does not seem to be in jeopardy. This conclusion neglects the difference between ex ante and ex post analysis. Before the results are known, there are not excessive profits on an expected value basis. After the one period has passed, either there will be $8,000 of cash flow and zero income or there will be $10,000 of cash flow and $2,000 of income leading to a return of .25 on the initial investment. This actual return of .25 is "clearly" excessive compared to the fair

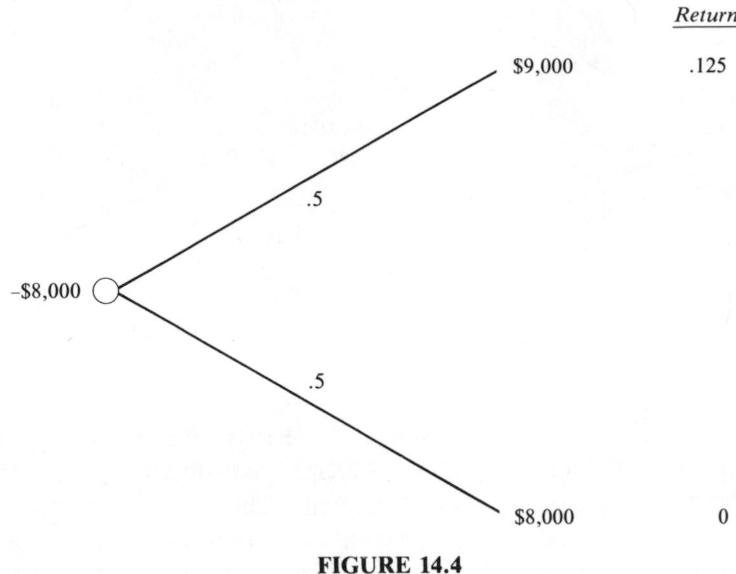

FIGURE 14.4

return of .125. If the income is reduced to $9,000, the return on investment of $8,000 is reduced to the allowed return of .125. Unfortunately this faulty application of the allowed return concept leads to an expected return of .0625 that is less than .125. Figure 14.4 shows the results that will occur after the "excessive" profits are reclaimed.

The ex ante average return is .0625. Given the firm's required return of .10, this investment is no longer acceptable, and investment capital will flow into industries that are not so closely controlled and where profits are not defined to be excessive merely because they exceed some arbitrary level.

The Capital Asset Pricing Model

The capital asset pricing model is an extension of the portfolio literature of the 1950s and early 1960s. The main change is that the model makes use of the prices that the market is setting for return-risk trade-offs instead of using subjective measures of attitudes toward risk (such as the utility functions of individual investors). The utility function of the individual investor will determine the split in the investor's portfolio between the market basket of risk assets and risk-free (or more accurately default-free) assets.

The capital asset pricing model says that investors have avail-

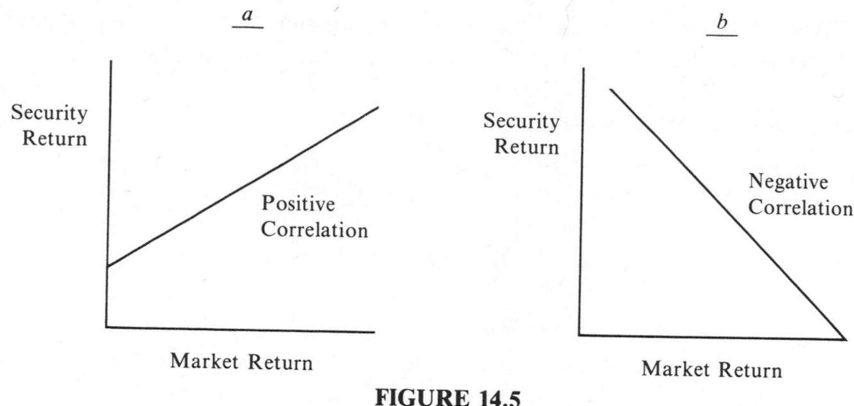

FIGURE 14.5

able a market basket of risky securities and the opportunity to invest in securities with no risk of default. Risk preferences of investors dictate a combination of the risky securities and the riskless securities. In equilibrium the return of any security must be such that the investor expects to earn a basic return equal to the return on a default-free security plus an adjustment that is heavily influenced by the "correlation" of the security's return and the market's return.

If the return from the investment is positively correlated with the market return, the equilibrium required return will be larger than the default-free return. If the correlation is negative, the equilibrium required return will be smaller than the default-free return. The correlation is positive if the two returns tend to move in the same direction (see Figure 14.5a) and negative if when one return goes up the other goes down (see Figure 14.5b). Negatively correlated investments tend to reduce risk.

Systematic Risk

Risk that cannot be eliminated by diversification is called systematic risk. The more that an investment is affected by changes in the market return, the larger is the systematic risk. The capital asset pricing model assumes that investors are widely diversified and the unsystematic risk is driven to zero by this policy of wide diversification. Thus an investment may have a large amount of risk, but if that risk is unsystematic it will not require a risk premium.

Consider a situation where investors require a return of .10 for investments with zero systematic risk. An investment costing $10,-

000,000 has two possible first-period outcomes that are independent of the market returns with the following probabilities:

Outcome	Probability	Return	Expected Return
20,000,000	.10	1.00	.10
10,000,000	.90	0	.00
		Expected return	.10

The expected return is .10, which is equal to the required return, and since the investment has zero systematic risk, the investment is acceptable. But the .90 probability of earning a zero return would discourage many corporations, even though the risk is defined to be all unsystematic. Theoretically, unsystematic risk should be ignored, but practically it tends to be considered by investors and financial managers. One reason for this is that many investors and even more importantly, managers, tend not to be perfectly diversified.

The Market Portfolio

The market portfolio includes some of all securities. While for empirical purposes the definition has tended to exclude investment opportunities that are not in the form of securities (e.g., real estate, art, gold), there is no reason why in theory these items should not be included.

The amount of each security included in the market portfolio is based on securities' current market prices. Securities are included in proportion to their market valuation. Thus if a specific common stock represented .001 of the total value of all investable assets, .001 of the market portfolio would be invested in this stock. In designing the market portfolio, no attention is paid to the prospects of the security or the risk preferences of the investor. The only place that the specific preferences of the investor come into play is in splitting the investment fund between the market portfolio and the default-free securities.

Capital Market Line

We will use the standard deviation of the investor's portfolio as the relevant measure of risk. The standard deviation is a measure of the spread of the distributions of outcomes about the expected value of the outcomes. The differences from the expected value are squared, weighted by their likelihood, and the products summed to obtain the variance. The standard deviation is the square root of the variance.

Figure 14.6 shows the capital market line. It is the locus of possible investment opportunities. At one extreme is an investment in a government security yielding r_f with a zero standard deviation (no default risk). At the other extreme is an investment in the market portfolio with an expected return of $\bar{r}_m$ and a standard deviation of σ_m. In between the two extreme points are all portfolios that are a mixture of the market portfolio and the default-free security. The preferences of the individual investor will determine where on the capital market line the investor will locate.

If borrowing is allowed at a rate of r_f, the capital market line extends upward to the right, meaning that higher expected returns with higher risk are feasible.

Define $\bar{r}_p$ as the expected return resulting from a combination of market portfolio and default-free securities. The combination has a standard deviation of σ_p, and the expected return may be written as:

$$\bar{r}_p = r_f + \left(\frac{\bar{r}_m - r_f}{\sigma_m}\right)\sigma_p$$

Assume that $\sigma_m = .04$ and that the investor wants only half of that much standard deviation (that is, $\sigma_p = 1/2\ \sigma_m = .02$). Also assume that $r_f = .08$ and $\bar{r}_m = .12$. We now have:

$$\bar{r}_p = .08 + \left(\frac{.12 - .08}{.04}\right).02 = .10$$

Given the investor's risk preferences, an expected return of .10 is feasible. This implies that .5 of the funds be invested in default-free securities. Let a represent the proportion invested in default-free securities; then:

$$.10 = a(.08) + (1 - a)(.12)$$

and

$$a = .5$$

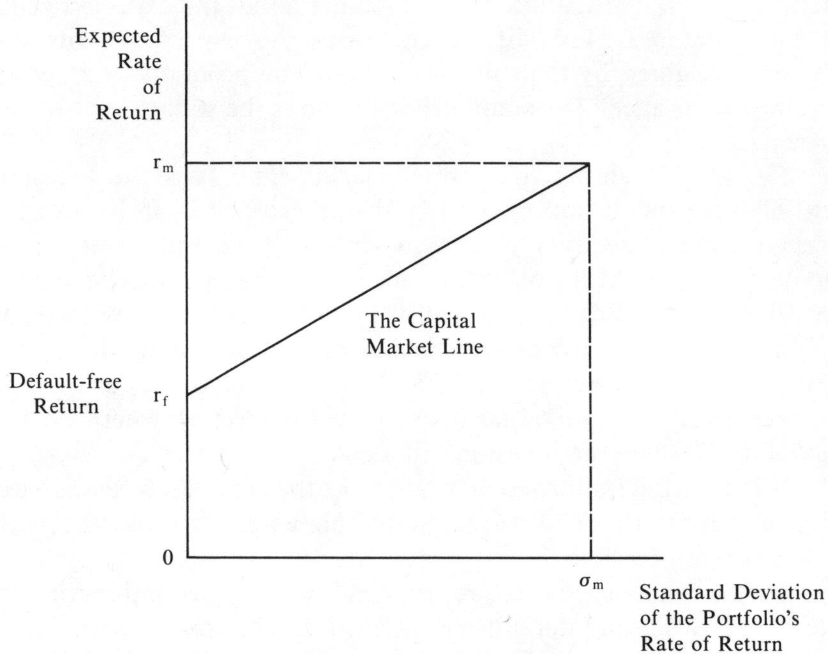

FIGURE 14.6. The Capital Market Line

The Security Market Line

Above, we assumed that the market was in equilibrium and that the investor merely combined a default-free asset with the market portfolio. For the market to be in equilibrium, it is necessary that each security also be in equilibrium, which implies that:

$$r_i = r_f + \frac{r_m - r_f}{\sigma^2_m} \mathrm{Cov}(r_i, r_m)$$

where

$\bar{r}_i$ = the expected required rate of return of security i if the market is in equilibrium

$\mathrm{Cov}(r_i, r_m)$ = the covariance of the return of security i and the market portfolio

The covariance measures how the changes in the returns of the security i and the market portfolio are linked together. It is common practice to define the beta (β) of a security as:

$$\beta = \frac{\text{Cov}(r_i, r_m)}{\sigma^2_m}$$

Substituting in the equation for $\bar{r}_i$, we have:

$$\bar{r}_i = r_f + (\bar{r}_m - r_f)\beta$$

This is the conventional formulation for the security market line. Figure 14.7 shows the security market line graphically. Note that when the beta of a security is equal to 1, the security must have a return equal to $\bar{r}_m$, the expected return of the market.

The security market line gives the required return for different amounts of risk, where risk is defined in terms of the investment's beta. The required expected rate is not affected by the investment's unsystematic risk.

The main significance of Figure 14.7 is that it shows that the required expected return for an investment is a function of how the investment's returns are correlated with the market's returns (that is, it depends on the beta of the investment). The use of a weighted average cost of capital for a firm with a beta of 1 is clearly not appropriate for a specific investment with a different beta.

FIGURE 14.7. The Security Market Line

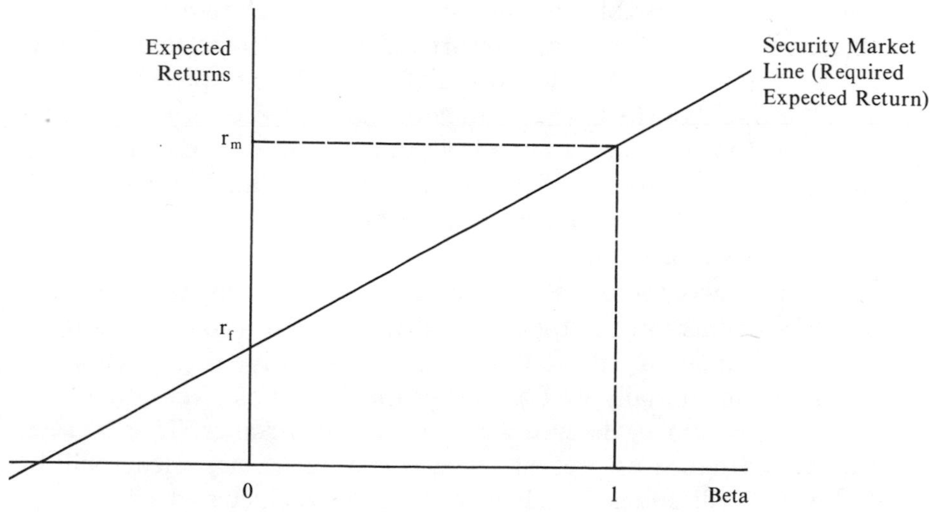

Implications for Financial Strategy

In evaluating investments, industry tends to use a weighted average cost of capital to implement the discounted cash flow capital budgeting techniques. This measure reflects average risks and average time value conditions and cannot be accurately applied to unique "marginal" situations, that is, to specific investments. There is no reason to think that the weighted average cost of capital of a firm can be inserted in a compound interest formula and then be applied to future cash flows to obtain a useful measure of net present value that takes both the time value and risk of the investment into consideration in an effective manner.

The capital asset pricing model offers hope for accomplishing a systematic calculation of risk-adjusted present value. The required return measure reflects the opportunities for investments with alternative return-risk trade-offs available to investors. This is analogous to the rate of interest on a government bond reflecting investment opportunities when there is no default risk. Unfortunately the model presently formulated is a one-period model, and the extension into a useful multiperiod tool requires further theoretical developments. Nevertheless, the model offers many useful insights that are presently applicable to financial decision making.

For example, an investment with a low or even negative expected return but desirable risk characteristics (e.g., the investment's return is independent or negatively correlated to the market's return) may become acceptable, and investments with high returns but more than average risk (e.g., their returns are highly correlated with the market returns) will find it more difficult to be accepted.

We find that the CAPM indicates it is not necessary to consider the spread in outcomes of the investment, nor even the risk of all the firm's assets joined together in one portfolio, but rather it is necessary to consider the relationship of the investment's return with the market's return.

Even where there is a reluctance to accept completely the specific theories illustrated in this chapter, there is likely to be a change in the way that management will look at alternative investments and discuss them. Initially we can expect the capital asset pricing model to affect investment decisions in a qualitative manner. That is, after the rate of return or present value is computed, arguments will be made that will attack or advance the investment based on its risk, where risk is defined in terms of market risk. In the long run we can expect the calculations of the capital asset model (or similar calculations) to be accepted because despite their limitations and complexity, they are better than many measures that are currently available, and they are likely to be improved in the future.

One important limitation of the capital asset pricing model should be kept in mind. The model assumes that the investors are very widely diversified, and even more important, it assumes that the managers of the firm are willing to make investment decisions with the objective of maximizing the well-being of this type of investor. This means that certain types of risk (for which the investor is well diversified) may be ignored in the evaluation of investments. These risks that are assumed not to affect risk premium of an investment are called "nonsystematic risks." By spreading the funds to be invested over a wide range of available opportunities, the nonsystematic risks are driven to zero for the portfolio. This assumes that the investor is widely diversified and that all single investments are a very small proportion of the market portfolio.

It is well known that objectives of firms and managers are complex and there will be a reluctance of managers to ignore types of risk just because they do not affect the well-diversified investor. The major asset many managers possess is their career in the specific firm for which they are working. The argument will not be persuasive to them that a major risk that jeopardizes the existence of the firm can be ignored since the investors in the firm are well diversified and the risk is unsystematic. Thus even if the importance of the capital asset pricing model is acknowledged, the financial manager will still want to consider risk factors that the formal capital asset model considers not to be relevant. The "nonsystematic" risk is not something that is likely to be ignored by a management which includes among its objectives the continuity of existence of the firm.

Conclusions

Risk can be studied at several different levels. The first and by far the most important error is to ignore risk completely. To have the type of tunnel vision that only allows the possibility of one event occurring in the future is likely to lead to disaster. One must allow for contingencies and buy insurance. Westinghouse assumed that uranium prices would stay the same or go down. It did not effectively consider the consequences of a large price rise. Chrysler bet that large gas guzzlers would always be in demand. This could be excused (if not admired) as a policy prior to 1973, but there is little excuse for the policy after 1973. The Rolls-Royce management was willing to bet the existence of the entire firm on its ability to develop a new engine (even though the necessary material input was not on hand) by a specific date without an alternative to fall back on.

Management has a responsibility to consider the risk implications of specific decisions, but more importantly it is strongly suggested in this chapter that the risk of a specific decision cannot be considered in isolation. It is necessary to consider, not the risk of the specific project, but rather its effect on the entire portfolio of the firm's assets if we are approaching the decision from the point of view of the corporation as an entity.

If we switch our focus from the legal fiction that is called a corporation to the individual investor and apply the logic of the capital asset pricing model, we find that we are not concerned with the diversification effects of the new investment on the firm. The statistical relationship of the investment's return and the market's return is of crucial importance.

It follows that for a widely diversified investor an investment should not be undertaken because it reduces the risk of the firm. All we have to know to make a decision is how the investment's risk-return characteristics compare to those of the market. The individual investor can achieve diversification by the use of the market portfolio, and the individual firm does not have to seek risk diversification for the investor. The justification for risk diversification at the firm level must be found either in the investor who is not well diversified or in the interests of the managers and workers, who have a major interest in the continuity of existence of the firm.

Chapter 15
Strategy: A State of Mind

"It is a theoretical question
And I am a practical man."
When you've used all your logical knowledge
*Common sense produces the plan.**

FMK

This is the last chapter in a book that purports to deal with corporate financial strategy. It is somewhat pretentious to talk about financial strategy rather than financial decisions, but there were several reasons for making the major thrust of this book strategy rather than decisions. First, there was a desire to avoid becoming bogged down with excessive details and the accompanying mathematical models. But even more importantly, there was a desire to establish a perspective, or, as the chapter heading indicates, a state of mind. Let each corporation map out a financial strategy. This implies that financial officers gain a realization that they have a wide range of choices and these choices can influence the basic nature of the corporation as well as influence the degree of attraction that the firm has to different groups of investors.

Keep It Simple

The accronym KISS ("Keep it simple, stupid") is a good place for any strategy to start. While complexity may sometimes necessarily accompany a decision, after a certain point more is lost than is gained by aiming at a better though much more complex formula-

* In response to a question by Harry Reasoner, a Russian TV executive said "It is a theoretical question. I am a practical man." "60 Minutes" January 6, 1980.

tion or solution to a problem. This is consistent with Simon's "satisficing" description of economic and managerial behavior.

A corporation installed an elaborate, complex, expensive computer-based management information system called SEMA (Sales, Engineering, Manufacturing, and Accounting). After a couple of years of efforts to make the system work, it was agreed that rather than SEMA, the company had A MES.

Setting the Objectives

Everyone knows that the primary objective of a business corporation is to "make money." Defining the objective more exactly, we can say that the objective is to maximize the present value of the stockholders' position. If the maximization is consistent with maximizing the "well-being" of the stockholders, there is no problem. These are possible inconsistencies, but it is sufficient for our purposes if one accepts the objective to be to make decisions in the interests of the stockholders.

The importance of setting this objective can be readily seen by considering other possible objectives. For example, one can define sales growth or percentage of market share as the objective. In themselves these are not valid objectives. Only if they have a desirable effect on the profits of the firm (properly measured) can we say that growth and increasing market share are desirable.

Consider the seemingly innocent procedure of awarding top management bonuses based on earnings per share and growth in earnings per share. After all, if earnings per share go up, the stockholders are better off. Well, that is not quite correct. If all things are equal and if earnings per share are increased, the stockholders are better off. But if the increase in the earnings per share results from increased investments and if the increased investments are not economically sound, the economic position of the stockholders is not improved even though the earnings per share have increased. Two factors should be noted. First, the accountant does not record the opportunity cost of stock equity capital. In fact, unless the capital is in the form of debt, no entry is made for capital costs. This means that a management being measured on the basis of earnings per share can profitably accept any investment earning a positive return as long as common stock capital is used. The second factor is that earnings per share can be increased by accounting changes or real decisions that increase the reported earnings even though the real earnings may not have changed for the better. For example, a decrease in research and development expenditures will increase the reported earnings, but the expected real earnings of the period are not affected by such a change.

Conflicts in Goals

To describe the primary goal of a corporation in terms of the stockholders' well-being is convenient but it is excessively simplified. There are other "clienteles" who have vital interests in the affairs of the corporation. One very important such group is management. Not only is management an important factor but normally the in-house management has a large amount of power. The stockholders are generally diffuse and their powers small because they are not organized. For many of the Fortune 500 firms no single investor owns over .05 of the common stock. With a disorganized, widely spread ownership it is not surprising that management has stepped into the vacuum. Another factor is that many investors have thought it inappropriate for common stock investors to exercise control. Thus universities and pension funds tend to vote their proxies consistent with the wishes of management.

It has implicitly been assumed that the objectives of management and the objectives of the stockholders are completely consistent with each other. Frequently managers are also shareholders; thus it would not be surprising if there were considerable overlaps in their objectives. On the other hand, it would also not be surprising if management, not controlled, would tend to manage a firm with the objective of maximizing the well-being of the managers rather than the well-being of the shareholders.

The chairman of one of America's largest corporations was asked to rationalize and justify his firm's latest and largest acquisition. He spoke of the necessity of keeping management's interest at a high level. This justification can be interpreted in either of two ways. One interpretation would be that if the company did not grow, good managers would be lost and the firm would suffer. A second interpretation is that business is a game and the managers want to have fun playing the game. In this case the former is probably the fairest interpretation. But it is easy to speak and act as if the corporation exists for its managers.

There is another extreme position that is equally faulty, namely, that the corporation exists to serve society. If the system works right, the corporation will serve society, but it serves society as it pursues its quest for larger profits. When a corporation abandons the profit objective and seeks to serve society independent of the direct interests of its shareholders, it is moving out on thin ice. Obviously, if the shareholders want such a policy, there is nothing wrong with the corporate entity pursuing such a course. But where the stockholders have not approved such an objective, it is questionable whether the managers have a right to spend the resources of the firm on such endeavors.

Other important clienteles of a corporation are its workers, its customers, and the locality where the firm does its business. The interrelationship of the well-being of the workers and the corporation has been well illustrated by the Chrysler recovery plan of 1979. The union (UAW) accepted a lower economic package from Chrysler than from Ford and GM. The company in turn placed the head of the UAW on its board of directors. The investment by the workers is implicit but real.

Implicitly the government represents the general interests of society, and when it guarantees debt for a corporation, it too is making an investment. While the normal profitable corporation does not make decisions with the specific objective of benefiting society, when it gets into financial difficulties the willingness of the different sectors to come forth with assistance is going to depend on the past record and future prospects of the corporation.

Success and Financial Strategy

Financial strategy can affect the magnitudes of the benefits, but only rarely is the basic profitability of the firm affected. When Chrysler incurs an operating loss of $1,000,000,000 in one year, this is not the result of its financial strategy. The strongest financial structure is going to be shattered by such a large loss. But it is true that the more debt, the smaller the loss has to be before the firm is pushed into a position of financial distress.

Thus financial strategy cannot turn an operating disaster into a dramatic success. It can enhance an operating success and increase the likelihood that the firm will survive long enough to attain that success. At the other extreme a large amount of debt can increase the probability of financial disaster, and a small amount of debt can decrease it.

Financial Personality

In the sixties the financial literature spoke extensively about growth companies. Also, traditionally, public utilities have been looked to for steady safe dividends with a little growth thrown in. But aside from these relatively minor exceptions, companies do not have strong financial personalities.

If a person shops for a suit, the type of suits to be found at Brooks Brothers is no surprise. If one shops for a common stock, it is much more difficult to know the type of financial strategy that one is obtaining.

In the marketing of products there is a realization that there are wide ranges of different customers and that it makes sense to go after a segment of the market. The marketing of a product should have a focus. Let us define the issuance of securities as a type of marketing. In the marketing of the common stock of a firm, there is frequently not the same focus as is found in the marketing of the firm's products. The marketing of securities other than common stock is generally well focused, but common stock is an exception.

Frequently a company with zero long-term debt will start adding debt. A company not paying a cash dividend will suddenly think it is a good idea to pay a dividend. There is little consistency through time in financial strategy and generally no attempt to target the company's common stock for a segment of the market.

From the point of view of investors trying to plan an investment strategy, it would be useful for firms to describe their financial strategies. This would make known the capital structure decisions but even more importantly the dividend decisions. While it would be indicated that events might necessitate a change in strategy, at least management's intentions would be revealed.

In many situations firms follow strategies that please few and annoy few. They are in a sense "minimax" strategies. Pay some dividends (say .4 of earnings) but not too much. Have some debt (say .35 of common stock) but not too much. The financial managers look at other firms and follow their lead. But since most managers are looking at each other, there are few leaders—we have a circle where each firm is looking at each other firm and is seeing itself.

This is, of course, an exaggeration, but it has too many elements of truth. If the financial managers of a firm deviate from the norm, the financial investing community will exert pressure via bond rating agencies and investment banking advisers which will tend to cause the firm to conform.

Unusual financial strategies are difficult to implement. There are many pressures toward conformity.

A few firms such as Teledyne do not act in conformance with the above, and do have a very special personality. We need more such firms, not necessarily following the same financial strategy as Teledyne, but following a financial strategy that is best for their investors. Investors with more or less common investment objectives will choose the common stock that fits their needs.

The Final Exam

Programmed learning uses the technique of asking a question and if the answer is wrong sending the student back to material where the necessary knowledge was presented so that this time the student can actually learn the material or alternatively have better luck with the next question.

Here you will receive your final examination in the form of one multiple-choice question. Assume preferred stock can be issued to yield .10 and common stock requires a yield of .14. Debt cannot be issued. Choose one of the following:

1. Preferred is cheaper than common stock and should be issued.
2. Preferred costs the same as common stock and there is indifference.
3. We cannot tell from the information.

You receive a passing grade if you did *not* choose statement 1. We cannot tell if preferred stock is cheaper than the common stock. An issuance of preferred stock creates prior claims to earning streams and thus results in higher costs to common stock. With the issuance of the preferred stock the common stockholders will require a higher yield than .14. If .14 is required without the preferred stock, with the issuance of preferred stock a higher return than .14 will be required. The amount of preferred stock issued will also affect the cost of the next issue of preferred stock (the number of dollars of earnings committed to investors will affect the required return since the risk changes).

Even though .10 is less than .14, we cannot be sure preferred stock is cheaper than common stock, since we do not yet know the effect on the weighted average cost of capital. We can also say that we do not know the marginal costs of the preferred stock and common stock where the marginal cost includes the effect on the cost of the other security.

Neither common stock nor preferred stock has any advantages at the corporate level where the basic cash flows are earned. There are good reasons for assuming that the two securities must have exactly the same cost (that is the weighted average cost is not affected by the choice). A difficulty arises if we consider the consequences to investors in the securities and define the cost or return from the investors' perspective. Since common stock returns and preferred stock returns are likely to be taxed differently, there could be a preference at the investor level where there is indifference at the firm level. Equilibrium analysis would require that the final yields of the two securities reflect not only the corporate tax structure but also the personal taxes that are imposed on investors.

If you answered that statement 1 was the correct statement, do not despair. The way the question is worded, it is easy to conclude (incorrectly) that the .10 and the .14 are fully descriptive measures of cost to the firm. Unfortunately, as is frequently the case, we must consider the dynamic elements of the decision. In this situation it is necessary to consider the consequences of the stock issuance on the costs of all other securities. The question must always be asked, What else is affected by the decision?

Conclusions

If we were to take all financial decisions out of the set of financial strategy considerations, we would be left with an empty box. If we were to take all strategy considerations out of the set of financial decisions, we would be left with a cookbook (the problems would be simplified so that exact and definite solutions could be obtained). A strategy approach to financial decisions is necessary, since exact normative financial decision recommendations are frequently a fiction based on simplified assumptions.

Financial strategy implies that the interconnection between

specific decisions be recognized. If debt is added to increase the earnings per share it has to be recognized that risk also increases, and that one has to be careful about not undertaking risky endeavors given the risky capital structure.

But perhaps an appropriate closing on strategy is:

Strategy: Confidence
Sapience
Watch expense
Dilligence
Excellence
Intelligence
Common sense
And Providence!

Notes

Chapter 1

1. J. J. Tarrant, *Drucker: The Man Who Invented the Corporate Society* (Boston: Cahners Books, 1976), p. 258.
2. H. A. Simon, *The New Science of Management Decision* (Englewood Cliffs, N.J.: Prentice-Hall, 1977), p. 53.
3. H. A. Simon, *Administrative Behavior,* 3rd ed. (New York: Free Press, 1976), p. xxviii.
4. Ibid., p. xxix.
5. Ibid., p. 6.
6. Peter F. Drucker, *Drucker on Management* (London: Management Publications Limited, 1970, p. 3.

Chapter 4

1. See Franco Modigliani and Merton H. Miller, "The Cost of Capital, Corporation Finance, and the Theory of Investment," *American Economic Review* (June 1958), pp. 261–297; "The Cost of Capital, Corporation Finance, and the Theory of Investment: Reply," *American Economic Review* (September 1959), pp. 655–669; and "Taxes and the Cost of Capital: A Correction," *American Economic Review* (June 1963), pp. 433–443. Also David Durand, "The Cost of Capital, Corporation Finance, and the Theory of Investment: Comment," *American Economic Review* (September 1959), pp. 640–654.

Chapter 7

1. See M. H. Miller and F. Modigliani, "Dividend Policy, Growth and the Valuation of Shares," *Journal of Business* (October 1961), pp. 411–433.

Chapter 8

1. See H. Bierman, Jr., and S. Smidt, *The Capital Budgeting Decision,* 5th ed. (New York: Macmillan, 1980), for the arguments.

Chapter 14

1. Harry M. Markowitz, *Portfolio: Efficient Diversification of Investments* (New York: Wiley, 1959).

Additional Reading

Chapter 1

ACKOFF, R. L. A Concept of Corporate Planning (New York: Wiley, 1970).

ANDREWS, K. R. *The Concept of Corporate Strategy* (Homewood: Irwin, 1971).

ANSOFF, H. I. *Corporate Strategy* (New York: McGraw-Hill, 1965).

CHANDLER, A. D. *Strategy and Structure* (Cambridge, Mass.: M.I.T. Press, 1962).

DRUCKER, P. F. *Concept of the Corporation* (New York: Day, 1972).

MCGREGOR, D. M. *The Human Side of Enterprise* (New York: McGraw-Hill, 1960).

SIMON, H. A. *The New Science of Management Decision* (Englewood Cliffs, N.J.: Prentice-Hall, 1977).

—— *Administrative Behavior,* 3rd ed. (New York: Free Press, 1976).

STEINER, G. A. *Top Management Planning* (New York, 1969).

TARRANT, J. J. *Drucker: The Man Who Invented the Corporate Society* (Boston: Cahners Books, 1976).

Chapter 2

BIERMAN, H., JR., AND HASS, J. "Normative Stock Price Models," *Journal of Financial and Quantitative Analysis* (September 1971), pp. 1135–1144.

BIERMAN, H., JR., DOWNES, D. H., AND HASS, J. "Closed Form Stock Price Models," *Journal of Financial and Quantitative Analysis* (June 1972), pp. 1797–1808.

BRIGHAM, EUGENE F., AND PAPPAS, JAMES L. "Duration of Growth, Change in Growth Rates, and Corporate Share Prices," *Financial Analysts Journal* (May–June 1966), pp. 157–162.

DURAND, DAVID. "Growth Stocks and the St. Petersburg Paradox," *Journal of Finance* (September 1957), pp. 348–363.

GORDON, MYRON J. *The Investment, Financing, and Valuation of the Corporation* (Homewood, Ill.: Irwin, 1962).

LORIE, J. H., AND HAMILTON, M. T. *The Stock Market, Theories and Evidence* (Homewood, Ill.: Irwin, 1973).

SOLOMON, EZRA. *The Theory of Financial Management* (New York: Columbia University Press, 1963).

WILLIAMS, JOHN BURR. *The Theory of Investment Values* (Cambridge, Mass.: Harvard University Press, 1938).

Chapter 3

DONALDSON, G. *Corporate Debt Capacity* (Boston: Harvard Graduate School of Business, 1961).

FISHER, L. "Determinants of Risk Premiums on Corporate Bonds," *Journal of Political Economy* (June 1959).

MALKIEL, BURTON G. *The Term Structure of Interest Rates* (Princeton, N.J.: Princeton University Press, 1966).

MODIGLIANI, F., AND MILLER, M. H. "The Cost of Capital, Corporation Finance and the Theory of Investment," *American Economic Review* (June 1958).

VAN HORNE, JAMES C. *Function and Analysis of Capital Market Rates* (Englewood Cliffs, N.J.: Prentice-Hall, 1970).

Chapter 4

ALTMAN, EDWARD I. "Corporate Bankruptcy Potential, Stockholder Returns, and Share Valuation," *Journal of Finance* (December 1969), pp. 887–900.

BAUMOL, WILLIAM, AND MALKIEL, BURTON G. "The Firm's Optimal Debt-Equity Combination and the Cost of Capital," *Quarterly Journal of Economics* (November 1967), pp. 547–578.

BAXTER, NEVINS D. "Leverage, Risk of Ruin, and the Cost of Capital," *Journal of Finance* (September 1967), pp. 395–404.

MILLER, M. H., AND MODIGLIANI, FRANCO. "Cost of Capital to Electric

Utility Industry," *American Economic Review* (June 1966), pp. 333-391.

MODIGLIANI, FRANCO, AND MILLER, M. H. "The Cost of Capital, Corporation Finance and the Theory of Investment," *American Economic Review* (June 1958), pp. 261–297.

——. "The Cost of Capital, Corporation Finance and the Theory of Investment: Reply," *American Economic Review* (September 1958), pp. 655–669; "Taxes and the Cost of Capital: A Correction," *American Economic Review* (June 1963), pp. 433–443; "Reply," *American Economic Review* (June 1965), pp. 524–527; "Reply to Heins and Sprenkle," *American Economic Review* (September 1969), pp. 592–595.

ROBICHEK, ALEXANDER A., AND MYERS, STEWART C. *Optimal Financing Decisions* (Englewood Cliffs, N.J.: Prentice-Hall, 1965).

SOLOMON, EZRA. "Leverage and the Cost of Capital," *Journal of Finance* (May 1963), pp. 273–279.

——. *The Theory of Financial Management* (New York: Columbia University Press, 1963).

VICKERS, DOUGLAS. "The Cost of Capital and the Structure of the Firm," *Journal of Finance* (March 1970), pp. 35–46.

Chapter 5

BILDERSEE, JOHN S. "Some Aspects of the Performance of Non-Convertible Preferred Stocks," *Journal of Finance* (December 1973), pp. 1187–1202.

DONALDSON, GORDON. "Financial Goals: Management vs. Stockholders," *Harvard Business Review* (May–June 1963), pp. 116–129.

"In Defense of Preferred Stock," *Harvard Business Review* (July–August 1962), pp. 123–136.

ELSAID, HUSSEIN H. " The Function of Preferred Stock in the Corporate Financial Plan," *Financial Analysts Journal* (July–August 1969), pp. 112–117.

FISHER, DONALD E., and GLENN A. WILT, JR. "Nonconvertible Preferred Stock as a Financing Instrument, 1950–1965," *Journal of Finance* (September 1968), pp. 611–624.

Chapter 6

BIERMAN, H., JR. *Financial Policy Decisions* (New York: Macmillan, 1970), chapters 16 and 17.

Brigham, E. F. "An Analysis of Convertible Debentures: Theory and Some Empirical Evidence," *Journal of Finance* (March 1966), pp. 35–54.

Ingersoll, J., "An Examination of Corporate Call Policies on Corporate Securities," *Journal of Finance,* May 1977, pp. 463–478.

Merton, Robert C. "On the Pricing of Corporate Debt," *Journal of Finance* (May 1974), pp. 449–470.

———. "A Rational Theory of Option Pricing," *Bell Journal of Economics and Management Science* (Spring 1973), pp. 141–183.

Pinches, George E. "Financing with Convertible Preferred Stocks, 1960–1967," *Journal of Finance* (March 1970), pp. 53–64.

Shelton, John P. "The Relation of the Price of a Warrant to the Price of Its Associated Stock," *Financial Analysts Journal* (May–June and July–August 1967), pp. 88–99 and 143–151.

Soldofsky, Robert M. "Yield-Risk Performance of Convertible Securities," *Financial Analysts Journal* (March–April 1971), pp. 61–65.

Chapter 7

Bierman, H., Jr., and West, R. "The Acquisition of Common Stock by the Corporate Issuer," *Journal of Finance* (December 1966).

———. "The Effect of Share Repurchase on the Value of the Firm: Some Further Comments," *Journal of Finance* (December 1968), pp. 865–869.

Brigham, Eugene. "The Profitability of a Firm's Repurchase of Its Own Common Stock," *California Management Review* (Winter 1964).

Donaldson, Gordon. "From the Thoughtful Businessman," *Harvard Business Review* (July–August 1965).

Ellis, Charles. "Repurchase Shares to Revitalize Equity," *Harvard Business Review* (July–August 1965).

Elton, E., and Gruber, M. "The Effects of Share Repurchase on the Value of the Firm," *Journal of Finance* (March 1968), pp. 135–149.

———. "Reply," *Journal of Finance* (December 1968), pp. 870–874.

Farrar, Donald E., and Selwyn, Lee L. "Taxes, Corporate Financial Policy and Return to Investors," *National Tax Journal* (December 1967), pp. 444–454.

Gordon, M. J. "Dividend, Earnings and Stock Prices," *Review of Economics and Statistics* (May 1959), pp. 99–105.

———. *The Investment, Financing, and Valuation of the Corporation* (Homewood, Ill.: Irwin, 1962).

Lintner, J. "Dividends, Earnings, Leverage, Stock Prices, and the Supply of Capital to Corporations," *Review of Economics and Statistics* (August 1962), pp. 243–270.

Miller, M. H. and Modigliani, F., "Dividend Policy, Growth and the Valuation of Shares," *Journal of Business* (October 1961), pp. 411–433.

——. *Dividend Policy and Enterprise Valuation* (Belmont, Calif.: Wadsworth, 1967).

West, R. R., and Bierman, H. Jr. "Corporate Dividend Policy and Preemptive Security Issues," *Journal of Business* (January 1968), pp. 71–75.

Chapter 8

Bierman, Harold, Jr., and Seymour Smidt. *The Capital Budgeting Decision* 5th edition (New York: Macmillan, 1980).

Hastie, K. Larry. "One Businessman's View of Capital Budgeting," *Financial Management* (Winter 1974), pp. 36–44.

Hertz, David B. "Risk Analysis in Capital Investment," *Harvard Business Review* (January–February 1964), pp. 95–106.

——. "Investment Policies That Pay Off," *Harvard Business Review* (January–February 1968), pp. 96–108.

Hespos, Richard, F., and Strassman, Paul A. "Stochastic Decision Trees for the Analysis of Investment Decisions," *Management Science* (August 1965), pp. 244–259.

Hillier, Frederick S. "The Derivation of Probabilistic Information for the Evaluation of Risky Investments," *Management Science* (April 1963), pp. 443–457.

——. "A Basic Model for Capital Budgeting of Risky Interrelated Projects," *Engineering Economist* (Fall 1971), pp. 1–30.

Magee, John F. "Decision Trees for Decision-Making," *Harvard Business Review* (July–August 1964), pp. 126–138.

Robichek, Alexander, and Myers, Stewart C. "Conceptual Problems in the Use of Risk-adjusted Discount Rates," *Journal of Finance* (December 1966), pp. 727–730.

——. *Optimal Financing Decisions* (Englewood Cliffs, N.J.: Prentice-Hall, 1965).

Solomon, Ezra. "The Arithmetic of Capital-Budgeting Decisions," *Journal of Business* (April 1956), pp. 124–129.

——. The Management of Corporate Capital (New York: Free Press, 1959).

Chapter 9

ALBERTS, W. W., and SEGALL, J. E. *The Corporate Merger* (Chicago: University of Chicago Press, 1966).

BIERMAN, HAROLD, JR., and HASS, JEROME E. "The Use and Misuse of the *P/E* Ratio in Acquisition and Merger Decisions," *Financial Executive* (October 1970), pp. 62–68.

BUTTERS, J. K., LINTNER, J., and CARY, W. S. *Effects of Taxation: Corporate Mergers* (Cambridge, Mass.: Harvard University Press, 1951).

DEWING, ARTHUR STONE. *The Financial Policy of Corporation,* 5th ed. (New York: Ronald, 1953), chapter 32.

MUELLER, DENNIS C. "A Theory of Conglomerate Mergers," *Quarterly Journal of Economics* (November 1969), pp. 643–659.

SMALTER, D. J., and LANCEY, R. C. "*P/E* Analysis in Acquisition Strategy," *Harvard Business Review* (November–December 1966), pp. 85–95.

VANCE, J. O. "Is Your Company a Take-over Target?" *Harvard Business Review* (May–June 1969), pp. 93–98.

WESTON, J. FRED (ed.). *Readings in Finance from Fortune* (New York: Henry Holt and Company, 1958), chapters IX and X.

Chapter 10

FISHER, IRVING. *The Theory of Interest* (New York: Macmillan, 1930).

HENDERSHOTT, P. H., and J. C. VAN HORNE. "Expected Inflation Implied by Capital Market Rates," *Journal of Finance* (May 1973), pp. 301–314.

MUNDELL, ROBERT. "Inflation and Real Interest," *Journal of Political Economy* (June 1963), pp. 280–283.

ROLL, RICHARD. "Interest Rates on Monetary Assets and Commodity Price Index Changes," *Journal of Finance* (May 1972), pp. 251–278.

STEINDL, FRANK G. "Price Expectations and Interest Rates," *Journal of Money, Credit and Banking* (November 1973), pp. 939–949.

Chapter 11

APB 15 (Opinion 15 of the Accounting Principles Board of the AICPA, 1969).

Chapter 12

BOWER, RICHARD S. "Issues in Lease Financing," *Financial Management* (Winter 1973), pp. 25–34.

SCHALL, LAWRENCE D. "The Lease-or-Buy and Asset Acquisition Decisions," *Journal of Finance* (September 1974), pp. 1203–1214.

VANCIL, RICHARD F. "Lease or Borrow: New Method of Analysis," *Harvard Business Review* (September–October 1961), pp. 122–136.

Chapter 13

DUFEY, GUNTER. "Corporate Finance and Exchange Rate Variations," *Financial Management* (Summer 1972), pp. 51–57.

ROBBINS, S. M., and STOBAUGH, R. B. "Financing Foreign Affiliates," *Financial Management* (Winter 1972), pp. 56–65.

RODRIGUES, RITA M., and CARTER, E. EUGENE. *International Financial Management* (Englewood Cliffs, N.J.: Prentice-Hall, 1979).

SOLNIK, BRUNO H. *European Capital Markets* (Boston: Lexington Books, 1973).

VERNON, RAYMOND. *Manager in the International Economy,* 2nd ed. (Englewood Cliffs, N.J.: Prentice-Hall, 1972).

WESTON, FRED, J., and B. W. SORGE, *International Managerial Finance,* R. D. Irwin, Inc., 1972.

ZENOFF, D. B., and JACK ZWICK, *International Financial Management,* Prentice-Hall, Inc., 1969.

Chapter 14

BIERMAN, H., and HASS, J. E. "Capital Budgeting under Uncertainty: A Reformulation," *Journal of Finance* (March 1973), pp. 119–129.

FAMA, E. "Risk, Return, and Equilibrium: Some Clarifying Comments," *Journal of Finance* (March 1968), pp. 29–40.

HAMADA, R. S. "Portfolio Analysis, Market Equilibrium and Corporation Finance," *Journal of Finance* (March 1969), pp. 13–31.

LINTNER, J. "The Valuation of Risk Assets and the Selection of Risky Investment in Stock Portfolios and Capital Budgets," *Review of Economics and Statistics* (February 1965), pp. 13–27.

——. "Security Prices, Risk, and Maximal Gains for Diversification," *Journal of Finance* (December 1965), pp. 587–613.

LITZENBERGER, R. H., and BUDD, A. P. "Corporate Investment Criteria and the Validation of Risk Assets," *Journal of Financial and Quantitative Analysis,* nos. 4 and 5 (December 1970), pp. 395–419.

MARKOWITZ, H. M. *Portfolio Selection: Efficient Diversification of Investments* (New York: Cowles Foundation Monograph No. 16, 1959).

MOSSIN, J. "Equilibrium in a Capital Asset Market," *Econometrica* (October 1966), pp. 768–775.

——. "Security Pricing and Investment Criteria in Competitive Markets," *American Economic Review* (December 1969), pp. 749–756.

ROBICHEK, A. A. "Risk and the Value of Securities," *Journal of Financial and Quantitative Analysis* (December 1969), pp. 513–538.

——. and MYERS, S. C. "Valuation of the Firm: Effects of Uncertainty in a Market Context," *Journal of Finance* (May 1966), pp. 215–227.

SHARPE, W. F. "Capital Asset Prices: A Theory of Market Equilibrium under Conditions of Risk," *Journal of Finance* (September 1964), pp. 425–442.

STAPLETON, R. C. "Portfolio Analysis, Stock Valuation and Capital Budgeting Decision Rules for Risky Projects," *Journal of Finance* (March 1971), pp. 95–117.

TOBIN, J. "Liquidity Preference as Behavior towards Risk," *Review of Economic Studies* (February 1958), pp. 65–86.

Chapter 15

ACKOFF, R. L. *A Concept of Corporate Planning* (New York: Wiley, 1970).

ANDREWS, K. R. *The Concept of Corporate Strategy* (Homewood: Irwin, 1971).

ANSOFF, H. I. *Corporate Strategy* (New York: McGraw-Hill, 1965).

CHANDLER, A. D. *Strategy and Structure* (Cambridge, Mass.: M.I.T. Press, 1962).

DRUCKER, P. F. *Concept of the Corporation* (New York: Day, 1972).

MCGREGOR, D. M. *The Human Side of Enterprise* (New York: McGraw-Hill, 1960).

SIMON, H. A. *The New Science of Management Decision* (Englewood Cliffs, N.J.: Prentice-Hall, 1977).

——. *Administrative Behavior,* 3rd ed. (New York: Free Press, 1976).

STEINER, G. A. *Top Management Planning* (New York, 1969).

TARRANT, J. J. *Drucker: The Man Who Invented the Corporate Society* (Boston: Cahners Books, 1976).

Index